NEW HORIZONS

NEW HORIZONS

An Anthology of Short Poems for Senior Students / *Revised Edition*

BERT CASE DILTZ / RONALD JOSEPH McMASTER

Copyright, Canada, 1955, by

McCLELLAND AND STEWART LIMITED

Revised edition © Canada, 1965, by

McCLELLAND AND STEWART LIMITED

Reprinted 1989

CANADIAN CATALOGUING IN PUBLICATION DATA

Main entry under title:

New horizons, an anthology of short poems for
senior students

First ed., 1954, edited by B.C. Diltz.
"List of books on poetry, its interpretation, appreciation
and enjoyment": p.
Includes index.

ISBN 0-7710-2736-2

1. British poetry.   2. American poetry.
3. Canadian poetry (English)*   I. Diltz, Bert
Case, 1894-   .   II. McMaster, Ronald Joseph,
1926-   .

PN6101.N49 1965   808.81   C65-1720

McClelland & Stewart Inc.
The Canadian Publishers
481 University Avenue, Toronto M5G 2E9

Printed and bound in Canada by The Alger Press Limited

ACKNOWLEDGEMENTS

This and the following six pages constitute an extension of the copyright page.

ATHENEUM PUBLISHERS: "The Woman at the Washington Zoo" by Randall Jarrell, reprinted by permission of the author and publisher.

BEHRMAN HOUSE INC.: "The Still Small Voice" and "Simeon Takes Hints from His Environs" from *Hath Not a Jew* by Abraham Moses Klein, reprinted by permission of the author and the publisher.

NATHANIEL A. BENSON: "Harvest," reprinted by permission of the author; "Canada" from *The Glowing Years*, copyright, 1937, by Thomas Nelson & Sons (Canada) Ltd., used by permission of the author and publisher.

EARLE BIRNEY: "Slug in Woods," by permission of the author; "Ellesmereland" from *Ice Cod Bell or Stone*, by permission of the author and McClelland and Stewart Limited.

THE BODLEY HEAD LTD.: "The Fight" from *Collected Poems, Volume I*, by Roy Campbell.

BRANDT & BRANDT: "when god lets my body be" from *Collected Poems* by E. E. Cummings, published by Harcourt, Brace & Company, Inc., copyright 1923, 1951, by E. E. Cummings; "Autumn," lines from "John Brown's Body" in *Selected Works of Stephen Vincent Benét*, published by Rinehart & Company, Inc., copyright, 1927, 1928, by Stephen Vincent Benét.

CHARLES BRUCE: "For All Who Remember" from *Grey Ship Moving* by Charles Bruce, reprinted by permission of the author.

BURNS, OATES & WASHBOURNE LTD.: "In No Strange Land" and "To a Snowflake" by Francis Thompson, reprinted by permission of Sir Francis Meynell, owner of the copyright, and Burns, Oates & Washbourne Ltd.

JONATHAN CAPE LIMITED: "The Kingfisher" from *The Collected Poems of W. H. Davies*, by permission of Mrs. W. H. Davies and the publisher; "Naming of Parts" from *A Map of Verona and Other Poems* by Henry Reed, by permission of the publisher; "Will It Be So Again" from *Collected Poems* by C. Day Lewis, by permission of the publisher.

CHATTO & WINDUS LTD.: "The Goal of Intellectual Man" from *Selected Poems* by Richard Eberhart, published by Chatto & Windus Ltd.; "Anthem for Doomed Youth," "Futility," and "Arms and the Boy" by Wilfred Owen, reprinted by permission of the author's heirs and the publisher; "Canterbury," "October," and "Canoe-Trip" from *The Wounded Prince and Other Poems* by Douglas Le Pan, reprinted by permission of the publisher.

JOHN CIARDI: "Elegy Just in Case," reprinted by permission of the author.

THE CLARENDON PRESS, OXFORD: "Nightingales" from *Poetical Works* of Robert Bridges.

LEONARD COHEN: "Story" from *Let Us Compare Mythologies*, published by McGill University Press.

ROBERT CUMBERLAND: "The Mulleins."

WALTER DE LA MARE: "All That's Past," "The Scribe," "Fare Well," and "The Listeners," reprinted by permission of the author and Faber and Faber Ltd.

J. M. DENT & SONS (CANADA) LTD.: "To a Poet a Thousand Years Hence" by James Elroy Flecker.

J. M. DENT & SONS LTD.: "The Donkey" by G. K. Chesterton; "Do Not Go Gentle into That Good Night" and "Fern Hill" by Dylan Thomas, reprinted by permission of the Literary Executors of the Dylan Thomas Estate and the publisher.

DODD, MEAD & COMPANY, INC.: "The Falconer of God" from *Golden Fleece* by William Rose Benét, copyright, 1927, by William Rose Benét.

DOUBLEDAY & COMPANY, INC.: "A Noiseless, Patient Spider" and "When I Heard the Learn'd Astronomer" from *Leaves of Grass* by Walt Whitman.

FABER & FABER LTD.: "Ballad," "The Unknown Citizen," and "Refugee Blues" from *Collected Shorter Poems*, and "The Average" from *New Year Letter* by W. H. Auden; "Journey of the Magi" and "Chorus" from "The Rock" from *Collected Poems 1909-1962* by T. S. Eliot, by permission of the publisher; "Suburban Dream" from *Collected Poems* by Edwin Muir; "The Sunlight on the Garden" and "Prayer Before Birth" from *Collected Poems* by Louis MacNeice.

FARRAR, STRAUS & COMPANY, INC.: "Women" and "Evening in the Sanitarium," reprinted from *Collected Poems* by Louise Bogan, by permission of Farrar, Straus and Giroux, Inc., copyright 1954 by Louise Bogan.

ROBERT FINCH: "The Reticent Phrase," by permission of the author.

HARCOURT, BRACE AND WORLD: "somewhere i have never travelled" and "anyone lived in a pretty how town" from *Poems 1923-1954* by E. E. Cummings; "As a Plane Tree by the Water" by Robert Lowell; "A Camp in the Prussian Forest" and "The Truth" by Randall Jarrell; "Advice to a Prophet" from *Advice to a Prophet and Other Poems* and "The Beautiful Changes" from *The Beautiful Changes and Other Poems* by Richard Wilbur; "The Drunken Fisherman" by Robert Lowell, reprinted by permission of the publisher.

vii

viii

OXFORD UNIVERSITY PRESS, TORONTO: "Comràde" by Robert Finch and "Toronto Crossing" from *Poems* by Robert Finch, reprinted by permission of the author and the publisher; "The Pool" and "Time in a Public Ward" from *The Cruising Auk* by George Johnston, by permission of the publisher.

OXFORD UNIVERSITY PRESS, INC.: "All Lovely Things" from *Collected Poems* by Conrad Aiken, copyright 1953 by Conrad Aiken, reprinted by permission of Oxford University Press, Inc.

MESSRS. PEARN, POLLINGER & HIGHAM: "Snake" by D. H. Lawrence, reprinted by permission of Mrs. Frieda Lawrence, William Heinemann Ltd., publishers; "Seascape" by Francis Brett Young, published by William Heinemann Ltd.

PUNCH: "In Flanders Fields" by John McCrae, reprinted by permission of the proprietors of *Punch*.

PUTNAM & COMPANY LTD.: "The Inarticulate" from *The Headlands* by Howard Sergeant, reprinted by permission of the publisher.

RANDOM HOUSE, INC.: "To the Stone-Cutters" from *Tamar and Other Poems* by Robinson Jeffers, copyright 1925 by Boni & Liveright Inc., 1953, by Robinson Jeffers, by permission of Random House, Inc.; "Auto Wreck" by Karl Shapiro, by permission of Random House, Inc.

THE RYERSON PRESS: "Winter Saturday," "Atlantic Door," and "Canada: Case History" from *The Strait of Anian* by Earle Birney; "The Paradox," "Take Beauty," and "The Negress" from *All Fool's Day* by Audrey Alexandra Brown; "Indian Summer" and "How One Winter Came in the Lake Region" from *The Poetical Work of Wilfred Campbell*; "A January Morning," "The Passing of Spring," "Late November," "Evening," and "Winter Uplands" from *The Selected Poems of Archibald Lampman*; "Admonition for Spring" from *Viper's Bugloss* by L. A. MacKay; "The Flight of the Geese" and "The Potato Harvest" from *Selected Poems of Sir Charles G. D. Roberts*; "The Cremation of Sam McGee" from *Songs of a Sourdough* by Robert W. Service; "Aunt Jane" and "Warren Pryor," reprinted from *Under the Ice* by Alden Nowlan; "To the Avon River Above Stratford, Canada," reprinted from *Twelve Letters to a Small Town* by James Reaney; "The Man Who Finds that His Son Has Become a Thief" and "Flight of the Roller-Coaster," reprinted from *The Colour of the Times* by Raymond Souster. By permission of the Ryerson Press, Toronto.

SIEGFRIED SASSOON: "Dreamers" and "Grandeur of Ghosts."

CHARLES SCRIBNER'S SONS: "Richard Cory," "The House on the Hill," "An Old Story," and "Calvary" from *The Children of the Night* by Edward Arlington Robinson; "O World" and "With You a Part of Me" from *Poems* by George Santayana, copyright 1923 by Charles Scribner's Sons, 1951 by George Santayana, used by permission of the publishers; "The Last Days of Alice" and "Death of Little Boys" are reprinted with the permission of Charles Scribner's Sons from *Poems* (1960) by Allen Tate.

GENERAL CONTENTS

TABLE OF CONTENTS

part one

BRITISH POETS

AMERICAN POETS

xiv

CANADIAN POETS

part two

BRITISH POETS

xvii

AMERICAN POETS

CANADIAN POETS

part three

BRITISH POETS

AMERICAN POETS

CANADIAN POETS

PREFACE TO THE REVISED EDITION

In preparing this edition, we have enjoyed the advice of Douglas Le Pan. Every attempt has been made to keep to the principles outlined in the Introduction as the bases of selection—variety, challenge, merit. Fidelity to these principles has made it possible to omit only ten of the poems that appeared in the original collection, and their exclusion has not been without reluctance. But in this, the computer age, other voices—some from the past—cry out to be heard, for their message is relevant to man's present situation. Accordingly, ninety additional poems, traditional and contemporary, appear in this edition.

The contemporary poets whose work we have selected must be read along with those older poets whose contribution to our literature is unquestioned. They, too, have something to say, and their urge to say it has been created by an experience that their predecessors could not have known. They have lived in a century which has suffered two world wars, a great depression, and is now undertaking the exploration of space. The explosive force of these events has shifted old patterns of belief. Change is everywhere. Consequently, the challenge of the reconstruction of significance facing the twentieth-century poet is different in degree, if not in kind, from that which confronted those who went before him.

Still, he must work with essentially the same language–words inherited from those earlier artists and burdened with the associations accumulated from centuries of use. Sensitive to new intellectual, moral, and social problems and possibilities, he quite naturally seeks to extend the dimensions of language. As a result, his poetry is often highly symbolic, complex, imagistic, subjective, and socially conscious. In exploring it, we may find in Eliot's words that:

> the end of all our exploring
> Will be to arrive where we started
> And know the place for the first time.

If so, if the something that appears to lie beyond even the newest horizon turns out to be the here and now, we shall have had the pleasure of an interesting journey and the joy of re-discovering truth.

B.C.D. / R.J.M.

INTRODUCTION

This anthology is compiled in three parts, and each part contains approximately fifty-five poems from the British Isles, ten from the United States, and seventeen from Canada. The poems in each part are arranged in rough chronological sequence, dating from the old ballad to the new lyrics of our own day. Of the eighty-two poems in each part, about forty were written during the past seventy-five years. As a consequence this anthology contains both some well-loved poems that have survived the test of time and some new and exciting moods and forms that are likely to be remembered in the years to come. At one and the same time, this collection of poems provides an introduction to the development of the art of poetic expression in English, and affords considerably more than a glimpse at the new poetry which reflects the search for new revelations of truth and sketches the landscape of a new culture. Although the parts are varied in content, their quality remains basically the same. Different parts may be used profitably in consecutive years of study with senior students.

Within the limits of space and suitability, this anthology of poems presents the greatest possible variety of authorship, theme, mood, idea, and form. The poetry of the sensibilities commingles with the poetry of the passions, and every poem has intrinsic poetic merit. The aim of selection has not been to appeal to immature and undisciplined minds, but rather to provide nourishment for the mind, to stimulate mental growth, to help students to see more, feel more, and think more as they read, and to lead them on to better disciplined judgements and more mature tastes. In no instance, however, is the basis of selection inconsistent with the accepted factors that determine the grading of materials for study. Properly presented, every poem will challenge the powers of the students for whom it is intended. It is in poetry that the imagination learns to dance its way along the uneven thoroughfares of life.

Every poem included is a work of art in which the content and the form complement each other, and every poem opens a clear way for the apprehension of poetic experience. Not only is each poem representative of some of the best effort of its author, but it reflects in some degree the artistic temper and tempo of the time in which it was written. Popularity alone is no proof of excellence in poetry. This anthology sets a standard of achievement for senior students in this branch of study.

In preparing the explanatory notes, care has been taken to provide assistance in the interpretation of difficult words and phrases – usages that a good dictionary cannot be expected to explain. Every effort has been made to keep close to the intentions of the various poets and to preclude the possibility of mere "busy-work" on the wrong things in literary study. A poem of genuine quality can speak for itself. The purpose of the notes is to secure understanding, stimulate the senses, and deepen insights. It is a mistake to think that second-rate poetry lays a good foundation for the reading of first-rate poetry. Every pupil has the right to see and feel the excellence of a masterpiece, whether or not he fully understands its meaning or significance.

The biographical notes supply a few salient facts concerning the lives of the poets. These facts, it is hoped, may suggest to the reader the range and depth of the interests and the tastes of each literary artist. Both the explanatory and the biographical notes should be examined in the course of the study of any poem. The serious study of great poetry can supply light for the mind, a valuable outlet for the emotions, and experiences shared. The enjoyment of poetry does not spring from the gathering of information, but rather from the experience of breaking old barriers to see new horizons.

B. C. D.

PART ONE

THE TWA CORBIES

As I was walking all alane,
I heard twa corbies making a mane;
The tane unto the t'other say,
"Whar sall we gang and dine to-day?"

"In behint yon auld fail dyke,
I wot there lies a new-slain knight;
And naebody kens that he lies there,
But his hawk, his hound, and lady fair.

"His hound is to the hunting gane,
His hawk to fetch the wild-fowl hame,   10
His lady's ta'en another mate,
So we may mak our dinner sweet.

"Ye'll sit on his white hause-bane,
And I'll pike out his bonny blue eyne:
Wi' ae lock o' his gowden hair,
We'll theek our nest when it grows bare.

"Mony a one for him makes mane,
But nane sall ken whar he is gane;
O'er his white banes, when they are bare,
The wind sall blaw for evermair."   20

Anonymous

1

SIR PATRICK SPENS

The king sits in Dumferling toune,
    Drinking the blude-reid wine:
"O whar will I get guid sailor,
    To sail this schip of mine?"

Up and spak an eldern knicht,
    Sat at the kings richt kne:
"Sir Patrick Spens is the best sailor,
    That sails upon the se."

The king has written a braid letter,
    And signd it wi his hand,   10
And sent it to Sir Patrick Spens,
    Was walking on the strand.

The first line that Sir Patrick red;
    A loud lauch lauched he;
The next line that Sir Patrick red,
    The teir blinded his ee.

"O wha is this has don this deid,
    This ill deid don to me,
To send me out this time o' the yeir,
    To sail upon the se!   20

"Mak hast, mak hast, my mirry men all,
    Our guid schip sails the morne:"
"O say na sae, my master deir,
    For I feir a deadlie storme.

"Late late yestreen I saw the new moone,
    Wi the auld moone in hir arme,
And I feir, I feir, my deir master,
    That we will cum to harme."

O our Scots nobles wer richt laith
    To weet their cork-heild schoone;   30
Bot lang owre a' the play wer playd,
    Thair hats they swam aboone.

O lang, lang may their ladies sit,
  Wi thair fans into their hand;
Or eir they se Sir Patrick Spens
  Cum sailing to the land.

O lang, lang may the ladies stand,
  Wi thair gold kems in their hair,
Waiting for thair ain deir lords,
  For they'll se thame na mair.   40

Haf owre, haf owre to Aberdour,
  It's fiftie fadom deip,
And thair lies guid Sir Patrick Spens,
  Wi the Scots lords at his feit.

Anonymous

THE CANTERBURY TALES

(Introduction, Knight)

The General Prologue

showers sweet	Whan that Aprille with his shourés sooté*
	The droghte of March hath percéd to the rooté
vein such moisture	And bathéd every veyne* in swich licour*
power flower	Of which vertu* engendered in the flour,*
also	Whan Zephirus eek* with his sweeté breeth
woodland heath	Inspiréd hath in every holt* and heeth*
shoots	The tendré croppés,* and the yongé sonné
	Hath in the Ram his halfé cours y-ronné,
birds make	And smalé fowelés maken* melodyé
eye	That slepen al the nyght with open yé,* 10
stirs them in their hearts	So priketh hem* Nature in hir coragés,*
Then long go	Thanne longen* folk to goon* on pilgrymagés,
pilgrims seeks	And palmeres* for to seken* straungé
strands	strondés,*
distant shrines known	To ferné halwés kouthe* in sondry londés.
	And specially, from every shirés endé
	Of Engélond, to Caunterbury they wendé,
	The holy, blisful martir for to seké
helped	That hem hath holpen* whan that they were
sick	seeké.*

3

It happened	Bifel* that in that sesoun on a day
lodged	In Southwerk at the Tabard, as I lay* 20
	Redy to wenden on my pilgrymagė
heart	To Caunterbury with ful devout coragė,*
	At nyght was come into that hostelryė
	Wel nyne-and-twenty in a compaignyė
by chance fallen	Of sondry folk by aventure y-fallė*
together	In felaweshipe, and pilgrymes were they allė
intended to	That toward Caunterbury wolden* rydė.
spacious	The chambrės and the stablės weren wydė,*
given the best *accommodation*	And wel we weren esėd attė bestė;*
	And shortly, whan the sonnė was to restė, 30
every one	So hadde I spoken with hem everichon*
their almost at once	That I was of hir* felaweshipe anon;*
agreement	And madė forward* erly for to rysė
where tell	To take oure wey ther-as* I yow devysė.*
nevertheless	But, nathėlees,* whil I have tyme and spacė,
Before go	Er that* I ferther in this talė pacė,*
It seems to me	Me thynketh it* acordant to resoun
	To tellė yow al the condicioun
them	Of ech of hem* so as it semėd me,
	And whiche they weren, and of what degree, 40
dress and equipage	And eek in what array* that they were innė;
will	And at a knyght that wol* I first bigynnė.
	A KNYGHT ther was, and that a worthy man,
	That, fro the tymė that he first bigan
ride (in expeditions)	To riden out,* he lovėd chivalryė,
generosity	Trouthe and honour, fredom* and curteisyė.
war	Ful worthy was he in his lordės werrė,*
farther	And thereto hadde he riden, no man ferrė,*
heathendom	As wel in Cristendom as in hethėnessė,*
	And evere honourėd for his worthynessė. 50
Alexandria (Egypt)	At Alisaundre* he was whan it was wonnė;
table headed	Ful oftė tyme he hadde the bord bigonnė*
Prussia	Aboven allė nacions in Prucė.*
Lithuania served *Russia*	In Lettow* hadde he reysėd,* and in Rucė,*
Granada (Spain) been *Algeciras Benmarin* *(Morocco)* *Ayas (Armenia) Adalia* *(Turkey)*	No Cristen man so ofte of his degree.
	In Gernade* at the seege eek hadde he be*
	Of Algezir,* and riden in Belmaryė.*
	At Lyeys* was he and at Satalyė*
Mediterranean	Whan they were wonne; and in the Gretė* See
armada	At many a noble armee* hadde he be. 60
	At mortal batailles hadde he been fiftenė,
Tlemçen (Algeria)	And foughten for oure feith at Tramyssenė*

4

In lystės* thriės, and ay* slayn his foo.
This ilkė* worthy Knyght hadde been also
Somtymė with the lord of Palatyė*
Agayn* another hethen in Turkyė;
   And evere moore* he hadde a sovereyn
     prys,*
And, though that he were worthy, he was wys,
And of his port* as meke as is a maydė.
He nevere yet no vileynye* ne saydė   70
In al his lyf unto no maner wight.*
He was a verray,* parfit, gentil knyght.
   But for to tellen yow of his array,
Hise hors* were goodė, but he was nat gay.*
Of fustian* he werėd a gypon*
Al bismoterėd* with his habergeon,*
Far he was late y-come from his viagė*
And wentė for to doon his pilgrymagė.

Geoffrey Chaucer

BENEDICITE

Blessed be the Lord God of Israel;
For he hath visited and redeemed his people,
And hath raised up an horn of salvation for us
In the house of his servant David;
And he spake by the mouth of his holy prophets,
Which have been since the world began:
That we should be saved from our enemies,
And from the hand of all that hate us;
To perform the mercy promised to our fathers,
And to remember his holy covenant;   10
The oath which he sware to our father Abraham,
That he would grant unto us,
That we being delivered out of the hand of our enemies
Might serve him without fear,
In holiness and righteousness before him,
All the days of our life.
And thou, child, shalt be called the prophet of the Highest:
For thou shalt go before the face of the Lord
To prepare his ways;
To give knowledge of salvation unto his people   20
By the remission of their sins,

Through the tender mercy of our God;
Whereby the dayspring from on high hath visited us,
To give light to them that sit in darkness
And in the shadow of death,
To guide our feet into the way of peace.

Luke 1: 68-79

A SEA PSALM

They that go down to the sea in ships,
That do business in great waters;
These see the works of the LORD,
And his wonders in the deep.

For he commandeth, and raiseth the stormy wind,
Which lifteth up the waves thereof.

They mount up to the heaven,
They go down again to the depths:
Their soul is melted because of trouble.

They reel to and fro, and stagger like a drunken man,   10
And are at their wit's end.

Then they cry unto the LORD in their trouble,
And he bringeth them out of their distresses.

He maketh the storm a calm,
So that the waves thereof are still.

Then are they glad because they be quiet;
So he bringeth them unto their desired haven.

Oh that men would praise the LORD for his goodness,
And for his wonderful works to the children of men!

Psalm 107: 23-31

EASTER

Most glorious Lord of Lyfe! that, on this day,
Didst make Thy triumph over death and sin;
And, having harrowd hell, didst bring away
Captivity thence captive, us to win:
This joyous day, deare Lord, with joy begin;
And grant that we, for whom thou diddest dye,
Being with Thy deare blood clene washt from sin,
May live for ever in felicity!
And that Thy love we weighing worthily,
May likewise love Thee for the same againe;   10
And for Thy sake, that all lyke deare didst buy,
With love may one another entertayne!
  So let us love, deare Love, lyke as we ought,
  – Love is the lesson which the Lord us taught.

Edmund Spenser

SONNET XXIX

When in disgrace with fortune and men's eyes
I all alone beweep my outcast state,
And trouble deaf heaven with my bootless cries,
And look upon myself, and curse my fate,
Wishing me like to one more rich in hope,
Featur'd like him, like him with friends possess'd,
Desiring this man's art, and that man's scope,
With what I most enjoy contented least;
Yet in these thoughts myself almost despising,
Haply I think on thee, – and then my state,   10
Like to the lark at break of day arising
From sullen earth, sings hymns at heaven's gate;
  For thy sweet love remember'd such wealth brings
  That then I scorn to change my state with kings.

William Shakespeare

SONNET LXXVI

Why is my verse so barren of new pride,
So far from variation or quick change?
Why with the time do I not glance aside
To new-found methods and to compounds strange?
Why write I still all one, ever the same,
And keep invention in a noted weed,
That every word doth almost tell my name,
Showing their birth, and where they did proceed?
O! know, sweet love, I always write of you,
And you and love are still my argument;   10
So all my best is dressing old words new,
Spending again what is already spent:
   For as the sun is daily new and old,
   So is my love still telling what is told.

William Shakespeare

SONNET CXVI

Let me not to the marriage of true minds
Admit impediments. Love is not love
Which alters when it alteration finds,
Or bends with the remover to remove:
O, no! it is an ever-fixèd mark,
That looks on tempests and is never shaken;
It is the star to every wandering bark,
Whose worth's unknown, although his height be taken.
Love's not Time's fool, though rosy lips and cheeks
Within his bending sickle's compass come;   10
Love alters not with his brief hours and weeks,
But bears it out even to the edge of doom: –
   If this be error and upon me proved,
   I never writ, nor no man ever loved.

William Shakespeare

O MISTRESS MINE

O Mistress mine, where are you roaming?
O! stay and hear! your true-love's coming,
    That can sing both high and low;
Trip no further, pretty sweeting;
Journeys end in lovers meeting,
    Every wise man's son doth know.

What is love? 'tis not hereafter;
Present mirth hath present laughter;
    What's to come is still unsure:
In delay there lies no plenty;   10
Then come kiss me, Sweet-and-twenty,
    Youth's a stuff will not endure.

William Shakespeare

FEAR NO MORE

Fear no more the heat o' the sun,
   Nor the furious winter's rages;
Thou thy worldly task hast done,
   Home art gone, and ta'en thy wages:
Golden lads and girls all must,
As chimney-sweepers, come to dust.

Fear no more the frown o' the great;
   Thou art past the tyrant's stroke;
Care no more to clothe and eat;
   To thee the reed is as the oak: 10
The sceptre, learning, physic, must
All follow this, and come to dust.

Fear no more the lightning-flash,
   Nor th' all-dreaded thunder-stone;
Fear not slander, censure rash;
   Thou hast finished joy and moan:
All lovers young, all lovers must
Consign to thee, and come to dust.

William Shakespeare

CHERRY RIPE

There is a garden in her face
Where roses and white lilies grow;
A heavenly paradise is that place
Wherein all pleasant fruits do flow.
    There cherries grow which none may buy,
    Till "Cherry Ripe" themselves do cry.

Those cherries fairly do enclose
Of orient pearl a double row,
Which when her lovely laughter shows,
They look like rose-buds filled with snow;   10
    Yet them nor peer nor prince can buy,
    Till "Cherry Ripe" themselves do cry.

Her eyes like angels watch them still,
Her brows like bended bows do stand,
Threatening with piercing frowns to kill
All that attempt with eye or hand
    Those sacred cherries to come nigh,
    Till "Cherry Ripe" themselves do cry.

Thomas Campion

DEATH, BE NOT PROUD

Death, be not proud, though some have callèd thee
Mighty and dreadful, for thou art not so:
For those, whom thou think'st thou dost overthrow,
Die not, poor Death; nor yet canst thou kill me.
From rest and sleep, which but thy picture be,
Much pleasure, then from thee much more must flow;
And soonest our best men with thee do go,
Rest of their bones and souls' delivery.
Thou'rt slave to fate, chance, kings, and desperate men,
And dost with poison, war, and sickness dwell;   10
And poppy or charms can make us sleep as well
And better than thy stroke; why swell'st thou then?
  One short sleep past, we wake eternally,
  And Death shall be no more: Death, thou shalt die!

John Donne

SONG

Go, lovely rose!
Tell her that wastes her time and me,
That now she knows,
When I resemble her to thee,
How sweet and fair she seems to be.

Tell her that's young,
And shuns to have her graces spied,
That hadst thou sprung
In deserts where no men abide,
Thou must have uncommended died.　　　　　10

Small is the worth
Of beauty from the light retired;
Bid her come forth,
Suffer herself to be desired,
And not blush so to be admired.

Then die! that she
The common fate of all things rare
May read in thee;
How small a part of time they share
That are so wondrous sweet and fair!

Edmund Waller

ON HIS BLINDNESS

When I consider how my light is spent
    Ere half my days, in this dark world and wide,
    And that one talent which is death to hide
    Lodged with me useless, though my soul more bent
To serve therewith my Maker, and present
    My true account, lest He returning chide;
    "Doth God exact day-labour, light denied?"
    I fondly ask. But Patience, to prevent
That murmur, soon replies, "God doth not need
    Either man's work or his own gifts. Who best   10
    Bear his mild yoke, they serve him best. His state
Is kingly: thousands at his bidding speed,
    And post o'er land and ocean without rest;
    They also serve who only stand and wait."

John Milton

BLIND AMONG ENEMIES

from "Samson Agonistes"

Blind among enemies, O worse than chains,
Dungeon, or beggary, or decrepit age!
Light the prime work of God to me is extinct,
And all her various objects of delight
Annull'd, which might in part my grief have eas'd,
Inferior to the vilest now become
Of man or worm; the vilest here excel me,
They creep, yet see, I dark in light expos'd
To daily fraud, contempt, abuse and wrong,
Within doors, or without, still as a fool,   10
In power of others, never in my own;
Scarce half I seem to live, dead more than half.
O dark, dark, dark, amid the blaze of noon,
Irrecoverably dark, total Eclipse
Without all hope of day!

John Milton

THE WORLD

For all that is in the world, the lust of the flesh, and the lust of the eyes, and the pride of life, is not of the Father, but is of the world. And the world passeth away, and the lust thereof: but he that doeth the will of God abideth for ever.
(1 John 2: 16-17)

I

I saw Eternity the other night,
Like a great ring of pure and endless light,
    All calm, as it was bright;
And round beneath it, Time in hours, days, years,
    Driven by the spheres
Like a vast shadow moved; in which the world
    And all her train were hurled.
The doting lover in his quaintest strain
    Did there complain;
Near him, his lute, his fancy, and his flights,   10
    Wit's sour delights;
With gloves, and knots, the silly snares of pleasure,
    Yet his dear treasure,
All scattered lay, while he his eyes did pour
    Upon a flower.

II

The darksome statesman, hung with weights and woe,
Like a thick midnight-fog, moved there so slow,
    He did nor stay, nor go;
Condemning thoughts – like sad eclipses – scowl
    Upon his soul,   20
And clouds of crying witnesses without
    Pursued him with one shout.
Yet digged the mole, and lest his ways be found,
    Worked under ground,
Where he did clutch his prey; but one did see
    That policy:
Churches and altars fed him; perjuries
    Were gnats and flies;
It rained about him blood and tears, but he
    Drank them as free.   30

III

The fearful miser on a heap of rust
Sate pining all his life there, did scarce trust
    His own hands with the dust,

Yet would not place one piece above, but lives
    In fear of thieves.
Thousands there were as frantic as himself,
    And hugged each one his pelf;
The downright epicure placed heaven in sense,
    And scorned pretense;
While others, slipped into a wide excess,   40
    Said little less;
The weaker sort slight, trivial wares enslave,
    Who think them brave;
And poor, despised Truth sate counting by
    Their victory.

IV

Yet some, who all this while did weep and sing,
And sing, and weep, soared up into the ring;
    But most would use no wing.
O fools – said I – thus to prefer dark night
    Before true light!   50
To live in grots and caves, and hate the day
    Because it shows the way;
The way, which from this dead and dark abode
    Leads up to God;
A way where you might tread the sun, and be
    More bright than he!
But as I did their madness so discuss,
    One whispered thus,
"This ring the Bridegroom did for none provide,
    But for His Bride."   60

Henry Vaughan

THE TURKEY AND THE ANT

In other men we faults can spy,
And blame the mote that dims their eye.
Each little speck and blemish find,
To our own stronger errors blind.
    A Turkey, tired of common food,
Forsook the barn and sought the wood.
Behind her ran her infant train,
Collecting here and there a grain.

"Draw near, my birds," the mother cries,
"This hill delicious fare supplies.   10
Behold the busy Negro race,
See millions blacken all the place,
Fear not! like me with freedom eat.
An ant is most delightful meat,
How blest, how envied were our life
Could we but 'scape the poult'rers knife.
But man, curst man on Turkeys preys,
And Christmas shortens all our days.
Sometimes with oysters we combine,
Sometimes assist the sav'ry chine,   20
From the low peasant to the lord,
The turkey smoaks on every board.
Sure men for gluttony are curst,
Of the seven deadly sins the worst."
    An ant who climbed beyond his reach
Thus answered from the neighbouring beech,
"Ere you remark another's sin,
By thy own conscience look within.
Control thy more voracious bill,
Nor for a breakfast nations kill."   30

John Gay

A LITTLE LEARNING

from "An Essay on Criticism"

A little learning is a dangerous thing;
Drink deep, or taste not the Pierian spring:
There shallow draughts intoxicate the brain,
And drinking largely sobers us again.
Fired at first sight with what the Muse imparts,
In fearless youth we tempt the heights of arts,
While from the bounded level of our mind,
Short views we take, nor see the lengths behind;
But more advanced, behold with strange surprise
New distant scenes of endless science rise!   10
So pleased at first the towering Alps we try,
Mount o'er the vales, and seem to tread the sky,
Th' eternal snows appear already past,
And the first clouds and mountains seem the last;

15

But, those attained, we tremble to survey
The growing labours of the lengthened way,
Th' increasing prospects tire our wandering eyes,
Hills peep o'er hills, and Alps on Alps arise!

Alexander Pope

AN ELEGY ON THE DEATH
OF A MAD DOG

Good people all, of every sort,
　Give ear unto my song;
And if you find it wondrous short,
　It cannot hold you long.

In Islington there was a man,
　Of whom the world might say,
That still a godly race he ran
　When'er he went to pray.

A kind and gentle heart he had,
　To comfort friends and foes;　　　　　　　　　10
The naked every day he clad,
　When he put on his clothes.

And in that town a dog was found,
　As many dogs there be,
Both mongrel, puppy, whelp, and hound,
　And curs of low degree.

This dog and man at first were friends;
　But when a pique began,
The dog, to gain his private ends,
　Went mad, and bit the man.　　　　　　　　　20

Around from all the neighbouring streets
　The wondering neighbours ran,
And swore the dog had lost his wits,
　To bite so good a man.

The wound it seemed both sore and sad
　To every Christian eye:
And while they swore the dog was mad,
　They swore the man would die.

But soon a wonder came to light,
   That showed the rogues they lied;   30
The man recovered of the bite,
   The dog it was that died.

Oliver Goldsmith

HOW SWEET I ROAMED

How sweet I roamed from field to field,
   And tasted all the summer's pride,
Till I the Prince of Love beheld
   Who in the sunny beams did glide!

He showed me lilies for my hair,
   And blushing roses for my brow;
He led me through his gardens fair
   Where all his golden pleasures grow.

With sweet May-dews my wings were wet,
   And Phœbus fired my vocal rage;   10
He caught me in his silken net,
   And shut me in his golden cage.

He loves to sit and hear me sing;
   Then, laughing, sports and plays with me;
Then stretches out my golden wing,
   And mocks my loss of liberty.

William Blake

TO A MOUSE

On Turning Her Up in Her Nest with the Plough,
November, 1785

Wee, sleekit, cow'rin', tim'rous beastie,
Oh, what a panic's in thy breastie!
Thou need na start awa sae hasty,
      Wi' bickering brattle!
I wad be laith to rin an' chase thee
      Wi' murd'ring pattle!

I'm truly sorry man's dominion
Has broken nature's social union,
An' justifies that ill opinion,
           Which makes thee startle   10
At me, thy poor, earth-born companion,
           An' fellow-mortal!

I doubt na, whyles, but thou may thieve;
What then? poor beastie, thou maun live!
A daimen-icker in a thrave
           'S a sma' request:
I'll get a blessin' wi' the lave,
           And never miss't!

Thy wee bit housie, too, in ruin!
Its silly wa's the win's are strewin'!   20
An' naething, now, to big a new ane,
           O' foggage green!
An' bleak December's winds ensuin',
           Baith snell an' keen!

Thou saw the fields laid bare and waste,
An' weary winter comin' fast,
An' cozie here, beneath the blast,
           Thou thought to dwell,
Till crash! the cruel coulter past
           Out thro' thy cell.   30

That wee bit heap o' leaves an' stibble
Has cost thee mony a weary nibble!
Now thou's turn'd out, for a' thy trouble,
           But house or hald,
To thole the winter's sleety dribble,
           An' cranreuch cauld!

But, Mousie, thou art no thy lane,
In proving foresight may be vain:
The best laid schemes o' mice an' men
           Gang aft a-gley,   40
An' lea'e us nought but grief an' pain,
           For promis'd joy.

Still thou art blest compar'd wi' me!
The present only toucheth thee:
But, och! I backward cast my e'e
      On prospects drear!
An' forward, tho' I canna see,
      I guess an' fear!

Robert Burns

LINES WRITTEN IN EARLY SPRING

I heard a thousand blended notes
    While in a grove I sate reclined,
In that sweet mood when pleasant thoughts
    Bring sad thoughts to the mind.

To her fair works did Nature link
    The human soul that through me ran;
And much it grieved my heart to think
    What man has made of man.

Through primrose tufts, in that green bower,
    The periwinkle trailed its wreaths;   10
And 'tis my faith that every flower
    Enjoys the air it breathes.

The birds around me hopped and played,
    Their thoughts I cannot measure, –
But the least motion which they made
    It seemed a thrill of pleasure.

The budding twigs spread out their fan
    To catch the breezy air;
And I must think, do all I can,
    That there was pleasure there.   20

If this belief from heaven be sent,
    If such be Nature's holy plan,
Have I not reason to lament
    What man has made of man?

William Wordsworth

SEPTEMBER, 1802

O Friend! I know not which way I must look
    For comfort, being, as I am, opprest,
    To think that now our life is only drest
For show; mean handy-work of craftsman, cook,
Or groom! – We must run glittering like a brook
    In the open sunshine, or we are unblest:
    The wealthiest man among us is the best:
No grandeur now in nature or in book
Delights us. Rapine, avarice, expense,
    This is idolatry; and these we adore.   10
    Plain living and high thinking are no more:
    The homely beauty of the good old cause
Is gone; our peace, our fearful innocence,
    And pure religion breathing household laws.

William Wordsworth

ROSABELLE

O listen, listen, ladies gay!
    No haughty feat of arms I tell;
Soft is the note, and sad the lay,
    That mourns the lovely Rosabelle.

"Moor, moor the barge, ye gallant crew!
    And, gentle ladye, deign to stay,
Rest thee in Castle Ravensheuch,
    Nor tempt the stormy firth to-day.

"The blackening wave is edged with white:
    To inch and rock the sea-mews fly;   10
The fishers have heard the Water-Sprite,
    Whose screams forebode that wreck is nigh.

"Last night the gifted Seer did view
    A wet shroud swathed round ladye gay;
Then stay thee, Fair, in Ravenscheuch:
    Why cross the gloomy firth to-day?" –

"'Tis not because Lord Lindesay's heir
   To-night at Roslin leads the ball,
But that my ladye-mother there
   Sits lonely in her castle-hall.   20

"'Tis not because the ring they ride,
   And Lindesay at the ring rides well,
But that my sire the wine will chide,
   If 'tis not fill'd by Rosabelle." –

O'er Roslin all that dreary night
   A wondrous blaze was seen to gleam;
'Twas broader than the watch-fire's light,
   And redder than the bright moonbeam.

It glared on Roslin's castled rock,
   It ruddied all the copse-wood glen;   30
'Twas seen from Dryden's groves of oak,
   And seen from cavern'd Hawthornden.

Seem'd all on fire that chapel proud,
   Where Roslin's chiefs uncoffin'd lie,
Each Baron, for a sable shroud,
   Sheathed in his iron panoply.

Seem'd all on fire, within, around,
   Deep sacristy and altar's pale,
Shone every pillar foliage-bound,
   And glimmer'd all the dead men's mail.   40

Blazed battlement and pinnet high,
   Blazed every rose-carved buttress fair –
So still they blaze when fate is nigh
   The lordly line of high St. Clair.

There are twenty of Roslin's barons bold
   Lie buried within that proud chapelle;
Each one the holy vault doth hold –
   But the sea holds lovely Rosabelle!

And each St. Clair was buried there,
   With candle, with book, and with knell;   50
But the sea-caves rung, and the wild winds sung
   The dirge of lovely Rosabelle.

Sir Walter Scott

TO NIGHT

Mysterious Night! when our first parent knew
Thee, from report divine, and heard thy name,
Did he not tremble for this lovely frame,
This glorious canopy of light and blue?
Yet 'neath a curtain of translucent dew,
Bathed in the rays of the great setting flame,
Hesperus, with the host of Heaven, came,
And lo! Creation widened in man's view.
Who could have thought such darkness lay concealed
Within thy beams, O sun! or who could find,   10
Whilst fly and leaf and insect stood revealed,
That to such countless orbs thou madst us blind!
     Why do we then shun Death with anxious strife?
     If Light can thus deceive, wherefore not Life?

Joseph Blanco White

LA BELLE DAME SANS MERCI

"O what can ail thee, knight-at-arms,
    Alone and palely loitering?
The sedge is withered from the lake,
    And no birds sing.

"O what can ail thee, knight-at-arms,
    So haggard and so woe-begone?
The squirrel's granary is full,
    And the harvest's done.

"I see a lily on thy brow
    With anguish moist and fever dew;   10
And on thy cheek a fading rose
    Fast withereth too."

"I met a lady in the meads,
    Full beautiful – a faery's child,
Her hair was long, her foot was light,
    And her eyes were wild.

"I made a garland for her head,
    And bracelets too, and fragrant zone;
She looked at me as she did love,
    And made sweet moan.   20

"I set her on my pacing steed
        And nothing else saw all day long,
For sideways would she bend, and sing
        A faery's song.

"She found me roots of relish sweet,
        And honey wild and manna dew,
And sure in language strange she said,
        'I love thee true!'

"She took me to her elfin grot,
        And there she wept and sighed full sore;   30
And there I shut her wild wild eyes
        With kisses four.

"And there she lullèd me asleep,
        And there I dreamed – Ah! woe betide!
The latest dream I ever dreamed
        On the cold hill's side.

"I saw pale kings and princes too,
        Pale warriors, death-pale were they all;
Who cried – 'La Belle Dame sans Merci
        Hath thee in thrall!'   40

"I saw their starved lips in the gloam
        With horrid warnings gapèd wide,
And I awoke and found me here
        On the cold hill's side.

"And this is why I sojourn here
        Alone and palely loitering,
Though the sedge is withered from the lake,
        And no birds sing."

                                        John Keats

ODE TO A NIGHTINGALE

My heart aches, and a drowsy numbness pains
    My sense, as though of hemlock I had drunk,
Or emptied some dull opiate to the drains
    One minute past, and Lethe-wards had sunk:
'Tis not through envy of thy happy lot,

23

But being too happy in thine happiness, –
　　That thou, light-wingèd Dryad of the trees,
　　　　In some melodious plot
　　Of beechen green, and shadows numberless,
　　　　Singest of summer in full-throated ease.　　　　10

O, for a draught of vintage! that hath been
　　Cool'd a long age in the deep-delvèd earth,
Tasting of Flora and the country green,
　　Dance, and Provençal song, and sunburnt mirth!
O for a beaker full of the warm South,
　　Full of the true, the blushful Hippocrene,
　　　　With beaded bubbles winking at the brim,
　　　　　　And purple-stainèd mouth;
　　That I might drink, and leave the world unseen,
　　　　And with thee fade away into the forest dim:　　　20

Fade far away, dissolve, and quite forget
　　What thou among the leaves hast never known,
The weariness, the fever, and the fret
　　Here, where men sit and hear each other groan;
Where palsy shakes a few, sad, last gray hairs,
　　Where youth grows pale, and spectre-thin, and dies;
　　　　Where but to think is to be full of sorrow
　　　　　　And leaden-eyed despairs,
　　Where Beauty cannot keep her lustrous eyes,
　　　　Or new Love pine at them beyond to-morrow.　　　30

Away! away! for I will fly to thee,
　　Not charioted by Bacchus and his pards,
But on the viewless wings of Poesy,
　　Though the dull brain perplexes and retards:
Already with thee; tender is the night,
　　And haply the Queen-Moon is on her throne,
　　　　Cluster'd around by all her starry Fays;
　　　　　　But here there is no light,
　　Save what from heaven is with the breezes blown
　　　　Through verdurous glooms and winding mossy ways.　40

I cannot see what flowers are at my feet,
　　Nor what soft incense hangs upon the boughs,
But, in embalmèd darkness, guess each sweet
　　Wherewith the seasonable month endows
The grass, the thicket, and the fruit-tree wild;

White hawthorn, and the pastoral eglantine;
   Fast-fading violets cover'd up in leaves;
      And mid-May's eldest child,
The coming musk-rose, full of dewy wine,
   The murmurous haunt of flies on summer eves.   50

Darkling I listen; and, for many a time
   I have been half in love with easeful Death,
Called him soft names in many a musèd rhyme,
   To take into the air my quiet breath;
Now more than ever seems it rich to die,
   To cease upon the midnight with no pain,
      While thou art pouring forth thy soul abroad
         In such an ecstasy!
Still wouldst thou sing, and I have ears in vain –
   To thy high requiem become a sod.   60

Thou wast not born for death, immortal bird!
   No hungry generations tread thee down;
The voice I hear this passing night was heard
   In ancient days by emperor and clown:
Perhaps the selfsame song that found a path
   Through the sad heart of Ruth, when, sick for home,
      She stood in tears amid the alien corn;
         The same that oft-times hath
Charmed magic casements, opening on the foam
   Of perilous seas, in faery lands forlorn.   70

Forlorn! the very word is like a bell
   To toll me back from thee to my sole self!
Adieu! the fancy cannot cheat so well
   As she is famed to do, deceiving elf.
Adieu! adieu! thy plaintive anthem fades
   Past the near meadows, over the still stream,
      Up the hill-side; and now 'tis buried deep
         In the next valley-glades:
Was it a vision, or a waking dream?
   Fled is that music: – do I wake or sleep?   80

John Keats

LEAD, KINDLY LIGHT

Lead, Kindly Light, amid the encircling gloom,
    Lead Thou me on;
The night is dark, and I am far from home,
    Lead Thou me on.
Keep Thou my feet; I do not ask to see
The distant scene; one step enough for me.

I was not ever thus, nor prayed that Thou
    Shouldst lead me on:
I loved to choose and see my path; but now
    Lead Thou me on.   10
I loved the garish day, and, spite of fears,
Pride ruled my will: remember not past years.

So long Thy power hath blest me, sure it still
    Will lead me on,
O'er moor and fen, o'er crag and torrent, till
    The night is gone;
And with the morn those angel faces smile
Which I have loved long since, and lost awhile.

John Henry Newman

IN MEMORIAM

LXIV

Dost thou look back on what hath been,
    As some divinely gifted man,
    Whose life in low estate began
And on a simple village green;

Who breaks his birth's invidious bar,
    And grasps the skirts of happy chance,
    And breasts the blows of circumstance,
And grapples with his evil star;

Who makes by force his merit known
    And lives to clutch the golden keys,   10
    To mould a mighty state's decrees,
And shape the whisper of the throne;

And moving up from high to higher,
    Becomes on Fortune's crowning slope
    The pillar of a people's hope,
The centre of a world's desire;

Yet feels, as in a pensive dream,
    When all his active powers are still,
    A distant dearness in the hill,
A secret sweetness in the stream,   20

The limit of his narrower fate,
    While yet beside its vocal springs
    He played at counsellors and kings,
With one that was his earliest mate;

Who ploughs with pain his native lea
    And reaps the labour of his hands,
    Or in the furrow musing stands;
"Does my old friend remember me?"

Alfred, Lord Tennyson

IN MEMORIAM

CXXIII

There rolls the deep where grew the tree.
    O earth, what changes hast thou seen!
    There where the long street roars, hath been
The stillness of the central sea.

The hills are shadows, and they flow
    From form to form, and nothing stands;
    They melt like mist, the solid lands,
Like clouds they shape themselves and go.

But in my spirit will I dwell,
    And dream my dream, and hold it true;   10
    For tho' my lips may breathe adieu,
I cannot think the thing farewell.

Alfred, Lord Tennyson

PROSPICE

Fear death? – to feel the fog in my throat,
    The mist in my face,
When the snows begin, and the blasts denote
    I am nearing the place,
The power of the night, the press of the storm,
    The post of the foe;
Where he stands, the Arch Fear in a visible form,
    Yet the strong man must go:
For the journey is done and the summit attained,
    and the barriers fall,   10
Though a battle's to fight ere the guerdon be gained,
    The reward of it all.
I was ever a fighter, so – one fight more,
    The best and the last!
I would hate that death bandaged my eyes and forbore
    And bade me creep past.
No! let me taste the whole of it, fare like my peers
    The heroes of old,
Bear the brunt, in a minute pay glad life's arrears
    Of pain, darkness and cold.   20
For sudden the worst turns the best to the brave,
    The black minute's at end,
And the elements' rage, the fiend-voices that rave,
    Shall dwindle, shall blend,
Shall change, shall become first a peace out of pain,
    Then a light, then thy breast,
O thou soul of my soul! I shall clasp thee again,
    And with God be the rest!

Robert Browning

SAY NOT THE STRUGGLE
NAUGHT AVAILETH

Say not the struggle naught availeth,
    The labour and the wounds are vain,
The enemy faints not, nor faileth,
    And as things have been they remain.

If hopes were dupes, fears may be liars;
    It may be, in yon smoke concealed,
Your comrades chase e'en now the fliers,
    And, but for you, possess the field.

For while the tired waves, vainly breaking,
   Seem here no painful inch to gain,   10
Far back, through creeks, and inlets making,
   Comes silent, flooding in, the main.

And not by eastern windows only,
   When daylight comes, comes in the light;
In front, the sun climbs slow, how slowly;
   But westward, look, the land is bright!

Arthur Hugh Clough

DOVER BEACH

The sea is calm tonight.
The tide is full, the moon lies fair
Upon the straits; – on the French coast the light
Gleams and is gone; the cliffs of England stand,
Glimmering and vast, out in the tranquil bay.
Come to the window, sweet is the night-air!
Only, from the long line of spray
Where the sea meets the moon-blanch'd land,
Listen! you hear the grating roar
Of pebbles which the waves draw back, and fling,   10
At their return, up the high strand,
Begin, and cease, and then again begin,
With tremulous cadence slow, and bring
The eternal note of sadness in.

Sophocles long ago
Heard it on the Ægean, and it brought
Into his mind the turbid ebb and flow
Of human misery; we
Find also in the sound a thought,
Hearing it by this distant northern sea.   20

The sea of faith
Was once, too, at the full, and round earth's shore
Lay like the folds of a bright girdle furl'd;
But now I only hear
Its melancholy, long, withdrawing roar,
Retreating, to the breath
Of the night-wind, down the vast edges drear
And naked shingles of the world.

Ah, love, let us be true
To one another! for the world, which seems   30
To lie before us like a land of dreams,
So various, so beautiful, so new,
Hath really neither joy, nor love, nor light,
Nor certitude, nor peace, nor help for pain;
And we are here, as on a darkling plain
Swept with confused alarms of struggle and flight,
Where ignorant armies clash by night.

Matthew Arnold

LIFE LAUGHS ONWARD

Rambling I looked for an old abode
Where, years back, one had lived I knew;
Its site a dwelling duly showed,
    But it was new.

I went where, not so long ago,
The sod had riven two breasts asunder;
Daisies throve gaily there, as though
    No grave were under.

I walked along a terrace where
Loud children gambolled in the sun;   10
The figure that had once sat there
    Was missed by none.

Life laughed and moved on unsubdued,
I saw that Old succumbed to Young:
'Twas well. My too regretful mood
    Died on my tongue.

Thomas Hardy

WEATHERS

I

This is the weather the cuckoo likes,
    And so do I;
When showers betumble the chestnut spikes,
    And nestlings fly;
And the little brown nightingale bills his best,
And they sit outside at *The Traveller's Rest*,
And maids come forth sprig-muslin drest,
And citizens dream of the south and west,
    And so do I;

II

This is the weather the shepherd shuns,   10
    And so do I;
When beeches drip in browns and duns,
    And thresh, and ply;
And hill-hid tides throb, throe on throe,
And meadow rivulets overflow,
And drops on gate-bars hang in a row,
And rooks in families homeward go,
    And so do I.

Thomas Hardy

WHEN I SET OUT
FOR LYONNESSE

When I set out for Lyonnesse,
    A hundred miles away,
    The rime was on the spray,
And starlight lit my lonesomeness
When I set out for Lyonnesse
    A hundred miles away.

What would bechance at Lyonnesse
    While I should sojourn there
    No prophet durst declare,
Nor did the wisest wizard guess   10
What would bechance at Lyonnesse
    While I should sojourn there.

When I came back from Lyonnesse
With magic in my eyes,
All marked with mute surmise
My radiance fair and fathomless,
When I came back from Lyonnesse
With magic in my eyes!

Thomas Hardy

SPRING AND FALL

To a Young Child

Márgarét, are you gríeving
Over Goldengrove unleaving?
Leáves, líke the things of man, you
With your fresh thoughts care for, can you?
Ah! ás the heart grows older
It will come to such sights colder
By and by, nor spare a sigh
Though worlds of wanwood leafmeal lie;
And yet you wíll weep and know why.
Now no matter, child, the name: 10
Sórrow's spríngs áre the same.
Nor mouth had, no nor mind, expressed
What heart heard of, ghost guessed:
It ís the blight man was born for,
It is Margaret you mourn for.

Gerard Manley Hopkins

NIGHTINGALES

Beautiful must be the mountains whence ye come,
And bright in the fruitful valleys the streams, wherefrom
Ye learn your song:
Where are those starry woods? O might I wander there,
Among the flowers, which in that heavenly air
Bloom the year long!

Nay, barren are those mountains and spent the streams:
Our song is the voice of desire, that haunts our dreams,
        A throe of the heart,
Whose pining visions dim, forbidden hopes profound,   10
No dying cadence nor long sigh can sound,
        For all our art.

Alone, aloud in the raptured ear of men
We pour our dark nocturnal secret; and then,
        As night is withdrawn
From these sweet-springing meads and bursting boughs of May,
Dream, while the innumerable choir of day
        Welcome the dawn.

                    Robert Bridges

IN NO STRANGE LAND

(The Kingdom of God is within you)

O world invisible, we view thee,
O world intangible, we touch thee,
O world unknowable, we know thee,
Inapprehensible, we clutch thee!

Does the fish soar to find the ocean,
The eagle plunge to find the air —
That we ask of the stars in motion
If they have rumour of thee there?

Not where the wheeling systems darken,
And our benumbed conceiving soars! —   10
The drift of pinions, would we hearken,
Beats at our own clay-shuttered doors.

The angels keep their ancient places; —
Turn but a stone, and start a wing!
'Tis ye, 'tis your estrangèd faces,
That miss the many-splendoured thing.

But (when so sad thou canst not sadder)
Cry; — and upon thy so sore loss
Shall shine the traffic of Jacob's ladder
Pitched betwixt Heaven and Charing Cross.   20

Yea, in the night, my Soul, my daughter,
Cry, — clinging Heaven by the hems;
And lo, Christ walking on the water
Not of Gennesareth, but Thames!

Francis Thompson

WHEN SMOKE STOOD UP
FROM LUDLOW

When smoke stood up from Ludlow,
    And mist blew off from Teme,
And blithe afield to ploughing
    Against the morning beam
    I stood beside my team,

The blackbird in the coppice
    Looked out to see me stride,
And hearkened as I whistled
    The trampling team beside,
    And fluted and replied: 10

"Lie down, lie down, young yeoman;
    What use to rise and rise?
Rise man a thousand mornings
    Yet down at last he lies
    And then the man is wise."

I heard the tune he sang me,
    And spied his yellow bill;
I picked a stone and aimed it
    And threw it with a will:
    Then the bird was still.   20

Then my soul within me
    Took up the blackbird's strain,
And still beside the horses
    Along the dewy lane
    It sang the song again:

"Lie down, lie down, young yeoman;
    The sun moves always west;
The road one treads to labour
    Will lead one home to rest,
    And that will be the best."   30

A. E. Housman

THE FIDDLER OF DOONEY

When I play on my fiddle in Dooney,
Folk dance like a wave of the sea;
My cousin is priest in Kilvarnet,
My brother in Moharabuiee.

I passed my brother and cousin:
They read in their books of prayer;
I read in my book of songs
I bought at the Sligo fair.

When we come at the end of time,
To Peter sitting in state,   10
He will smile on the three old spirits,
But call me first through the gate;

For the good are always the merry,
Save by an evil chance,
And the merry love the fiddle,
And the merry love to dance:

And when the folk there spy me,
They will all come up to me,
With, "Here is the fiddler of Dooney!"
And dance like a wave of the sea.   20

William Butler Yeats

THE LEADERS OF THE CROWD

They must to keep their certainty accuse
All that are different of a base intent;
Pull down established honour; hawk for news
Whatever their loose phantasy invent
And murmur it with bated breath, as though
The abounding gutter had been Helicon
Or calumny a song. How can they know
Truth flourishes where the student's lamp has shone,
And there alone, that have no solitude?
So the crowd come they care not what may come.   10
They have loud music, hope every day renewed
And heartier loves; that lamp is from the tomb.

William Butler Yeats

TO A FRIEND WHOSE WORK
HAS COME TO NOTHING

Now all the truth is out,
Be secret and take defeat
From any brazen throat,
For how can you compete,
Being honour bred, with one
Who, were it proved he lies,
Were neither shamed in his own
Nor in his neighbours' eyes?
Bred to a harder thing
Than Triumph, turn away   10
And like a laughing string
Whereon mad fingers play
Amid a place of stone,
Be secret and exult,
Because of all things known
That is most difficult.

William Butler Yeats

FOR THE FALLEN

With proud thanksgiving, a mother for her children,
England mourns for her dead across the sea.
Flesh of her flesh they were, spirit of her spirit,
Fallen in the cause of the free.

Solemn the drums thrill: Death august and royal
Sings sorrow up into immortal spheres.
There is music in the midst of desolation
And a glory that shines upon our tears.

They went with songs to the battle, they were young,
Straight of limb, true of eye, steady and aglow.   10
They were staunch to the end against odds uncounted,
They fell with their faces to the foe.

They shall not grow old, as we that are left grow old:
Age shall not weary them, nor the years condemn.
At the going down of the sun and in the morning
We will remember them.

They mingle not with their laughing comrades again;
They sit no more at familiar tables at home;
They have no lot in our labour of the day-time;
They sleep beyond England's foam.   20

But where our desires are and our hopes profound,
Felt as a well-spring that is hidden from sight,
To the innermost heart of their own land they are known
As the stars are known to the Night;

As the stars that shall be bright when we are dust,
Moving in marches upon the starry plain,
As the stars that are starry in the time of our darkness,
To the end, to the end, they remain.

Laurence Binyon

THE KINGFISHER

It was the Rainbow gave thee birth,
   And left thee all her lovely hues;
And, as her mother's name was Tears,
   So runs it in thy blood to choose
For haunts the lonely pools, and keep
In company with trees that weep.

Go you and, with such glorious hues,
   Live with proud peacocks in green parks;
On lawns as smooth as shining glass,
   Let every feather show its marks;   10
Get thee on boughs and clap thy wings
Before the windows of proud kings.

Nay, lovely Bird, thou art not vain;
   Thou hast no proud, ambitious mind;
I also love a quiet place
   That's green, away from all mankind;
A lonely pool, and let a tree
Sigh with her bosom over me.

W. H. Davies

THE ROAD

"Now where are ye goin'," ses I, "wid the shawl
An' cotton umbrella an' basket an' all?
Would ye not wait for McMullen's machine,
Wid that iligant instep befittin' a queen?
   Oh, you wid the wind-soft grey eye wid a wile in it,
   You wid the lip wid the troublesome smile in it,
   Sure, the road's wet, ivery rain-muddied mile in it – "
"Ah, the Saints 'll be kapin' me petticoats clean!"

"But," ses I, "would ye like it to meet Glancy's bull,
Or the tinks poachin' rabbits above Slieve-na-coul?   10
An' the ford at Kilmaddy is big wid the snows,
An' the whisht Little People that wear the green close,
   They'd run from the bog to be makin' a catch o' ye,
   The king o' them's wishful o' weddin' the match o' ye,
   'Twould be long, if they did, 'ere ye lifted the latch o' ye – "
"What fairy's to touch her that sings as she goes!"

"Ah, where are ye goin'," ses I, "wid the shawl,
An' the grey eyes a-dreamin' beneath it an' all?
The road by the mountain's a long one, depend
Ye'll be done for, alannah, ere reachin' the end;   20
   Ye'll be bate wid the wind on each back-breakin' bit on it,
   Wet wid the puddles and lamed with the grit on it, –
   Since lonesome ye're layin' yer delicut fit on it – "
"Sure whin's a road lonesome that's stepped wid a friend?"
   That's stepped wid a friend?
   Who did Bridgy intend?
Still 't was me that went wid her right on to the end!

                      Patrick R. Chalmers

ALL THAT'S PAST

Very old are the woods:
   And the buds that break
Out of the brier's boughs,
   When March winds wake,

So old with their beauty are –
   Oh, no man knows
Through what wild centuries
   Roves back the rose.

Very old are the brooks;
   And the rills that rise   10
Where snow sleeps cold beneath
   The azure skies
Sing such a history
   Of come and gone,
Their every drop is as wise
   As Solomon.

Very old are we men;
   Our dreams are tales
Told in dim Eden
   By Eve's nightingales;   20
We wake and whisper awhile,
   But, the day gone by,
Silence and sleep like fields
   Of Amaranth lie.

Walter de la Mare

THE DONKEY

When fishes flew and forests walked
   And figs grew upon thorn,
Some moment when the moon was blood
   Then surely I was born;

With monstrous head and sickening cry
   And ears like errant wings,
The devil's walking parody
   On all four-footed things.

The tattered outlaw of the earth,
   Of ancient crooked will;   10
Starve, scourge, deride me; I am dumb,
   I keep my secret still.

Fools! For I also had my hour;
   One far fierce hour and sweet:
There was a shout about my ears,
   And palms before my feet.

G. K. Chesterton

CHRISTMAS EVE AT SEA

A wind is rustling "south and soft,"
    Cooing a quiet country tune,
The calm sea sighs, and far aloft
    The sails are ghostly in the moon.

Unquiet ripples lisp and purr,
    A block there pipes and chirps i' the sheave,
The wheel-ropes jar, the reef-points stir
    Faintly – and it is Christmas Eve.

The hushed sea seems to hold her breath,
    And o'er the giddy, swaying spars,   10
Silent and excellent as Death,
    The dim blue skies are bright with stars.

Dear God – they shone in Palestine
    Like this, and yon pale moon serene
Looked down among the lowing kine
    On Mary and the Nazarene.

The angels called from deep to deep,
    The burning heavens felt the thrill,
Startling the flocks of silly sheep
    And lonely shepherds on the hill.   20

To-night beneath the dripping bows
    Where flashing bubbles burst and throng,
The bow-wash murmurs and sighs and soughs
    A message from the angels' song.

The moon goes nodding down the west,
    The drowsy helmsman strikes the bell;
Rex Judæorum natus est,
    I charge you, brothers, sing *Nowell, Nowell,*
Rex Judæorium natus est.

John Masefield

THE GIRL I LEFT BEHIND ME

She watched the blaze,
And so I said the thing I'd come to say,
Pondered for days.

Her lips moved slow,
And the wide eye she flashed on me
Was sudden as a blow.

She turned again,
Her hands clasping her knees, and did not speak
– She did not deign.

And I, poor gnome!   10
A chided cur crawls to a hole to hide!
. . . I toddled home!

          James Stephens

THE OLD SHIPS

I have seen old ships sail like swans asleep
Beyond the village which men still call Tyre,
With leaden age o'ercargoed, dipping deep
For Famagusta and the hidden sun
That rings black Cyprus with a lake of fire;
And all those ships were certainly so old
Who knows how oft with squat and noisy gun,
Questing brown slaves or Syrian oranges,
The pirate Genoese
Hell-raked them till they rolled   10
Blood, water, fruit and corpses up the hold.
But now through friendly seas they softly run,
Painted the mid-sea blue or shore-sea green,
Still patterned with the vine and grapes in gold.

But I have seen
Pointing her shapely shadows from the dawn
And image tumbled on a rose-swept bay,
A drowsy ship of some yet older day;
And, wonder's breath indrawn,

Thought I – who knows – who knows – but in that   20
    same
(Fished up beyond Æææ, patched up new
– Stern painted brighter blue –)
That talkative, bald-headed seaman came
(Twelve patient comrades sweating at the oar)
From Troy's doom-crimson shore,
And with great lies about his wooden horse
Set the crew laughing, and forgot his course.

It was so old a ship – who knows, who knows?
– And yet so beautiful, I watched in vain
To see the mast burst open with a rose,   30
And the whole deck put on its leaves again.

James Elroy Flecker

SEASCAPE

Over that morn hung heaviness, until,
Near sunless noon, we heard the ship's bell beating
A melancholy staccato on dead metal;
Saw the bare-footed watch come running aft;
Felt, far below, the sudden telegraph jangle
Its harsh metallic challenge, thrice repeated:
Stand to. Half-speed ahead. Slow. Stop her!
                              They stopped.
The plunging pistons sank like a stopped heart:
She held, she swayed, a bulk, a hollow carcass   10
Of blistered iron that the gray-green, waveless,
Unruffled tropic waters slapped languidly.
And, in that pause, a sinister whisper ran;
Burial at Sea! a Portuguese official . . . .
Poor fever-broken devil from Mozambique:
Came on half tight: the doctor calls it heat-stroke.
Why do they travel steerage? It's the exchange:
So many million *reis* to the pound!
What did he look like? No one ever saw him:
Took to his bunk, and drank and drank and died.   20
They're ready! Silence!
                    We clustered to the rail,
Curious and half-ashamed. The well-deck spread
A comfortable gulf of segregation

Between ourselves and death. *Burial at sea* . . . .
The master holds a black book at arm's length;
His droning voice comes for'ard: *This our brother* . . . .
We therefore commit his body to the deep
To be turned into corruption. . . . The bo's'n whispers
Hoarsely behind his hand: *Now, all together!*   30
The hatch-cover is tilted; a mummy of sailcloth
Well ballasted with iron shoots clear of the poop;
Falls, like a diving gannet. The green sea closes
Its burnished skin; the snaky swell smoothes over. . . .

While he, the man of the steerage, goes down, down,
Feet foremost, sliding swiftly down the dim water,
Swift to escape
Those plunging shapes with pale, empurpled bellies
That swirl and veer about him. He goes down
Unerringly, as though he knew the way   40
Through green, through gloom, to absolute watery darkness,
Where no weed sways nor curious fin quivers:
To the sad, sunless deeps where, endlessly,
A downward drift of death spreads its wan mantle
In the wave-moulded valleys that shall enfold him
Till the sea gives up its dead.

There shall he lie dispersed amid great riches:
Such gold, such arrogance, so many bold hearts!
All the sunken armadas pressed to powder
By weight of incredible seas! That mingled wrack   50
No living sun shall visit till the crust
Of earth be riven, or this rolling planet
Reel on its axis; till the moon-chained tides,
Unloosed, deliver up that white Atlantis
Whose naked peaks shall beach above the slaked
Thirst of Sahara, fringed by weedy tangles
Of Atlas's drowned cedars, frowning eastward
To where the sands of India lie cold,
And heaped Himalaya's a rib of coral,
Slowly uplifted, grain on grain. . . .   60
                              We dream
Too long! Another jangle of alarum
Stabs at the engines: *Slow. Half-speed. Full-speed!*
The great bearings rumble; the screw churns, frothing
Opaque water to downward-swelling plumes
Milky as wood-smoke. A shoal of flying-fish
Spurts out like animate spray. The warm breeze wakens;
And we pass on, forgetting,

Toward the solemn horizon of bronzed cumulus
That bounds our brooding sea, gathering gloom
That, when night falls, will dissipate in flaws
Of watery lightning, washing the hot sky,
Cleansing all hearts of heat and restlessness,
Until, with day, another blue be born.

Francis Brett Young

THE GREY SQUIRREL

Like a small grey
coffee-pot,
sits the squirrel.
He is not

all he should be,
kills by dozens
trees, and eats
his red-brown cousins.

The keeper, on the
other hand   10
, who shot him, is
a Christian, and

loves his enemies,
which shows
the squirrel was not
one of those.

Humbert Wolfe

THE SOLDIER

If I should die, think only this of me:
    That there's some corner of a foreign field
That is for ever England. There shall be
    In that rich earth a richer dust concealed;
A dust whom England bore, shaped, made aware,
    Gave, once, her flowers to love, her ways to roam,
A body of England's, breathing English air,
    Washed by the rivers, blest by suns of home.

44

And think, this heart, all evil shed away,
    A pulse in the eternal mind, no less   10
        Gives somewhere back the thoughts by England given;
Her sights and sounds; dreams happy as her day;
    And laughter, learnt of friends; and gentleness,
        In hearts at peace, under an English heaven.

Rupert Brooke

THE HOLLOW MEN

Mistah Kurtz – he dead
A penny for the Old Guy

I

We are the hollow men
We are the stuffed men
Leaning together
Headpiece filled with straw. Alas!
Our dried voices, when
We whisper together
Are quiet and meaningless
As wind in dry grass
Or rats' feet over broken glass
In our dry cellar   10

Shape without form, shade without colour,
Paralysed force, gesture without motion;

Those who have crossed
With direct eyes, to death's other Kingdom
Remember us – if at all – not as lost
Violent souls, but only
As the hollow men
The stuffed men.

II

Eyes I dare not meet in dreams
In death's dream kingdom   20
These do not appear:
There, the eyes are
Sunlight on a broken column

There, is a tree swinging
And voices are
In the wind's singing
More distant and more solemn
Than a fading star.

Let me be no nearer
In death's dream Kingdom   30
Let me also wear
Such deliberate disguises —
Rat's coat, crowskin, crossed staves
In a field
Behaving as the wind behaves
No nearer —

Not that final meeting
In the twilight kingdom.

III

This is the dead land
This is cactus land   40
Here the stone images
Are raised, here they receive
The supplication of a dead man's hand
Under the twinkle of a fading star.

Is it like this
In death's other kingdom?
Waking alone
At the hour when we are
Trembling with tenderness,
Lips that would kiss   50
Form prayers to broken stone.

IV

The eyes are not here
There are no eyes here
In this valley of dying stars
In this hollow valley
This broken jaw of our lost kingdoms

In this last of meeting places
We grope together
And avoid speech
Gathered on this beach of the tumid river   60

Sightless, unless
The eyes reappear
As the perpetual star
Multifoliate rose
Of death's twilight kingdom
The hope only
Of empty men.

V

Here we go round the prickly pear
Prickly pear prickly pear
Here we go round the prickly pear   70
At five o'clock in the morning.

Between the idea
And the reality
Between the motion
And the act
Falls the Shadow

        For Thine is the Kingdom

Between the conception
and the creation
Between the emotion   80
And the response
Falls the Shadow

        Life is very long

Between the desire
And the spasm
Between the potency
And the existence
Between the essence
And the descent
Falls the Shadow   90

        For Thine is the Kingdom

For Thine is
Life is
For Thine is the

This is the way the world ends
This is the way the world ends
This is the way the world ends
Not with a bang but a whimper.

        T. S. Eliot

CHORUS

from "The Rock"

The Eagle soars in the summit of Heaven,
The Hunter with his dogs pursues his circuit.
O perpetual revolution of configured stars,
O perpetual recurrence of determined seasons,
O world of spring and autumn, birth and dying!
The endless cycle of idea and action,
Endless invention, endless experiment,
Brings knowledge of motion, but not of stillness;
Knowledge of speech, but not of silence;
Knowledge of words, and ignorance of the Word.   10
All our knowledge brings us nearer to our ignorance,
All our ignorance brings us nearer to death,
But nearness to death no nearer to GOD.
Where is the Life we have lost in living?
Where is the wisdom we have lost in knowledge?
Where is the knowledge we have lost in information?
The cycles of Heaven in twenty centuries
Bring us farther from GOD and nearer to the Dust.
I journeyed to London, to the timekept City,
Where the River flows, with foreign flotations.   20
There I was told: we have too many churches,
And too few chop-houses. There I was told:
Let the vicars retire. Men do not need the Church
In the place where they work, but where they spend
    their Sundays.
In the City, we need no bells:
Let them waken the suburbs.
I journeyed to the suburbs, and there I was told:
We toil for six days, on the seventh we must motor
To Hindhead, or Maidenhead.
If the weather is foul we stay at home and read the   30
    papers.
In industrial districts, there I was told
Of economic laws.
In the pleasant countryside, there it seemed
That the country now is only fit for picnics.
And the Church does not seem to be wanted
In country or in suburb; and in the town
Only for important weddings.

T. S. Eliot

ANTHEM FOR DOOMED YOUTH

What passing-bells for these who die as cattle?
    Only the monstrous anger of the guns.
    Only the stuttering rifles' rapid rattle
Can patter out their hasty orisons.
No mockeries for them; no prayers nor bells,
    Nor any voice of mourning save the choirs, –
The shrill, demented choirs of wailing shells;
    And bugles calling for them from sad shires.

What candles may be held to speed them all?
    Not in the hands of boys, but in their eyes   10
Shall shine the holy glimmers of goodbyes.
    The pallor of girls' brows shall be their pall;
Their flowers the tenderness of patient minds,
And each slow dusk a drawing-down of blinds.

Wilfred Owen

THE FIGHT

One silver-white and one of scarlet hue,
Storm hornets humming in the wind of death,
Two aeroplanes were fighting in the blue
Above our town; and if I held my breath,
It was because my youth was in the Red
While in the White an unknown pilot flew –
And that the White had risen overhead.

From time to time the crackle of a gun
Far into flawless ether faintly railed,
And now, mosquito-thin, into the Sun,   10
And now like mating dragonflies they sailed:
And, when like eagles near the earth they drove,
The Red, still losing what the White had won,
The harder for each lost advantage strove.

So lovely lay the land – the towers and trees
Taking the seaward counsel of the stream:
The city seemed, above the far-off seas,
The crest and turret of a Jacob's dream,
And those two gun-birds in their frantic spire
At death-grips for its ultimate regime –   20
Less to be whirled by anger than desire.

Till (Glory!) from his chrysalis of steel
The Red flung wide the fatal fans of fire:
I saw the long flames ribboning, unreel,
And slow bitumen trawling from his pyre.
I knew the ecstasy, the fearful throes,
And the white phoenix from his scarlet sire
As silver in the Solitude he rose.

The towers and trees were lifted hymns of praise,
The city was a prayer, the land a nun: 30
The noonday azure strumming all its rays
Sang that a famous battle had been won,
As signing his white Cross, the very Sun,
The Solar Christ and captain of my days
Zoomed to the zenith; and his will was done.

Roy Campbell

IN HEAVEN, I SUPPOSE,
LIE DOWN TOGETHER

In heaven, I suppose, lie down together
Agonized Pilate and the boa-constrictor
That swallows anything: but we must seize
One horn or the other of our antitheses.
When I consider each independent star
Wearing its world of darkness like a fur
And rubbing shoulders with infinity,
I am content experience should be
More discontinuous than the points pricked
Out by the mazy course of a derelict,   10
Iceberg, or Flying Dutchman, and the heart
Stationary and passive as a chart.
In such star-frenzy I could boast, betwixt
My yester and my morrow self are fixed
All the birds carolling and all the seas
Groaning from Greenwich to the Antipodes.

But an eccentric hour may come, when systems
Not stars divide the dark; and then life's pistons
Pounding into their secret cylinder
Begin to tickle the most anchorite ear   20
With hints of mechanisms that include
The man. And once that rhythm arrests the blood,

50

Who would be satisfied his mind is no
Continent but an archipelago?
They are preposterous paladins and prance
From myth to myth, who take an Agag stance
Upon the needle points of here and now,
Where only angels ought to tread. Allow
One jointure feasible to man, one state
Squared with another – then he can integrate   30
A million selves and where disorder ruled
Straddle a chaos and beget a world.

Peals of the New Year once for me came tumbling
Out of the narrow night like clusters of humming-
Birds loosed from a black bag, and rose again
Irresponsibly to silence: but now I strain
To follow them and see for miles around
Men square or shrug their shoulders at the sound.
Then I remember the pure and granite hills
Where first I caught an ideal tone that stills,   40
Like the beloved's breath asleep, all din
Of earth at traffic: silence's first-born,
Carrying over each sensual ravine
To inform the seer and uniform the seen.
So from this ark, this closet of the brain,
The dove emerges and flies back again
With a Messiah sprig of certitude –
Promise of ground below the sprawling flood.

C. Day Lewis

WILL IT BE SO AGAIN?

Will it be so again
That the brave, the gifted are lost from view,
And empty, scheming men
Are left in peace their lunatic age to renew?
Will it be so again?

Must it be always so
That the best are chosen to fall and sleep
Like seeds, and we too slow
In claiming the earth they quicken, and the old
    usurpers reap
What they could not sow?   10

Will it be so again –
The jungle code and the hypocrite gesture?
A poppy wreath for the slain
And a cut-throat world for the living? that
    stale imposture
Played on us once again?

Will it be as before –
Peace, with no heart or mind to ensue it,
Guttering down to war
Like a libertine to his grave? We should not be
    surprised: we knew it
Happen before.   20

Shall it be so again?
Call not upon the glorious dead
To be your witnesses then.
The living alone can nail to their promise the
    ones who said
It shall not be so again.

C. Day Lewis

A SUBALTERN'S LOVE-SONG

Miss J. Hunter Dunn, Miss J. Hunter Dunn,
Furnish'd and burnish'd by Aldershot sun,
What strenuous singles we played after tea,
We in the tournament – you against me!

Love-thirty, love-forty, oh! weakness of joy,
The speed of a swallow, the grace of a boy,
With carefullest carelessness, gaily you won,
I am weak from your loveliness, Joan Hunter Dunn.

Miss Joan Hunter Dunn, Miss Joan Hunter Dunn,
How mad I am, sad I am, glad that you won.   10
The warm-handled racket is back in its press,
But my shock-headed victor, she loves me no less.

Her father's euonymus shines as we walk,
And swing past the summer-house, buried in talk,
And cool the verandah that welcomes us in
To the six-o'clock news and a lime-juice and gin.

The scent of the conifers, sound of the bath,
The view from my bedroom of moss-dappled path,
As I struggle with double-end evening tie,
For we dance at the Golf Club, my victor and I.   20

On the floor of her bedroom lie blazer and shorts
And the cream-coloured walls are be-trophied with sports,
And westering, questioning settles the sun
On your low-leaded window, Miss Joan Hunter Dunn.

The Hillman is waiting, the light's in the hall,
The pictures of Egypt are bright on the wall,
My sweet, I am standing beside the oak stair
And there on the landing's the light on your hair.

By roads "not adopted," by woodlanded ways,
She drove to the club in the late summer haze,   30
Into nine-o'clock Camberley, heavy with bells
And mushroomy, pine-woody, evergreen smells.

Miss Joan Hunter Dunn, Miss Joan Hunter Dunn,
I can hear from the car-park the dance has begun.
Oh! full Surrey twilight! importunate band!
Oh! strongly adorable tennis-girl's hand!

Around us are Rovers and Austins afar,
Above us, the intimate roof of the car,
And here on my right is the girl of my choice,
With the tilt of her nose and the chime of her voice,   40

And the scent of her wrap, and the words never said,
And the ominous, ominous dancing ahead.
We sat in the car-park till twenty to one
And now I'm engaged to Miss Joan Hunter Dunn.

John Betjeman

THE UNKNOWN CITIZEN

*(To JS/07/M/378 – This Marble Monument
Is Erected by the State)*

He was found by the Bureau of Statistics to be
One against whom there was no official complaint,
And all the reports on his conduct agree
That, in the modern sense of an old-fashioned word, he
    was a saint,
For in everything he did he served the Greater Community.
Except for the War till the day he retired
He worked in a factory and never got fired,
But satisfied his employers, Fudge Motors Inc.
Yet he wasn't a scab or odd in his views,
For his Union reports that he paid his dues,   10
(Our report on his Union shows it was sound)
And our Social Psychology workers found
That he was popular with his mates and liked a drink.
The Press are convinced that he bought a paper every day
And that his reactions to advertisements were normal in
    every way.
Policies taken out in his name prove that he was fully
    insured,
And his Health-card shows he was once in hospital but
    left it cured.
Both Producers Research and High-Grade Living declare
He was fully sensible to the advantages of the Instalment
    Plan
And had everything necessary to the Modern Man,   20
A phonograph, a radio, a car and a frigidaire.
Our researchers into Public Opinion are content
That he held the proper opinions for the time of year;
When there was peace, he was for peace; when there was
    war, he went.
He was married and added five children to the population,
Which our Eugenist says was the right number for a parent
    of his generation,
And our teachers report that he never interfered with their
    education.
Was he free? Was he happy? The question is absurd:
Had anything been wrong, we should certainly have heard.

W. H. Auden

PRAYER BEFORE BIRTH

I am not yet born; O hear me.
Let not the bloodsucking bat or the rat or the stoat or the
    clubfooted ghoul come near me.

I am not yet born; console me.
I fear that the human race may with tall walls wall me,
    with strong drugs dope me, with wise lies lure me,
        on black racks rack me, in blood-baths roll me.

I am not yet born; provide me
With water to dandle me, grass to grow for me, trees to talk
    to me, sky to sing to me, birds and a white light   10
        in the back of my mind to guide me.

I am not yet born; forgive me
For the sins that in me the world shall commit, my words
    when they speak me, my thoughts when they think me,
        my treason engendered by traitors beyond me,
            my life when they murder by means of my
                hands, my death when they live me.

I am not yet born; rehearse me
In the parts I must play and the cues I must take when
    old men lecture me, bureaucrats hector me, mountains   20
        frown at me, lovers laugh at me, the white
            waves call me to folly and the desert calls
                me to doom and the beggar refuses
                    my gift and my children curse me.

I am not yet born; O hear me,
Let not the man who is beast or who thinks he is God
    come near me.

I am not yet born; O fill me
With strength against those who would freeze my
    humanity, would dragoon me into a lethal automaton,   30
        would make me a cog in a machine, a thing with
            one face, a thing, and against all those
                who would dissipate my entirety, would
                    blow me like thistledown hither and
                      thither or hither and thither
                        like water held in the
                        hands would spill me
Let them not make me a stone and let them not spill me.
Otherwise kill me.

                                        Louis MacNeice

THE INVADING SPRING

Man has fenced the wilderness back in the hills;
Tamed in the town he walks on concrete blocks;
And in the park his heart with pleasure fills –
But not at Wordsworth's school-book daffodils.
No, his delight is catching up with clocks
And turning knobs and pressing Button A –
The train is due; there's half a minute to go
But the lift's gone down and the escalator's slow –
Praise God for the Underground this lark-song day!

Breathing, yet dead, his life is caged with steel –   10
Wire, wheel, and cable – automatic aids
To living – he exists but cannot feel
The slow barbaric beauty that invades
A world at Spring. He moves in crowds and queues
And reads the *Morning Star* and the *Evening News*
But cannot read the sky though April beats
A golden fanfare down the dusty streets
And breathes a green breath through the petrol fumes.

Yet a third-floor room is powerless to deny
The feel of leaves, the pollen-smell behind   20
New flowered cretonnes where a rebel wind
Is strong and blue with ranging through the sky.
And though the files of his mind are entered up
Like office ledgers, unknowing he holds the cup
Brimmed with the light of moons beyond his reach.
The street is thronged with more than he can know –
The Invisibles who know him; without speech
They call him; without form they come and go
And catch him by the sleeve until the slow
Unwilling flesh is beckoned from its task.   30
Released, he finds the vital stream that spills
A primrose light on sullen window-sills.

Phoebe Hesketh

THE HAND THAT SIGNED
THE PAPER FELLED A CITY

The hand that signed the paper felled a city;
Five sovereign fingers taxed the breath,
Doubled the globe of dead and halved a country;
These five kings did a king to death.

The mighty hand leads to a sloping shoulder,
The finger joints are cramped with chalk;
A goose's quill has put an end to murder
That put an end to talk.

The hand that signed the treaty bred a fever,
And famine grew, and locusts came;   10
Great is the hand that holds dominion over
Man by a scribbled name.

The five kings count the dead but do not soften
The crusted wound nor pat the brow;
A hand rules pity as a hand rules heaven;
Hands have no tears to flow.

Dylan Thomas

A NOISELESS, PATIENT SPIDER

A noiseless, patient spider,
I mark'd, where, on a little promontory, it stood, isolated;
Mark'd how, to explore the vacant, vast surrounding,
It launch'd forth filament, filament, filament, out of itself;
Ever unreeling them, ever tirelessly speeding them.

And you, O my Soul, where you stand,
Surrounded, detached, in measureless oceans of space,
Ceaselessly musing, venturing, throwing, – seeking the spheres,
   to connect them;
Till the bridge you will need, be form'd, till the ductile anchor
   hold;
Till the gossamer thread you fling, catch somewhere, O my Soul. 10

Walt Whitman

THE SNAKE

A narrow fellow in the grass
Occasionally rides;
You may have met him, – did you not,
His notice sudden is.

The grass divides as with a comb,
A spotted shaft is seen;
And then it closes at your feet
And opens farther on.

He likes a boggy acre,
A floor too cool for corn.   10
Yet when a child, and barefoot,
I more than once, at morn,

Have passed, I thought, a whip-lash
Unbraiding in the sun, –
When, stooping to secure it,
It wrinkled, and was gone.

Several of nature's people
I know, and they know me;
I feel for them a transport
Of cordiality;   20

But never met this fellow,
Attended or alone,
Without a tighter breathing,
And zero at the bone.

Emily Dickinson

WONDER IS NOT PRECISELY KNOWING

Wonder is not precisely knowing,
And not precisely knowing not;
A beautiful but bleak condition
He has not lived who has not felt.

Suspense is his maturer sister;
Whether adult delight is pain
Or of itself a new misgiving –
This is the gnat that mangles men.

Emily Dickinson

BECAUSE I COULD NOT STOP FOR DEATH

Because I could not stop for Death,
He kindly stopped for me;
The carriage held but just ourselves
And Immortality.

We slowly drove, he knew no haste,
And I had put away
My labour, and my leisure too,
For his civility.

We passed the school where children played
At wrestling in a ring;   10
We passed the fields of gazing grain,
We passed the setting sun.

We paused before a house that seemed
A swelling of the ground;
The roof was scarcely visible,
The cornice but a mound.

Since then 'tis centuries; but each
Feels shorter than the day
I first surmised the horses' heads
Were toward eternity.   20

Emily Dickinson

RICHARD CORY

Whenever Richard Cory went down town,
    We people on the pavement looked at him:
He was a gentleman from sole to crown,
    Clean favoured, and imperially slim.

And he was always quietly arrayed,
    And he was always human when he talked;
But still he fluttered pulses when he said,
    "Good-morning," and he glittered when he walked.

And he was rich – yes, richer than a king –
    And admirably schooled in every grace: 10
In fine, we thought that he was everything
    To make us wish that we were in his place.

So on we worked, and waited for the light,
    And went without the meat, and cursed the bread;
And Richard Cory, one calm summer night,
    Went home and put a bullet through his head.

Edwin Arlington Robinson

MADONNA OF THE EVENING FLOWERS

All day I have been working,
Now I am tired.
I call: "Where are you?"
But there is only the oak tree rustling in the wind.
The house is very quiet,
The sun shines in on your books,
On your scissors and thimble just put down,
But you are not there.

Suddenly I am lonely:
Where are you? 10
I go about searching.
Then I see you,
Standing under a spire of pale blue larkspur,
With a basket of roses on your arm.
You are cool, like silver,
And you smile.

I think the Canterbury bells are playing little tunes,
You tell me that the peonies need spraying,
That the columbines have overrun all bounds,
That the pyrus japonica should be cut back and rounded. 20
You tell me these things.
But I look at you, heart of silver,
White heart-flame of polished silver,
Burning beneath the blue steeples of the larkspur,
And I long to kneel instantly at your feet,
While all about us peal the loud, sweet *Te Deums* of the
  Canterbury bells.

Amy Lowell

THE ROAD NOT TAKEN

Two roads diverged in a yellow wood,
And sorry I could not travel both
And be one traveller, long I stood
And I looked down one as far as I could
To where it bent in the undergrowth;

Then took the other, as just as fair,
And having perhaps the better claim,
Because it was grassy and wanted wear;
Though as for that the passing there
Had worn them really about the same.   10

And both that morning equally lay
In leaves no step had trodden black.
Oh, I kept the first for another day!
Yet knowing how way leads on to way,
I doubted if I should ever come back.

I shall be telling this with a sigh
Somewhere ages and ages hence:
Two roads diverged in a wood, and I –
I took the one less travelled by,
And that has made all the difference.   20

Robert Frost

THE WOOD-PILE

Out walking in the frozen swamp one grey day,
I paused and said, "I will turn back from here.
No, I will go on farther – and we shall see."
The hard snow held me, save where now and then
One foot went through. The view was all in lines
Straight up and down of tall slim trees
Too much alike to mark or name a place by
So as to say for certain I was here
Or somewhere else: I was just far from home.
A small bird flew before me. He was careful   10
To put a tree between us when he lighted,
And say no word to tell me who he was
Who was so foolish as to think what *he* thought.
He thought that I was after him for a feather –
The white one in his tail; like one who takes
Everything said as personal to himself.
One flight out sideways would have undeceived him.
And then there was a pile of wood for which
I forgot him and let his little fear
Carry him off the way I might have gone,   20
Without so much as wishing him good-night.
He went behind it to make his last stand.

It was a cord of maple, cut and split
And piled – and measured, four by four by eight.
And not another like it could I see.
No runner tracks in this year's snow looped near it.
And it was older sure than this year's cutting,
Or even last year's or the year's before.
The wood was grey and the bark warping off it
And the pile somewhat sunken. Clematis   30
Had wound strings round and round it like a bundle.
What held it though on one side was a tree
Still growing, and on one a stake and prop,
These latter about to fall. I thought that only
Someone who lived in turning to fresh tasks
Could so forget his handiwork on which
He spent himself, the labour of his axe,
And leave it there far from a useful fireplace
To warm the frozen swamp as best it could
With the slow smokeless burning of decay.   40

Robert Frost

THE WIDOW'S LAMENT IN SPRINGTIME

Sorrow in my own yard
where the new grass
flames as it has flamed
often before but not
with the cold fire
that closes round me this year.
Thirtyfive years
I lived with my husband.
The plumtree is white today
with masses of flowers.   10
Masses of flowers
loaded the cherry branches
and colour some bushes
yellow and some red
but the grief in my heart
is stronger than they
for though they were my joy
formerly, today I notice them
and turned away forgetting.
Today my son told me   20
that in the meadows,

at the edge of the heavy woods
in the distance, he saw
trees of white flowers.
I feel that I would like
to go there
and fall into those flowers
and sink into the marsh near them.

William Carlos Williams

A GRAVE

Man looking into the sea
taking the view from those who have as much right to it as you have
    to it yourself,
it is human nature to stand in the middle of a thing,
but you cannot stand in the middle of this;
the sea has nothing to give but a well-excavated grave.
The firs stand in a procession, each with an emerald turkey-foot at
    the top,
reserved as their contours, saying nothing;
repression, however, is not the most obvious characteristic of the sea;
the sea is a collector, quick to return a rapacious look.
There are others besides you who have worn that look—   10
whose expression is no longer a protest; the fish no longer investigate
    them
for their bones have not lasted:
men lower nets, unconscious of the fact that they are desecrating a
    grave,
and row quickly away—the blades of the oars
moving together like the feet of water-spiders as if there were no
    such thing as death.
The wrinkles progress among themselves in a phalanx—beautiful
    under networks of foam,
and fade breathlessly while the sea rustles in and out of the seaweed;
the birds swim through the air at top speed, emitting cat-calls as
    heretofore—
the tortoise-shell scourges about the feet of the cliffs, in motion
    beneath them;
and the ocean, under the pulsation of lighthouses and noise of
    bell-buoys,   20

advances as usual, looking as if it were not that ocean in which
    dropped things are bound to sink–
into which if they turn and twist, it is neither with volition nor
    consciousness.

Marianne Moore

BLUE GIRLS

Twirling your blue skirts, travelling the sward
Under the towers of your seminary,
Go listen to your teachers old and contrary
Without believing a word.

Tie the white fillets then about your lustrous hair
And think no more of what will come to pass
Than bluebirds that go walking on the grass
And chattering on the air.

Practise your beauty, blue girls, before it fail;
And I will cry with my loud lips and publish   10
Beauty which all our power shall never establish,
It is so frail.

For I could tell you a story which is true:
I know a lady with a terrible tongue,
Blear eyes fallen from blue,
All her perfections tarnished – yet it is not long
Since she was lovelier than any of you.

John Crowe Ransom

ALL LOVELY THINGS

All lovely things will have an ending,
    All lovely things will fade and die,
And youth, that's now so bravely spending,
    Will beg a penny by and by.

Fine ladies all are soon forgotten,
    And goldenrod is dust when dead,
The sweetest flesh and flowers are rotten
    And cobwebs tent the brightest head.

Come back, true love! Sweet youth, return! –
    But time goes on, and will, unheeding,   10
Though hands will reach, and eyes will yearn,
    And the wild days set true hearts bleeding.

Come back, true love! Sweet youth, remain! –
    But goldenrod and daisies wither,
And over them blows autumn rain,
    They pass, they pass, and know not whither.

Conrad Aiken

SAY WHAT YOU WILL

Say what you will, and scratch my heart to find
The roots of last year's roses in my breast;
I am as surely riper in my mind
As if the fruit stood in the stalls confessed.
Laugh at the unshed leaf, say what you will,
Call me in all things what I was before,
A flutterer in the wind, a woman still;
I tell you I am what I was and more.
My branches weigh me down, frost cleans the air,
My sky is black with small birds bearing south;   10
Say what you will, confuse me with fine care,
Put by my word as but an April truth –
Autumn is no less on me than a rose
Hugs the brown bough and sighs before it goes.

Edna St. Vincent Millay

WITH AGE WISDOM

At twenty, stooping round about,
I thought the world a miserable place,
Truth a trick, faith in doubt,
Little beauty, less grace.

Now at sixty what I see,
Although the world is worse by far
Stops my heart in ecstasy.
God, the wonders that there are!

Archibald MacLeish

somewhere i have never travelled, gladly beyond
any experience, your eyes have their silence:
in your most frail gesture are things which enclose me,
or which i cannot touch because they are too near

your slightest look easily will unclose me
though i have closed myself as fingers,
you open always petal by petal myself as Spring opens
(touching skilfully, mysteriously) her first rose

or if your wish be to close me, i and
my life will shut very beautifully, suddenly,   10
as when the heart of this flower imagines
the snow carefully everywhere descending;

nothing which we are to perceive in this world equals
the power of your intense fragility: whose texture
compels me with the colour of its countries,
rendering death and forever with each breathing

(i do not know what it is about you that closes
and opens; only something in me understands
the voice of your eyes is deeper than all roses)
nobody, not even the rain, has such small hands   20

E. E. Cummings

THE LAST DAYS OF ALICE

Alice grown lazy, mammoth but not fat,
Declines upon her lost and twilight age,
Above in the dozing leaves the grinning cat
Quivers forever with his abstract rage;

Whatever light swayed on the perilous gate
Forever sways, nor will the arching grass
Caught when the world clattered undulate
In the deep suspension of the looking-glass.

Bright Alice! always pondering to gloze
The spoiled cruelty she had meant to say   10
Gazes learnedly down her airy nose
At nothing, nothing thinking all the day:

67

Turned absent-minded by infinity
She cannot move unless her double move,
The All-Alice of the world's entity
Smashed in the anger of her hopeless love,

Love for herself who as an earthly twain
Pouted to join her two in a sweet one:
No more the second lips to kiss in vain
The first she broke, plunged through the glass alone – 20

Alone to the weight of impassivity
Incest of spirit, theorem of desire
Without will as chalky cliffs by the sea
Empty as the bodiless flesh of fire;

All space that heaven is a dayless night
A nightless day driven by perfect lust
For vacancy, in which her bored eyesight
Stares at the drowsy cubes of human dust.

We, too, back to the world shall never pass
Through the shattered door, a dumb shade-harried   30
    crowd,
Being all infinite, function, depth and mass
Without figure; a mathematical shroud

Hurled at the air – blessèd without sin!
O God of our flesh, return us to Your wrath
Let us be evil could we enter in
Your grace, and falter on the stony path!

Allen Tate

THE GOAL OF
INTELLECTUAL MAN

The goal of intellectual man
Striving to do what he can
To bring down out of uncreated light
Illumination to our night

Is not possession of the fire
Annihilation of his own desire
To the source a secret soaring
And all his self outpouring

Nor is it an imageless place
Wherein there is no human face   10
Nor laws, nor hierarchies, nor dooms
And only the cold weight of the tomb

But it is human love, love
Concrete, specific,'in a natural move
Gathering goodness, it is free
In the blood as in the mind's harmony,

It is love discoverable here
Difficult, dangerous, pure, clear,
The truth of the positive hour
Composing all of human power.   20

Richard Eberhart

THE DEATH OF THE
BALL TURRET GUNNER

From my mother's sleep I fell into the State,
And I hunched in its belly till my wet fur froze.
Six miles from earth, loosed from its dream of life,
I woke to black flak and the nightmare fighters.
When I died they washed me out of the turret with a hose.

Randall Jarrell

THE TRUTH

When I was four my father went to Scotland.
They *said* he went to Scotland.

When I woke up I think I thought that I was dreaming –
I was so little then that I thought dreams
Are in the room with you, like the cinema.
That's why you don't dream when it's still light –
They pull the shades down when it is, so you can sleep.
I thought that then, but that's not right.
Really it's in your head.

And it was light then – light at *night*.   10
I heard Stalky bark outside.
But really it was Mother crying –
She coughed so hard she cried.
She kept shaking Sister,
She shook her and shook her.
I thought Sister had had her nightmare.
But he wasn't barking, he had died.
There was dirt all over Sister.
It was all streaks, like mud. I cried.
She didn't, but she was older.   20
                              I thought she didn't
Because she was older, I thought Stalky had just gone.
I got *everything* wrong.
I didn't get one single thing right.
It seems to me that I'd have thought
It didn't happen, like a dream,
Except that it was light. At night.
They burnt our house down, they burnt down London.

Next day my mother cried all day, and after that
She said to me when she would come to see me: 30
"Your father has gone away to Scotland.
He will be back after the war."

The war then was different from the war now.
The war now is *nothing*.

I used to live in London till they burnt it.
What was it like? It was just like here.
No, that's the truth.
My mother would come here, some, but she would cry.
She said to Miss Elise, "He's not himself";
She said, "Don't you love me any more at all?"   40
I was *my*self.
Finally she wouldn't come at all.
She never said one thing my father said, or Sister.
Sometimes she did,
Sometimes she was the same, but that was when I
         dreamed it.
I could tell I was dreaming, she was just the same.

That Christmas she bought me a toy dog.

I asked her what was its name, and when she didn't know
I asked her over, and when she didn't know
I said, "You're not my mother, you're not my mother.   50
She *hasn't* gone to Scotland, she is dead!"
And she said, "Yes, he's dead, he's dead!"
And cried and cried; she *was* my mother,
She put her arms around me and we cried.

Randall Jarrell

THE DRUNKEN FISHERMAN

Wallowing in this bloody sty,
I cast for fish that pleased my eye
(Truly Jehovah's bow suspends
No pots of gold to weight its ends);
Only the blood-mouthed rainbow trout
Rose to my bait. They flopped about
My canvas creel until the moth
Corrupted its unstable cloth.

A calendar to tell the day;
A handkerchief to wave away   10
The gnats; a couch unstuffed with storm
Pouching a bottle in one arm;
A whiskey bottle full of worms;
And bedroom slacks: are these fit terms
To mete the worm whose molten rage
Boils in the belly of old age?

Once fishing was a rabbit's foot –
O wind blow cold, O wind blow hot,
Let suns stay in or suns step out:
Life danced a jig on the sperm-whale's spout –   20
The fisher's fluent and obscene
Catches kept his conscience clean.
Children, the raging memory drools
Over the glory of past pools.

Now the hot river, ebbing, hauls
Its bloody waters into holes;
A grain of sand inside my shoe
Mimics the moon that might undo

71

Man and Creation too; remorse
Stinking, has puddled up its source;   30
Here tantrums thrash to a whale's rage.
This is the pot-hole of old age.

Is there no way to cast my hook
Out of this dynamited brook?
The Fisher's sons must cast about
When shallow waters peter out.
I will catch Christ with a greased worm,
And when the Prince of Darkness stalks
My bloodstream to its Stygian term . . .
On water the Man-Fisher walks.   40

Robert Lowell

ELEGY JUST IN CASE

Here lie Ciardi's pearly bones
In their ripe organic mess.
Jungle blown, his chromosomes
Breed to a new address.

Was it bullets or a wind
Or a rip-cord fouled on Chance?
Artifacts the natives find
Decorate them when they dance.

Here lies the sgt.'s mortal wreck
Lily spiked and termite kissed,   10
Spiders pendant from his neck
And a beetle on his wrist.

Bring the tic and southern flies
Where the land crabs run unmourning
Through a night of jungle skies
To a climeless morning.

And bring the chalked eraser here
Fresh from rubbing out his name.
Burn the crew-board for a bier.
(Also Colonel what's-his-name.)   20

Let no dice be stored and still.
Let no poker deck be torn.
But pour the smuggled rye until
The barracks threshold is outworn.

File the papers, pack the clothes,
Send the coded word through air –
"We regret and no one knows
Where the sgt. goes from here."

"Missing as of inst. oblige,
Deepest sorrow and remain—"   30
Shall I grin at persiflage?
Could I have my skin again

Would I choose a business form
Stilted mute as a giraffe,
Or a pinstripe unicorn
On a cashier's epitaph?

Darling, darling, just in case
Rivets fail or engines burn,
I forget the time and place
But your flesh was sweet to learn.   40

Swift and single as a shark
I have seen you churn my sleep;
Now if beetles hunt my dark
What will beetles find to keep?

Fractured meat and open bone –
Nothing single or surprised.
Fragments of a written stone,
Undeciphered but surmised.

John Ciardi

EGO

When I was on Night Line,
flying my hands to park
a big-bird B-29,
I used to command the dark:
four engines were mine

to jazz; I was ground-crew,
an unfledged pfc,
but when I waved planes through
that flight line in Tennessee,
my yonder was wild blue.   10

Warming up, I was hot
on the throttle, logging an hour
of combat, I was the pilot
who rogered the tower.
I used to take off a lot.

With a flat-hat for furlough
and tin wings to sleep on,
I fueled my high-octane ego:
I buzzed, I landed my jeep on
the ramp, I flew low.   20

When a cross-country hop
let down, I was the big deal
who signaled big wheels to stop.
That's how I used to feel.
I used to get all revved up.

Philip Booth

THE POTATO HARVEST

A high bare field, brown from the plough, and borne
   Aslant from sunset; amber wastes of sky
   Washing the ridge; a clamour of crows that fly
In from the wide flats where the spent tides mourn
To yon their rocking roosts in pines wind-torn;
   A line of grey snake-fence, that zigzags by
   A pond, and cattle; from the homestead nigh
The long deep summonings of the supper horn.

Black on the ridge, against that lonely flush,
   A cart, and stoop-necked oxen; ranged beside   10
   Some barrels; and the day-worn harvest-folk,
Here emptying their baskets, jar the hush
   With hollow thunders. Down the dusk hillside
   Lumbers the wain; and day fades out like smoke.

Charles G. D. Roberts

A JANUARY MORNING

The glittering roofs are still with frost; each worn
Black chimney builds into the quiet sky
Its curling pile to crumble silently.
Far out to westward on the edge of morn,
The slender misty city towers up-borne
Glimmer faint rose against the pallid blue;
And yonder on those northern hills, the hue
Of amethyst, hang fleeces dull as horn.
And here behind me come the woodmen's sleighs
With shouts and clamorous squeakings; might and main 10
Up the steep slope the horses stamp and strain,
Urged on by hoarse-tongued drivers – cheeks ablaze,
Iced beards and frozen eyelids – team by team,
With frost-fringed flanks, and nostrils jetting steam.

Archibald Lampman

THE LARGEST LIFE

There is a beauty at the goal of life,
A beauty growing since the world began,
Through every age and race, through lapse and strife
Till the great human soul complete her span.
Beneath the waves of storm that lash and burn,
The currents of blind passion that appal,
To listen and keep watch till we discern
The tide of sovereign truth that guides it all;
So to address our spirits to the height,
And so attune them to the valiant whole,   10
That the great light be clearer for our light,
And the great soul the stronger for our soul:
To have done this is to have lived, though fame
Remember us with no familiar name.

Archibald Lampman

THE DREAMER

Whence came the sweet insurgence of the Spring
That loosed the wild bird songs, the willow buds,
The twilight chorus in the marsh, and shone
Within the visionary soul of Man? . . .
When we behold in August on a day
The goldenrod upon a thousand trails,
The asters in blue drifts through clearings wild,
And every roadside gay with meadow rue –
The poet's recompense and traveller's joy –
When, thrilled by beauty passing thought, we sense 10
That harmony which is the artist's peace
And presage of creation, then we know
One walked with love among the misty hills
In a grey cloak of rain, and dreamed a dream.

Bliss Carman

A SUMMER STORM

Last night a storm fell on the world
    From heights of drouth and heat,
The surly clouds for weeks were furled,
    The air could only sway and beat.

The beetles clattered at the blind,
    The hawks fell twanging from the sky,
The west unrolled a feathery wind,
    And the night fell sullenly.

The storm leaped roaring from its lair,
    Like the shadow of doom,   10
The poignard lightning searched the air,
    The thunder ripped the shattered gloom.

The rain came down with a roar like fire,
    Full-voiced and clamorous and deep,
The weary world had its heart's desire,
    And fell asleep.

Duncan Campbell Scott

PÈRE LALEMANT

I lift the Lord on high,
Under the murmuring hemlock boughs, and see
The small birds of the forest lingering by
And making melody.
These are mine acolytes and these my choir,
And this mine altar in the cool green shade,
Where the wild soft-eyed does draw nigh
Wondering, as in the byre
Of Bethlehem the oxen heard Thy cry
And saw Thee, unafraid.   10

My boatmen sit apart,
Wolf-eyed, wolf-sinewed, stiller than the trees.
Help me, O Lord, for very slow of heart
And hard of faith are these.
Cruel are they, yet Thy children. Foul are they.
Yet wert Thou born to save them utterly.

Then make me as I pray
Just to their hates, kind to their sorrows, wise
After their speech, and strong before their free
Indomitable eyes.   20

Do the French lilies reign
Over Mont Royal and Stadacona still?
Up the St. Lawrence comes the spring again,
Crowning each southward hill
And blossoming pool with beauty, while I roam
Far from the perilous folds that are my home,
There where we built St. Ignace for our needs,
Shaped the rough roof-tree, turned the first sweet sod,
St. Ignace, and St. Louis, little beads
On the rosary of God.   30

Pines shall Thy pillars be,
Fairer than those Sidonian cedars brought
By Hiram out of Tyre, and each birch-tree
Shines like a holy thought.
But come no worshippers; shall I confess,
St. Francis-like, the birds of the wilderness?
O, with Thy love my lonely head uphold,
A wandering shepherd I, who hath no sheep;
A wandering soul, who hath no scrip, nor gold,
Nor anywhere to sleep.   40

My hour of rest is done;
On the smooth ripple lifts the long canoe;
The hemlocks murmur sadly as the sun
Slants his dim arrows through.
Whither I go I know not, nor the way,
Dark with strange passions, vexed with heathen charms,
Holding I know not what of life or death;
Only be Thou beside me day by day,
Thy rod my guide and comfort, underneath
Thy everlasting arms.

                                    Marjorie Pickthall

THE PRIZE CAT

Pure blood domestic, guaranteed,
Soft-mannered, musical in purr,
The ribbon had declared the breed,
Gentility was in the fur.

Such feline culture in the gads,
No anger ever arched her back –
What distance since those velvet pads
Departed from the leopard's track!

And when I mused how Time had thinned
The jungle strains within the cells,   10
How human hands had disciplined
Those prowling optic parallels;

I saw the generations pass
Along the reflex of a spring,
A bird had rustled in the grass,
The tab had caught it on the wing:

Behind the leap so furtive-wild
Was such ignition in the gleam,
I thought an Abyssinian child
Had cried out in the whitethroat's scream.   20

E. J. Pratt

EROSION

It took the sea a thousand years,
A thousand years to trace
The granite features of this cliff,
In crag and scarp and base.

It took the sea an hour one night,
An hour of storm to place
The sculpture of these granite seams
Upon a woman's face.

E. J. Pratt

79

TORONTO CROSSING

The well-drest woman in the costly car
Stares at the busfolk waiting in the wet,
The soldiers thumbing rides; her cigarette
Impeccably finds where lighter and ashtray are.

The well-drest car round the costly woman purrs
At its quiver of light shopping, its corner full
Of the new books, its driver a furred fruit on wool;
The purr the car purrs is both its and hers.

If she were those people waiting, she wouldn't, she'd walk.
This has been an unusually exhausting day.   10
The lights have been against her all the way.
She flicks her unfinished smoke onto the sidewalk

As the lights change and the changed eyes of the starer
Release the crowd for a double glance at the mirror.

Robert Finch

ADMONITION FOR SPRING

Look away now from the high lonesome hills
So hard on the hard sky since the swift shower;
See where among the restless daffodils
The hyacinth sets his melancholy tower.

Draw in your heart from vain adventurings;
Float slowly, swimmer, slowly drawing breath.
See, in this wild green foam of growing things
The heavy hyacinth remembering death.

L. A. Mackay

HARVEST

There is a quietness in autumn fields
To soothe the driven spirit, for it seems
These dowered lands, golden with ample yields,
Lie resting, having filled their April dreams.
These have upborne, like men, the bitter frost,
The furious lash of heaven, and in need
Panted for dark warm rain, thought summer lost,
Yet to fruition at last have borne their seed.
   So it may be with me – despite all stress,
All strange uncertain fears and curious pain,   10
Long winters of the heart, lost happiness,
I shall complete this mortal year, and gain
Some golden still September of the soul
Whose harvest-tide brings ripeness of the whole.

Nathaniel Benson

CANADA: CASE HISTORY

This is the case of a high-school land,
deadset in adolescence,
loud treble laughs and sudden fists,
bright cheeks, the gangling presence.
This boy is wonderful at sports
and physically quite healthy;
he's taken to church on Sunday still
and keeps his prurience stealthy.
He doesn't like books except about bears,
collects new coins and model planes,   10
and never refuses a dare.
His Uncle spoils him with candy, of course,
yet shouts him down when he talks at table.
You will note he's got some of his French mother's looks,
though he's not so witty and no more stable.
He's really much more like his father and yet
if you say so he'll pull a great face.
He wants to be different from everyone else
and daydreams of winning the global race.

Parents unmarried and living abroad,   20
relatives keen to bag the estate,
schizophrenia not excluded,
will he learn to grow up before it's too late?

Earle Birney

SLUG IN WOODS

For eyes he waves greentipped
taut horns of slime. They dipped,
hours back, across a reef,
a salmonberry leaf.
Then strained to grope past fin
of spruce. Now eyes suck in
as through the hemlock butts
of his day's ledge there cuts
a vixen chipmunk. Stilled
is he – green mucus chilled,   10
or blotched and soapy stone,
pinguid in moss, alone.
Hours on, he will resume
his silver scrawl, illume
his palimpsest, emboss
his diver's line across
that waving green illim-
itable seafloor. Slim
young jay his sudden shark;
the wrecks he skirts are dark   20
and fungussed firlogs, whom
spirea sprays emplume,
encoral. Dew his shell,
while mounting boles foretell
of isles in dappled air
fathoms above his care.
Azygous muted life,
himself his viscid wife,
foodward he noses cold beneath his sea.
So spends a summer's jasper century.   30

Earle Birney

THE PARADOX

In the high blaze of noon my heart grew sick
To hear the tapping of the blind man's stick;
– Where the gold gorse beggars its treasury,
To pass and never see!
To walk and never look upon his way . . .
For him there is no day.
But in a moonless darkness muffled deep
With fog, his tapping signalled through my sleep;
I heard him pass, secure as would have done
A seeing man in sun   10
Treading erectly down a road of light . . .
For him there is no night.

Audrey Alexandra Brown

THE STILL SMALL VOICE

The candles splutter; and the kettle hums;
The heirloomed clock enumerates the tribes,
Upon the wine-stained table-cloth lie crumbs
Of matzoh whose wide scattering describes
Jews driven in far lands upon this earth.
The kettle hums; the candles splutter; and
Winds whispering from shutters tell re-birth
Of beauty rising in an eastern land,
Of paschal sheep driven in cloudy droves;
Of almond-blossoms colouring the breeze;   10
Of vineyards upon verdant terraces;
Of golden globes in orient orange-groves.
And those assembled at the table dream
Of small schemes that an April wind doth scheme,
And cry from out the sleep assailing them:
Jerusalem, next year! Next year, Jerusalem!

A. M. Klein

MRS. FORNHEIM, REFUGEE

Very merciful was the cancer
Which first blinding you altogether
Afterwards stopped up your hearing;
At the end when Death was nearing,
Black-gloved, to gather you in
You did not demur, or fear
One you could not see or hear.
I taught you Shakespeare's tongue, not knowing
The time and manner of your going;
Certainly if with ghosts to dwell,   10
German would have served as well.
Voyaging lady, I wish for you
An Englishwoman to talk to,
An unruffled listener,
And green words to say to her.

Irving Layton

THE POOL

A boy gazing in a pool
Is all profound; his eyes are cool
And he's as though unborn, he's gone;
He's the abyss he gazes on.

A man searches the pool in vain
For his profundity again;
He finds it neither there nor here
And all between is pride and fear.

His eyes are warm with love and death,
Time makes a measure of his breath;   10
The world is now profound and he
Fearful, on its periphery.

George Johnston

SISTERS

These children split each other open like nuts,
break and crack in the small house,
are doors slamming.
Still, on the whole, are gentle for mother, take
her simple comfort like a drink of milk.

Fierce on the street they own the sun and spin
on separate axes
attract about them in their motion all
the shrieking neighbourhood of little earths;
in violence hold hatred in their mouths.   10

With evening their joint gentle laughter leads
them into pastures of each other's eyes;
beyond, the world is barren; they contract
tenderness from each other like disease
and talk as if each word had just been born
a butterfly, and soft from its cocoon.

                                        P. K. Page

FLIGHT OF THE ROLLER-COASTER

Once more around should do it, the man confided . . . .

And sure enough, when the roller-coaster reached the peak
Of the giant curve above me, screech of its wheels
Almost drowned by the shriller cries of the riders –

Instead of the dip and plunge with its landslide of screams
It rose in the air like a movieland magic carpet, some
    wonderful bird,

And without fuss or fanfare swooped slowly across the
    amusement park,
Over Spook's Castle, ice-cream booths, shooting gallery;
    and losing no height

Made the last yards above the beach, where the cucumber-cool
Brakeman in the last seat saluted   10
A lady about to change from her bathing-suit.

Then, as many witnesses duly reported, headed leisurely
   over the water,
Disappearing mysteriously all too soon behind a low-flying
   flight of clouds.

Raymond Souster

AUNT JANE

Aunt Jane, of whom I dreamed the nights it thundered,
was dead at ninety, buried at a hundred.
We kept her corpse a decade, hid upstairs,
where it ate porridge, slept and said its prayers

And every night before I went to bed
they took me in to worship with the dead.
Christ Lord, if I should die before I wake,
I pray thee Lord my body take.

Alden Nowlan

PART TWO

THE DAEMON LOVER

"O where have you been, my long, long love,
 This long seven years and mair?" –
"O I'm come to seek my former vows
 Ye granted me before." –

"O hold your tongue of your former vows,
 For they will breed sad strife;
O hold your tongue of your former vows,
 For I am become a wife."

He turned him right and round about,
 And the tear blinded his ee: 10
"I wad never hae trodden on Irish ground,
 If it had not been for thee.

"I might hae had a king's daughter,
 Far, far beyond the sea;
I might hae had a king's daughter,
 Had it not been for love o' thee."

"If ye might hae had a king's daughter,
 Yersel ye had to blame;
Ye might have taken the king's daughter,
 For ye kend that I was nane!   20

"If I was to leave my husband dear,
 And my two babes also,
O what have you to take me to,
 If with you I should go?"

"I hae seven ships upon the sea –
 The eighth brought me to land –
With four-and-twenty bold mariners,
 And music on every hand."

She has taken up her two little babes,
    Kissed them baith cheek and chin;   30
"O fair ye well, my ain two babes,
    For I'll never see you again."

She set her foot upon the ship.
    No mariners could she behold;
But the sails were o' the taffetie,
    And the masts o' the beaten gold.

She had not sailed a league, a league,
    A league, but barely three,
When dismal grew his countenance,
    And drumlie grew his ee.   40

They had not sailed a league, a league,
    A league, but barely three,
Until she espied his cloven foot,
    And she wept right bitterlie.

"O hold your tongue of your weeping," says he,
    "Of your weeping now let me be;
I will show you how the lilies grow
    On the banks of Italy!" –

"O what hills are yon, yon pleasant hills,
    That the sun shines sweetly on?"   50
"O yon are the hills of heaven," he said,
    "Where you will never win." –

"O whaten a mountain is yon," she said,
    "All so dreary wi' frost and snow?"
"O yon is the mountain of hell," he cried,
    "Where you and I will go."

He strack the top-mast wi' his hand,
    The fore-mast wi' his knee,
And he brake that gallant ship in twain,
    And sank her in the sea.   60

Anonymous

HYND HORN

Near the King's court was a young child born,
  With a high lillelu and a high lo lan;
And his name it was called Young Hynd Horn,
  And the birk and the broom blooms bonnie.

Seven lang years he served the King,
And it's a' for the sake o' his daughter Jean.

The King an angry man was he,
He sent Young Hynd Horn to the sea.

O his love gave him a gay gold ring,
With three shining diamonds set therein;   10

"As lang as these diamonds keep their hue,
Ye'll know I am a lover true,

"But when your ring turns pale and wan,
Then I'm in love with another man."

He's gone to the sea and far away,
And he's stayed for seven lang years and a day.

Seven lang years by land and sea,
And he's aften look'd how his ring may be.

One day when he look'd this ring upon,
The shining diamonds were pale and wan.   20

He hoisted sails, and hame cam' he,
Hame unto his ain countrie.

He's left the sea and he's come to land,
And the first he met was an auld beggar-man.

"What news, what news, my silly auld man?
For it's seven lang years since I saw this land."

"No news, no news," doth the beggar-man say,
"But our King's ae daughter she'll wed to-day."

"Wilt thou give to me thy begging coat?
And I'll give to thee my scarlet cloak.   30

"Give me your auld pike-staff and hat,
And ye sall be right weel paid for that."

The auld beggar-man cast off his coat,
And he's ta'en up the scarlet cloak.

He's gi'en him his auld pike-staff and hat,
And he was right weel paid for that.

The auld beggar-man was bound for the mill,
But Young Hynd Horn for the King's ain hall.

When he came to the King's ain gate,
He asked a drink for Young Hynd Horn's sake.   40

These news unto the bonnie bride cam',
That at the gate there stands an auld man,

There stands an auld man at the King's gate,
He asketh a drink for Young Hynd Horn's sake.

The bride cam' tripping down the stair,
The combs o' fine goud in her hair;

A cup o' the red wine in her hand,
And that she gave to the beggar-man.

Out o' the cup he drank the wine,
And into the cup he dropt the ring.   50

"O gat thou this by sea or by land?
Or gat thou it aff a dead man's hand?"

"I gat it neither by sea nor land,
Nor gat I it from a dead man's hand;

"But I gat it at my wooing gay,
And I gie it to you on your wedding day."

"I'll cast aside my satin goun,
And I'll follow you frae toun to toun;

"I'll tak' the fine goud frae my hair,
And follow you for evermair."   60

He let his cloutie cloak doun fa',
Young Hynd Horn shone above them a'.

The Bridegroom thought he had her wed,
With a high lillelu and a high lo lan;
But she is Young Hynd Horn's instead,
And the birk and the broom blooms bonnie.

Anonymous

THE CANTERBURY TALES

The General Prologue

(*Squire, Yeoman*)

	With hym ther was his sone, a yong SQUYER,
aspirant to knighthood	A lovyere and a lusty bacheler,*
curled as if curlers	With lokkės crulle as* they were leyd in pressė.*
	Of twenty yeer of age he was, I gessė.
average height	Of his stature he was of evene lengthė.*
agile	And wonderly delyvere,* and of greet strengthė,
cavalry expeditions	And he hadde been somtyme in chivachyė* In Flaundrės, in Artoys, and Picardyė,
conducted time	And born* hym wel, as of so litel spacė,*
stand lady's	In hope to stonden* in his lady* gracė. 10
Embroidered meadow	Embrouded* was he as it were a meedė* Al ful of fresshė flourės white and reedė.
fluting or whistling	Syngynge he was or floytynge* al the day. He was as fressh as is the monthe of May. Short was his gowne with slevės longe and wydė.
gracefully	Wel koude he sitte on hors and fairė* rydė.
composed words for tunes	He koudė songės make and wel enditė,*
Joust also draw	Juste,* and eek* daunce, and wel purtreye,* and writė.
nighttime	So hoote he lovėde that by nyghtertalė* He slepte namoore than dooth a nyghtyn- 20 galė.
	Curteys he was, lowely, and servysablė,
carved	And carf* biforn his fader at the tablė.

93

A YEMAN* hadde he* and servantz namo*
At that tyme, for hym listé* rydé so,
And he was clad in cote and hood of grené.
A sheef of pecok arwés* bright and kené
Under his belt he bar* ful thriftily* –
Wel koude he dresse* his takel* yemanly;
His arwés droupéd noght with fetherés lowé –
And in his hand he bar a myghty bowé.   30
A not*-heed hadde he, with a broun visagé.
Of wodécraft wel koude* he al the usagé.
Upon his arm he bar a gay* bracer,*
And by his syde a swerd* and a bokeler,*
And on that* oother syde a gay* daggeré,
Harneyséd* wel, and sharp as poynt of speré,
A Cristofre* on his brest of silver shené.*
An horn he bar, the bawdryk* was of grené.
A forster* was he soothly,* as I gessé.

Margin glosses (left column, matched to asterisked words):
- yeoman   he (the knight)
- no more
- he liked to
- arrows
- carried   ready for service
- prepare   equipment
- close-cropped
- knew
- bright   archer's guard
- sword   buckler (shield)
- the flashy
- Mounted
- a St. Christopher's image bright
- carrying-belt, baldric
- forester   truly

Geoffrey Chaucer

CHARITY

Though I speak with the tongues of men and of angels,
And have not charity,
I am become as sounding brass,
Or a tinkling cymbal.

And though I have the gift of prophecy,
And understand all mysteries, and all knowledge;
And though I have all faith, so that I could remove mountains,
And have not charity,
I am nothing.

And though I bestow all my goods to feed the poor,   10
And though I give my body to be burned,
And have not charity,
It profiteth me nothing.

1 Corinthians 13: 1-3

THE MAGNIFICAT

And Mary said,
My soul doth magnify the Lord,
And my spirit hath rejoiced in God my Saviour.
For he hath regarded the low estate of his handmaiden:
For, behold, from henceforth all generations
Shall call me blessed.
For he that is mighty hath done to me great things;
And holy is his name.
And his mercy is on them that fear him
From generation to generation.   10

He hath shewed strength with his arm;
He hath scattered the proud in the imagination of their hearts.
He hath put down the mighty from their seats,
And exalted them of low degree.
He hath filled the hungry with good things;
And the rich he hath sent empty away.
He hath holpen his servant Israel,
In remembrance of his mercy;
As he spake to our fathers,
To Abraham, and to his seed for ever.   20

Luke 1: 46-55

THE LORD IS MY SHEPHERD

The Lord is my shepherd;
I shall not want.

He maketh me to lie down in green pastures:
He leadeth me beside the still waters.
He restoreth my soul:
He leadeth me in the paths of righteousness for
   his name's sake.

Yea, though I walk through the valley of the shadow
   of death,
I will fear no evil:
For thou art with me;
Thy rod and thy staff they comfort me.   10

Thou preparest a table before me
In the presence of mine enemies:
Thou anointest my head with oil;
My cup runneth over.

Surely goodness and mercy shall follow me all
    the days of my life:
And I will dwell in the house of the LORD for ever.

Psalm 23

THE PASSIONATE SHEPHERD
TO HIS LOVE

Come live with me and be my Love,
And we will all the pleasures prove
That hills and valleys, dale and field,
And all the craggy mountains yield.

There will we sit upon the rocks
And see the shepherds feed their flocks,
By shallow rivers, to whose falls
Melodious birds sing madrigals.

There will I make thee beds of roses
And a thousand fragrant posies,   10
A cap of flowers, and a kirtle
Embroidered all with leaves of myrtle.

A gown made of the finest wool,
Which from our pretty lambs we pull,
Fair linèd slippers for the cold,
With buckles of the purest gold.

A belt of straw and ivy buds
With coral clasps and amber studs.
And if these pleasures may thee move,
Come live with me and be my Love.   20

Thy silver dishes for thy meat
As precious as the gods do eat,
Shall on an ivory table be
Prepared each day for thee and me.

The shepherd swains shall dance and sing
For thy delight each May-morning:
If these delights thy mind may move,
Then live with me and be my Love.

Christopher Marlowe

SONNET XXX

When to the sessions of sweet silent thought
I summon up remembrance of things past,
I sigh the lack of many a thing I sought,
And with old woes new wail my dear time's waste:
Then can I drown an eye, unus'd to flow,
For precious friends hid in death's dateless night,
And weep afresh love's long since cancell'd woe,
And moan the expense of many a vanish'd sight:
Then can I grieve at grievances foregone,
And heavily from woe to woe tell o'er   10
The sad account of fore-bemoaned moan,
Which I new pay as if not paid before.
    But if the while I think on thee, dear friend,
    All losses are restor'd and sorrows end.

William Shakespeare

SONNET LXV

Since brass, nor stone, nor earth, nor boundless sea,
But sad mortality o'ersways their power,
How with this rage shall beauty hold a plea,
Whose action is no stronger than a flower?
O, how shall summer's honey breath hold out
Against the wreckful siege of battering days,
When rocks impregnable are not so stout,
Nor gates of steel so strong, but Time decays?
O fearful meditation! where, alack!
Shall Time's best jewel from Time's chest lie hid?   10
Or what strong hand can hold his swift foot back?
Or who his spoil of beauty can forbid?
    O, none, unless this miracle have might,
    That in black ink my love may still shine bright.

William Shakespeare

SONNET LXXI

No longer mourn for me when I am dead
Than you shall hear the surly sullen bell
Give warning to the world that I am fled
From this vile world, with vilest worms to dwell.
Nay, if you read this line, remember not
The hand that writ it; for I love you so,
That I in your sweet thoughts would be forgot,
If thinking on me then should make you woe.
O, if, I say, you look upon this verse
When I perhaps compounded am with clay,   10
Do not so much as my poor name rehearse,
But let your love even with my life decay!
   Lest the wise world should look into your moan,
   And mock you with me after I am gone.

William Shakespeare

SONNET LXXIII

That time of year thou mayst in me behold
When yellow leaves, or none, or few, do hang
Upon those boughs which shake against the cold,
Bare ruined choirs, where late the sweet birds sang.
In me thou see'st the twilight of such day
As after sunset fadeth in the west,
Which by and by black night doth take away,
Death's second self, that seals up all in rest.
In me thou see'st the glowing of such fire
That on the ashes of his youth doth lie,   10
As the death-bed whereon it must expire,
Consum'd with that which it was nourish'd by.
   This thou perceiv'st, which makes thy love
      more strong
   To love that well which thou must leave ere long.

William Shakespeare

SILVIA

Who is Silvia? what is she,
 That all our swains commend her? –
Holy, fair, and wise is she;
 The heaven such grace did lend her,
That she might admired be.

Is she kind as she is fair?
 For beauty lives with kindness;
Love doth to her eyes repair,
 To help him of his blindness;
And, being helped, inhabits there.   10

Then to Silvia let us sing,
 That Silvia is excelling;
She excels each mortal thing,
 Upon the dull earth dwelling:
To her let us garlands bring.

        William Shakespeare

A HYMN TO GOD THE FATHER

Wilt Thou forgive that sin where I begun,
 Which was my sin, though it were done before?
Wilt Thou forgive that sin, through which I run,
 And do run still, though still I do deplore?
  When Thou hast done, Thou hast not done;
   For I have more.

Wilt Thou forgive that sin which I have won
 Others to sin, and made my sin their door?
Wilt Thou forgive that sin which I did shun
 A year or two, but wallowed in a score?   10
  When Thou hast done, Thou hast not done;
   For I have more.

I have a sin of fear, that when I've spun
 My last thread, I shall perish on the shore;
But swear by Thyself, that at my death Thy Son
 Shall shine as He shines now, and heretofore;
  And, having done that, Thou hast done;
   I fear no more.

        John Donne

THE PULLEY

When God at first made man,
Having a glass of blessings standing by,
   "Let us," said He, "pour on him all we can;
Let the world's riches, which dispersèd lie,
   Contract into a span."

   So strength first made a way;
Then beauty flowed, then wisdom, honour, pleasure,
   When almost all was out, God made a stay,
Perceiving that, alone of all His treasure,
   Rest in the bottom lay.   10

   "For if I should," said He,
"Bestow this jewel also on My creature,
   He would adore my gifts instead of Me,
And rest in Nature, not the God of Nature;
   So both should losers be.

   "Yet let him keep the rest,
But keep them with repining restlessness:
   Let him be rich and weary, that at least,
If goodness lead him not, yet weariness
   May toss him to My breast."   20

George Herbert

HOW SOON HATH TIME

How soon hath Time, the subtle thief of youth,
   Stolen on his wing my three-and-twentieth year!
   My hasting days fly on with full career,
   But my late spring no bud or blossom shew'th.
Perhaps my semblance might deceive the truth
   That I to manhood am arrived so near;
   And inward ripeness doth much less appear,
   That some more timely-happy spirits endu'th.
Yet, be it less or more, or soon or slow,
   It shall be still in strictest measure even   10
   To that same lot, however mean or high,
Toward which Time leads me, and the will of Heaven.
   All is, if I have grace to use it so,
   As ever in my great Task-Master's eye.

John Milton

ON TIME

Fly, envious Time, till thou run out thy race:
Call on the lazy leaden-stepping Hours,
Whose speed is but the heavy plummet's pace;
And glut thyself with what thy womb devours,
Which is no more than what is false and vain,
And merely mortal dross;
So little is our loss,
So little is thy gain!
For, whenas each thing bad thou hast entombed,
And, last of all, thy greedy self consumed,   10
Then long Eternity shall greet our bliss
With an individual kiss,
And Joy shall overtake us as a flood;
When every thing that is sincerely good
And perfectly divine,
With Truth, and Peace, and Love, shall ever shine
About the supreme throne
Of Him, to whose happy-making sight alone
When once our heavenly-guided soul shall climb,
Then, all this earthly grossness quit,   20
Attired with stars we shall for ever sit,
Triumphing over Death, and Chance, and thee,
    O Time!
                              John Milton

TO LUCASTA,
ON GOING TO THE WARS

Tell me not, Sweet, I am unkind,
    That from the nunnery
Of thy chaste breast and quiet mind,
    To war and arms I fly.

True, a new mistress now I chase,
    The first foe in the field;
And with a stronger faith embrace
    A sword, a horse, a shield.

Yet this inconstancy is such
    As you too shall adore;   10
I could not love thee, Dear, so much,
    Loved I not Honour more.

                        Richard Lovelace

THE PEACOCK, THE TURKEY, AND THE GOOSE

In beauty faults conspicuous grow,
The smallest speck is seen on snow.
   As near a barn, by hunger led,
A Peacock with the poultry fed,
All viewed him with an envious eye,
And mocked his gaudy pageantry.
He, conscious of superior merit,
Contemns their base reviling spirit;
His state and dignity assumes,
And to the sun displays his plumes,   10
Which, like the Heavens' o'er-arching skies,
Are spangled with a thousand eyes.
The circling rays, and varied light,
At once confound their dazzled sight;
On every tongue detraction burns,
And malice prompts their spleen by turns.
   "Mark with what insolence and pride,
The creature takes his haughty stride,"
The Turkey cries. "Can spleen contain?
Sure never bird was half so vain!   20
But, were intrinsic merit seen,
We Turkeys have the whiter skin."
   From tongue to tongue they caught abuse;
And next was heard the hissing Goose:
"What hideous legs! What filthy claws!
I scorn to censure little flaws.
Then what a horrid squalling throat!
Ev'n owls are frighted at the note."
   "True. Those are faults," the Peacock cries;
"My scream, my shanks, you may despise;   30
But such blind critics rail in vain.
What! Overlook my radiant train!
Know, did my legs (your scorn and sport)
The Turkey or the Goose support,
And did ye scream with harsher sound,
Those faults in you had ne'er been found.
To all apparent beauties blind,
Each blemish strikes an envious mind."
   Thus in assemblies have I seen
A nymph of brightest charm and mien   40
Wake envy in each ugly face,
And buzzing scandal fills the place.

John Gay

THE QUIET LIFE

Happy the man, whose wish and care
   A few paternal acres bound,
Content to breathe his native air
    In his own ground.

Whose herds with milk, whose fields with bread,
   Whose flocks supply him with attire;
Whose trees in summer yield him shade,
    In winter fire.

Blest, who can unconcern'dly find
   Hours, days, and years slide soft away   10
In health of body, peace of mind,
    Quiet by day,

Sound sleep by night; study and ease
   Together mix'd; sweet recreation,
And innocence, which most does please
    With meditation.

Thus let me live, unseen, unknown;
   Thus unlamented let me die;
Steal from the world, and not a stone
    Tell where I lie.   20

                       Alexander Pope

THE WINTER MORNING WALK

From *The Task*

'Tis morning; and the sun, with ruddy orb
Ascending, fires the horizon; while the clouds
That crowd away before the driving wind,
More ardent as the disk emerges more,
Resemble most some city in a blaze,
Seen through the leafless wood. His slanting ray
Slides ineffectual down the snowy vale,
And, tingeing all with his own rosy hue,
From every herb and every spiry blade
Stretches a length of shadow o'er the field.   10
Mine, spindling into longitude immense,
In spite of gravity, and sage remark

That I myself am but a fleeting shade,
Provokes me to a smile. With eye askance
I view the muscular proportioned limb
Transformed to a lean shank. The shapeless pair
As they designed to mock me at my side
Take step for step; and as I near approach
The cottage, walk along the plastered wall,
Preposterous sight! the legs without the man.   20
The verdure of the plain lies buried deep
Beneath the dazzling deluge; and the bents
And coarser grass, upspearing o'er the rest,
Of late unsightly and unseen, now shine
Conspicuous, and in bright apparel clad,
And fledged with icy feathers, nod superb.
The cattle mourn in corners where the fence
Screens them, and seem half petrified to sleep
In unrecumbent sadness. There they wait
Their wonted fodder, not like hungering man,   30
Fretful if unsupplied, but silent, meek,
And patient of the slow-paced swain's delay.
He from the stack carves out the accustomed load,
Deep-plunging and again deep-plunging oft,
His broad keen knife into the solid mass:
Smooth as a wall the upright remnant stands,
With such undeviating and even force
He severs it away: no needless care,
Lest storms should overset the leaning pile
Deciduous, or its own unbalanced weight.   40

William Cowper

THE NEW JERUSALEM

And did those feet in ancient time
    Walk upon England's mountain green?
And was the holy Lamb of God
    On England's pleasant pasture seen?

And did the Countenance Divine
    Shine forth upon our clouded hills?
And was Jerusalem builded here
    Among these dark Satanic Mills?

Bring me my bow of burning gold!
   Bring me my arrows of desire!   10
Bring me my spear: O clouds, unfold!
   Bring me my chariot of fire!

I will not cease from mental fight,
   Nor shall my sword sleep in my hand,
Till we have built Jerusalem
   In England's green and pleasant land.

William Blake

From EPISTLE TO JOHN LAPRAIK,

An Old Scottish Bard
April 1, 1785

I am nae poet, in a sense,
But just a rhymer, like, by chance,
An' hae to learning nae pretence,
     Yet what the matter?
Whene'er my Muse does on me glance,
     I jingle at her.

Your critic-folk may cock their nose,
And say "How can you e'er propose,
You wha ken hardly verse frae prose,
     To mak a sang?"   10
But, by your leaves, my learnèd foes,
     Ye're maybe wrang.

What's a' your jargon o' your schools,
Your Latin names for horns an' stools;
If honest nature made you fools,
     What sairs your grammars?
Ye'd better ta'en up spades and shools,
     Or knappin'-hammers.

A set o' dull conceited hashes
Confuse their brains in college classes!   20
They gang in stirks, and come out asses,
     Plain truth to speak;
An' syne they think to climb Parnassus
     By dint o' Greek!

Gie me ae spark o' Nature's fire,
That's a' the learning I desire;
Then tho' I drudge thro' dub an' mire
    At pleugh or cart,
My Muse, though hamely in attire,
    May touch the heart.   30

Robert Burns

A SLUMBER DID MY SPIRIT SEAL

A slumber did my spirit seal;
    I had no human fears:
She seemed a thing that could not feel
    The touch of earthly years.

No motion has she now, no force;
    She neither hears nor sees;
Rolled round in earth's diurnal course,
    With rocks, and stones, and trees.

William Wordsworth

COMPOSED UPON WESTMINSTER BRIDGE

Earth has not anything to show more fair:
    Dull would he be of soul who could pass by
    A sight so touching in its majesty:
This City now doth, like a garment, wear
The beauty of the morning; silent, bare,
    Ships, towers, domes, theatres, and temples lie
    Open unto the fields, and to the sky;
All bright and glittering in the smokeless air.
Never did sun more beautifully steep
    In his first splendour, valley, rock, or hill;   10
Ne'er saw I, never felt, a calm so deep!
    The river glideth at his own sweet will:
Dear God! the very houses seem asleep;
    And all that mighty heart is lying still!

William Wordsworth

IT IS NOT TO BE THOUGHT OF

It is not to be thought of that the Flood
    Of British freedom, which, to the open sea
    Of the world's praise, from dark antiquity
Hath flowed, "with pomp of waters, unwithstood,"
Roused though it be full often to a mood
    Which spurns the check of salutary bands,
    That this most famous stream in bogs and sands
Should perish; and to evil and to good
Be lost for ever. In our halls is hung
    Armoury of the invincible Knights of old: 10
We must be free or die, who speak the tongue
    That Shakespeare spake; the faith and morals hold
Which Milton held. – In everything we are sprung
    Of Earth's first blood, have titles manifold.

William Wordsworth

PROUD MAISIE

From *The Heart of Midlothian*

Proud Maisie is in the wood,
    Walking so early;
Sweet Robin sits on the bush,
    Singing so rarely.

"Tell me, thou bonny bird,
    When shall I marry me?"
"When six braw gentlemen
    Kirkward shall carry ye."

"Who makes the bridal bed,
    Birdie, say truly?"   10
"The grey-headed sexton
    That delves the grave duly.

"The glow-worm o'er grave and stone
    Shall light thee steady.
The owl from the steeple sing,
    'Welcome, proud lady'."

Sir Walter Scott

OZYMANDIAS

I met a traveller from an antique land
Who said: Two vast and trunkless legs of stone
Stand in the desert. Near them, on the sand,
Half sunk, a shattered visage lies, whose frown,
And wrinkled lip, and sneer of cold command,
Tell that its sculptor well those passions read
Which yet survive, stamped on these lifeless things,
The hand that mocked them, and the heart that fed;
And on the pedestal these words appear:
"My name is Ozymandias, king of kings: 10
Look on my works, ye Mighty, and despair!"
Nothing beside remains. Round the decay
Of that colossal wreck, boundless and bare
The lone and level sands stretch far away.

Percy Bysshe Shelley

ON FIRST LOOKING INTO
CHAPMAN'S HOMER

Much have I travelled in the realms of gold,
  And many goodly states and kingdoms seen;
  Round many western islands have I been
Which bards in fealty to Apollo hold.
Oft of one wide expanse had I been told
  That deep-browed Homer ruled as his demesne;
  Yet did I never breathe its pure serene
Till I heard Chapman speak out loud and bold:
Then felt I like some watcher of the skies
  When a new planet swims into his ken;   10
Or like stout Cortez when with eagle eyes
  He stared at the Pacific – and all his men
Looked at each other with a wild surmise –
  Silent, upon a peak in Darien.

John Keats

TO AUTUMN

Season of mists and mellow fruitfulness!
    Close bosom-friend of the maturing sun;
Conspiring with him how to load and bless
    With fruit the vines that round the thatch-eves run;
To bend with apples the mossed cottage-trees,
    And fill all fruit with ripeness to the core;
        To swell the gourd, and plump the hazel shells
With a sweet kernel; to set budding more,
    And still more, later flowers for the bees,
    Until they think warm days will never cease,   10
        For summer has o'er-brimmed their clammy cells.

Who hath not seen thee oft amid thy store?
    Sometimes whoever seeks abroad may find
Thee sitting careless on a granary floor,
    Thy hair soft-lifted by the winnowing wind;
Or on a half-reaped furrow sound asleep,
    Drowsed with the fumes of poppies, while thy hook
        Spares the next swath and all its twinèd flowers:
And sometimes like a gleaner thou dost keep
    Steady thy laden head across a brook;   20
    Or by a cider-press, with patient look,
        Thou watchest the last oozings hours by hours.

Where are the songs of Spring? Ay, where are they?
    Think not of them, thou hast thy music too, –
While barred clouds bloom the soft-dying day,
    And touch the stubble-plains with rosy hue;
Then in a wailful choir the small gnats mourn
    Among the river sallows, borne aloft
        Or sinking as the light wind lives or dies;
And full-grown lambs loud bleat from hilly bourn;   30
    Hedge-crickets sing; and now with treble soft
    The redbreast whistles from a garden-croft;
        And gathering swallows twitter in the skies.

John Keats

SILENCE

There is a silence where hath been no sound,
  There is a silence where no sound may be,
  In the cold grave – under the deep, deep sea,
Or in wide desert where no life is found,
Which hath been mute, and still must sleep profound;
  No voice is hush'd – no life treads silently,
  But clouds and cloudy shadows wander free,
That never spoke, over the idle ground:
But in green ruins, in the desolate walls
  Of antique palaces where Man hath been,   10
Though the dun fox or wild hyaena calls,
  And owls, that flit continually between,
Shriek to the echo, and the low winds moan –
There the true Silence is, self-conscious and alone.

Thomas Hood

From THE RUBÁIYÁT OF OMAR KHAYYÁM

Alas, that Spring should vanish with the Rose!
That Youth's sweet-scented Manuscript should close!
  The Nightingale that in the Branches sang,
Ah, whence, and whither flown again, who knows!

Ah, Love! could thou and I with Fate conspire
To grasp this sorry Scheme of Things entire,
  Would not we shatter it to bits – and then
Re-mould it nearer to the Heart's Desire!

Ah, Moon of my Delight who know'st no wane,
The Moon of Heav'n is rising once again: 10
  How oft hereafter rising shall she look
Through this same Garden after me – in vain!

And when Thyself with shining Foot shall pass
Among the Guests Star-scatter'd on the Grass,
  And in the joyous Errand reach the Spot
Where I made one – turn down an empty Glass!

Edward FitzGerald

IN MEMORIAM
LIV

Oh yet we trust that somehow good
    Will be the final goal of ill,
    To pangs of nature, sins of will,
Defects of doubt, and taints of blood;

That nothing walks with aimless feet;
    That not one life shall be destroyed,
    Or cast as rubbish to the void,
When God hath made the pile complete;

That not a worm is cloven in vain;
    That not a moth with vain desire   10
    Is shrivelled in a fruitless fire,
Or but subserves another's gain.

Behold, we know not anything;
    I can but trust that good shall fall
    At last – far off – at last, to all,
And every winter change to spring.

So runs my dream; but what am I?
    An infant crying in the night:
    An infant crying for the light:
And with no language but a cry.   20

Alfred, Lord Tennyson

IN MEMORIAM
CXV

Now fades the last long streak of snow,
    Now burgeons every maze of quick
    About the flowering squares, and thick
By ashen roots the violets blow.

Now rings the woodland loud and long,
    The distance takes a lovelier hue,
    And drown'd in yonder living blue
The lark becomes a sightless song.

Now dance the lights on lawn and lea,
    The flocks are whiter down the vale,   10
    And milkier every milky sail
On winding stream or distant sea,

Where now the seamew pipes, or dives
  In yonder greening gleam, and fly
  The happy birds, that change their sky
To build and brood; that live their lives

From land to land; and in my breast
  Spring wakens too; and my regret
  Becomes an April violet,
And buds and blossoms like the rest.   20

Alfred, Lord Tennyson

ULYSSES

It little profits that an idle king,
By this still hearth, among these barren crags,
Match'd with an agèd wife, I mete and dole
Unequal laws unto a savage race,
That hoard, and sleep, and feed, and know not me.
I cannot rest from travel: I will drink
Life to the lees: All times I have enjoy'd
Greatly, have suffer'd greatly, both with those
That loved me, and alone; on shore, and when
Thro' scudding drifts the rainy Hyades   10
Vext the dim sea: I am become a name;
For always roaming with a hungry heart
Much have I seen and known; cities of men
And manners, climates, councils, governments,
Myself not least, but honour'd of them all;
And drunk delight of battle with my peers,
Far on the ringing plains of windy Troy.
I am a part of all that I have met;
Yet all experience is an arch wherethro'
Gleams that untravell'd world whose margin fades   20
For ever and for ever when I move.
How dull it is to pause, to make an end,
To rust unburnish'd, not to shine in use!
As tho' to breathe were life! Life piled on life
Were all too little, and of one to me
Little remains: but every hour is saved
From that eternal silence, something more,
A bringer of new things; and vile it were
For some three suns to store and hoard myself
And this gray spirit yearning in desire   30

To follow knowledge like a sinking star,
Beyond the utmost bound of human thought.
　　This is my son, mine own Telemachus,
To whom I leave the sceptre and the isle, –
Well-loved of me, discerning to fulfil
This labour, by slow prudence to make mild
A rugged people, and thro' soft degrees
Subdue them to the useful and the good.
Most blameless is he, centred in the sphere
Of common duties, decent not to fail　　　　　　　40
In offices of tenderness, and pay
Meet adoration to my household gods,
When I am gone. He works his work, I mine.
　　There lies the port: the vessel puffs her sail:
There gloom the dark broad seas. My mariners,
Souls that have toil'd, and wrought, and thought
　　　　with me –
That ever with a frolic welcome took
The thunder and the sunshine, and opposed
Free hearts, free foreheads – you and I are old;
Old age hath yet his honour and his toil;　　　　　50
Death closes all: but something ere the end,
Some work of noble note, may yet be done,
Not unbecoming men that strove with Gods.
The lights begin to twinkle from the rocks:
The long day wanes: the slow moon climbs: the deep
Moans round with many voices. Come, my friends,
'Tis not too late to seek a newer world.
Push off, and sitting well in order smite
The sounding furrows; for my purpose holds
To sail beyond the sunset, and the baths　　　　　60
Of all the western stars, until I die.
It may be that the gulfs will wash us down:
It may be we shall touch the Happy Isles,
And see the great Achilles, whom we knew.
Tho' much is taken, much abides: and tho'
We are not now that strength which in old days
Moved earth and heaven; that which we are, we are;
One equal temper of heroic hearts,
Made weak by time and fate, but strong in will
To strive, to seek, to find, and not to yield.　　　70

Alfred, Lord Tennyson

MY LAST DUCHESS

Ferrara

That's my last Duchess painted on the wall,
Looking as if she were alive. I call
That piece a wonder, now: Fra Pandolf's hands
Worked busily a day, and there she stands.
Will't please you sit and look at her? I said
"Fra Pandolf" by design, for never read
Strangers like you that pictured countenance,
The depth and passion of its earnest glance,
But to myself they turned (since none puts by
The curtain I have drawn for you, but I),   10
And seemed as they would ask me, if they durst,
How such a glance came there; so, not the first
Are you to turn and ask thus. Sir, t'was not
Her husband's presence only, called that spot
Of joy into the Duchess' cheek; perhaps
Fra Pandolf chanced to say, "Her mantle laps
Over my lady's wrist too much," or "Paint
Must never hope to reproduce the faint
Half-flush that dies along her throat": such stuff
Was courtesy, she thought, and cause enough   20
For calling up that spot of joy. She had
A heart – how shall I say? – too soon made glad,
Too easily impressed; she liked whate'er
She looked on, and her looks went everywhere.
Sir, 'twas all one! My favour at her breast,
The dropping of the daylight in the West,
The bough of cherries some officious fool
Broke in the orchard for her, the white mule
She rode with round the terrace – all and each
Would draw from her alike the approving speech,   30
Or blush, at least. She thanked men, – good! but
        thanked
Somehow – I know not how – as if she ranked
My gift of a nine-hundred-years-old name
With anybody's gift. Who'd stoop to blame
This sort of trifling? Even had you skill
In speech – (which I have not) – to make your will
Quite clear to such an one, and say, "Just this
Or that in you disgusts me; here you miss,
Or there exceed the mark" – and if she let
Herself be lessoned so, nor plainly set   40
Her wits to yours, forsooth, and made excuse,

114

– E'en then would be some stooping; and I choose
Never to stoop. Oh sir, she smiled, no doubt,
Whene'er I passed her; but who passed without
Much the same smile? This grew; I gave commands;
Then all smiles stopped together. There she stands
As if alive. Will't please you rise? We'll meet
The company below, then. I repeat,
The Count your master's known munificence
Is ample warrant that no just pretence   50
Of mine for dowry will be disallowed;
Though his fair daughter's self, as I avowed
At starting, is my object. Nay, we'll go
Together down, sir. Notice Neptune, though,
Taming a sea-horse, thought a rarity,
Which Claus of Innsbruck cast in bronze for me!

Robert Browning

THE PATRIOT

An Old Story

I

It was roses, roses, all the way,
   With myrtle mixed in my path like mad:
The house-roofs seemed to heave and sway,
   The church-spires flamed, such flags they had,
A year ago on this very day.

II

The air broke into a mist with bells,
   The old walls rocked with the crowd and cries.
Had I said, "Good folks, mere noise repels –
   But give me your sun from yonder skies!"
They had answered, "And afterward, what else?"   10

III

Alack, it was I who leaped at the sun
   To give it my loving friends to keep!
Nought man could do, have I left undone:
   And you see my harvest, what I reap
This very day, now a year is run.

IV

There's nobody on the house-tops now –
  Just a palsied few at the windows set;
For the best of the sight is, all allow,
  At the Shamble's Gate –or, better yet,
By the very scaffold's foot, I trow.   20

V

I go in the rain, and, more than needs,
  A rope cuts both my wrists behind;
And I think, by the feel, my forehead bleeds,
  For they fling, whoever has a mind,
Stones at me for my year's misdeeds.

VI

Thus I entered, and thus I go!
  In triumphs, people have dropped down dead.
"Paid by the world, what dost thou owe
  Me?" – God might question; now instead,
'Tis God shall repay: I am safer so.   30

Robert Browning

LAST LINES

No coward soul is mine,
No trembler in the world's storm-troubled sphere:
  I see Heaven's glories shine,
And faith shines equal, arming me from fear.

O God within my breast,
Almighty, ever-present Deity!
  Life – that in me has rest,
As I – undying Life – have power in Thee!

Vain are the thousand creeds
That move men's hearts: unutterably vain;   10
  Worthless as wither'd weeds,
Or idlest froth amid the boundless main,

To waken doubt in one
Holding so fast by Thine Infinity;
  So surely anchor'd on
The steadfast rock of immortality.

With wide-embracing love
The Spirit animates eternal years,
   Pervades and broods above,
Changes, sustains, dissolves, creates, and rears.   20

   Though earth and man were gone,
And suns and universes cease to be,
   And Thou wert left alone,
Every existence would exist in Thee.

   There is not room for Death,
Nor atom that his might could render void;
   Thou – Thou art Being and Breath,
And what Thou art may never be destroyed.

Emily Brontë

UP-HILL

Does the road wind up-hill all the way?
   Yes, to the very end.
Will the day's journey take the whole long day?
   From morn to night, my friend.

But is there for the night a resting-place?
   A roof for when the slow, dark hours begin.
May not the darkness hide it from my face?
   You cannot miss that inn.

Shall I meet other wayfarers at night?
   Those who have gone before.   10
Then must I knock, or call when just in sight?
   They will not keep you standing at that door.

Shall I find comfort, travel-sore and weak?
   Of labour you shall find the sum.
Will there be beds for me and all who seek?
   Yea, beds for all who come.

Christina Rossetti

SUMMER SCHEMES

When friendly summer calls again,
    Calls again
Her little fifers to these hills,
We'll go – we two – to that arched fane
Of leafage where they prime their bills
Before they start to flood the plain
With quavers, minims, shakes, and thrills.
    "– We'll go," I sing; but who shall say
    What may not chance before that day!

And we shall see the waters spring,   10
    Waters spring
From chinks the scrubby copses crown;
And we shall trace their oncreeping
To where the cascade tumbles down
And sends the bobbing growths aswing,
And ferns not quite but almost drown.
    "– We shall," I say; but who may sing
    Of what another moon may bring!

Thomas Hardy

GREAT THINGS

Sweet cyder is a great thing,
    A great thing to me,
Spinning down to Weymouth town
    By Ridgway thirstily,
And maid and mistress summoning
    Who tend the hostelry:
O cyder is a great thing,
    A great thing to me!

The dance is a great thing,
    A great thing to me,   10
With candles lit and partners fit
    For night-long revelry;
And going home when day-dawning
    Peeps pale upon the lea:
O dancing is a great thing,
    A great thing to me!

Love is, yea, a great thing,
    A great thing to me,
When, having drawn across the lawn
    In darkness silently,   20
A figure flits like one a-wing
    Out from the nearest tree:
O love is, yes, a great thing,
    A great thing to me!

Will these be always great things,
    Great things to me? . . .
Let it befall that One will call,
    "Soul, I have need of thee";
What then? Joy-jaunts, impassioned flings,
    Love, and its ecstasy,   30
Will always have been great things,
    Great things to me!

Thomas Hardy

AFTERWARDS

When the Present has latched its postern behind my tremulous stay,
    And the May month flaps its glad green leaves like wings,
Delicate-filmed as new-spun silk, will the neighbours say,
    "He was a man who used to notice such things"?

If it be in the dusk when, like an eyelid's soundless blink,
    The dewfall-hawk comes crossing the shades to alight
Upon the wind-warped upland thorn, a gazer may think,
    "To him this must have been a familiar sight."

If I pass during some nocturnal blackness, mothy and warm,
    When the hedgehog travels furtively over the lawn,   10
One may say, "He strove that such innocent creatures should come
       to no harm,
    But he could do little for them; and now he is gone."

If, when hearing that I have been stilled at last, they stand at the
      door,
    Watching the full-starred heavens that winter sees,
Will this thought rise on those who will meet my face no more,
    "He was one who had an eye for such mysteries"?

say when my bell of quittance is heard in the gloom,
  crossing breeze cuts a pause in its outrollings,
  rise again, as they were a new bell's boom,
  he hears it not now, but used to notice such things"?   20

Thomas Hardy

THE WINDHOVER

To Christ Our Lord

I caught this morning morning's minion, king-
    dom of daylight's dauphin, dapple-dawn-drawn Falcon, in his
      riding
Of the rolling, level underneath him steady air, and striding
High there, how he rung upon the rein of a wimpling wing
In his ecstasy! then off, off forth on swing,
    As a skate's heel sweeps smooth on a bow-bend: the hurl and
      gliding
Rebuffed the big wind. My heart in hiding
Stirred for a bird, – the achieve of, the mastery of the thing!

Brute beauty and valour and act, oh, air, pride, plume here
    Buckle! AND the fire that breaks from thee then, a billion   10
Times told lovelier, more dangerous, O my chevalier!

No wonder of it: shéer plód makes plough down sillion
Shine, and blue-bleak embers, ah my dear,
    Fall, gall themselves, and gash gold-vermilion.

Gerard Manley Hopkins

TO A SNOWFLAKE

What heart would have thought you? –
Past our devisal
O filagree petal!
Fashioned so purely,
Fragilely, surely,
From that Paradisal
Imagineless metal,
Too costly for cost?
Who hammered you, wrought you,

From argentine vapour? – 10
"God was my shaper.
Passing surmisal,
He hammered. He wrought me.
From curled silver vapour,
To lust of His mind: –
Thou could'st not have thought me!
So purely, so palely,
Tinily, surely,
 Mightily, frailly,
Inscupīed and embossed, 20
With His hammer of wind,
And His graver of frost."

Francis Thompson

REVEILLÉ

Wake: the silver dusk returning
    Up the beach of darkness brims,
And the ship of sunrise burning
    Strands upon the eastern rims.

Wake: the vaulted shadow shatters,
    Trampled to the floor it spanned,
And the tent of night in tatters
    Straws the sky-pavilioned land.

Up, lad, up, 'tis late for lying:
    Hear the drums of morning play; 10
Hark, the empty highways crying
    "Who'll beyond the hills away?"

Towns and countries woo together,
    Forelands beacon, belfries call;
Never lad that trod on leather
    Lived to feast his heart with all.

Up, lad: thews that lie and cumber
    Sunlit pallets never thrive;
Morns abed and daylight slumber
    Were not meant for man alive. 20

Clay lies still, but blood's a rover;
    Breath's a ware that will not keep.
Up, lad: when the journey's over
    There'll be time enough to sleep.

A. E. Housman

RECESSIONAL

June 22, 1897

God of our fathers, known of old,
    Lord of our far-flung battle-line,
Beneath whose awful Hand we hold
    Dominion over palm and pine –
Lord God of Hosts, be with us yet,
Lest we forget – lest we forget!

The tumult and the shouting dies;
    The captains and the kings depart:
Still stands Thine ancient sacrifice,
    An humble and a contrite heart.   10
Lord God of Hosts, be with us yet,
Lest we forget – lest we forget!

Far-called, our navies melt away;
    On dune and headland sinks the fire:
Lo, all our pomp of yesterday
    Is one with Nineveh and Tyre!
Judge of the Nations, spare us yet,
Lest we forget – lest we forget!

If, drunk with sight of power, we loose
    Wild tongues that have not Thee in awe,   20
Such boastings as the Gentiles use,
    Or lesser breeds without the Law –
Lord God of Hosts, be with us yet,
Lest we forget – lest we forget!

For heathen heart that puts her trust
    In reeking tube and iron shard,
All valiant dust that builds on dust,
    And guarding, calls not Thee to guard,
For frantic boast and foolish word –
Thy Mercy on Thy People, Lord!   30

Rudyard Kipling

THE LAKE ISLE OF INNISFREE

I will arise and go now, and go to Innisfree,
And a small cabin build there, of clay and wattles made;
Nine bean rows will I have there, a hive for the honey bee,
    And live alone in the bee-loud glade.

And I shall have some peace there, for peace comes
        dropping slow,
Dropping from the veils of the morning to where the cricket
        sings;
There midnight's all a glimmer, and noon a purple glow,
    And evening full of the linnet's wings.

I will arise and go now, for always night and day
I hear lake water lapping with low sounds by the shore;   10
While I stand on the roadway, or on the pavements grey,
    I hear it in the deep heart's core.

William Butler Yeats

THE SCHOLARS

Bald heads forgetful of their sins,
Old, learned, respectable bald heads
Edit and annotate the lines
That young men, tossing on their beds,
Rhymed out in love's despair
To flatter beauty's ignorant ear.

All shuffle there; all cough in ink;
All wear the carpet with their shoes;
All think what other people think;
All know the man their neighbour knows.   10
Lord, what would they say
Did their Catullus walk that way?

William Butler Yeats

GHOUL CARE

Sour fiend, go home and tell the Pit
For once you met your master, —
A man who carried in his soul
Three charms against disaster,
The Devil and disaster.

Away, away, and tell the tale
And start your whelps a-whining,
Say "In the greenwood of his soul
A lizard's eye was shining,
A little eye kept shining."   10

Away, away, and salve your sores,
And set your hags a-groaning,
Say "In the greenwood of his soul
A drowsy bee was droning,
A dreamy bee was droning."

Prodigious Bat! Go start the walls
Of Hell with horror ringing,
Say "In the greenwood of his soul
There was a goldfinch singing,
A pretty goldfinch singing."   20

And then come back, come, if you please,
A fiercer ghoul and ghaster,
With all the glooms and smuts of Hell
Behind you, I'm your master!
You know I'm still your master.

Ralph Hodgson

THE SCRIBE

What lovely things
Thy hand hath made:
The smooth-plumed bird
In its emerald shade,
The seed of the grass,
The speck of stone
Which the wayfaring ant
Stirs – and hastes on!

124

Though I should sit
By some tarn in Thy hills,   10
Using its ink
As the spirit wills
To write of Earth's wonders,
Its live, willed things,
Flit would the ages
On soundless wings
Ere unto Z
My pen drew nigh;
Leviathan told,
And the honey-fly: 20
And still would remain
My wit to try –
My worn reeds broken,
The dark tarn dry,
All words forgotten –
Thou, Lord, and I.

Walter de la Mare

FARE WELL

When I lie where shades of darkness
Shall no more assail mine eyes,
Nor the rain make lamentation
    When the wind sighs;
How will fare the world whose wonder
Was the very proof of me?
Memory fades, must the remembered
    Perishing be?

Oh, when this my dust surrenders
Hand, foot, lip, to dust again,   10
May these loved and loving faces
    Please other men!
May the rusting harvest hedgerow
Still the Traveller's Joy entwine,
And as happy children gather
    Posies once mine.

Look thy last on all things lovely
Every hour. Let no night
Seal thy sense in deathly slumber
      Till to delight   20
Thou have paid thy utmost blessing;
Since that all things thou wouldst praise
Beauty took from those who loved them
      In other days.

Walter de la Mare

THE ICE-CART

Perched on my city office-stool
I watched with envy, while a cool
And lucky carter handled ice. . . .
And I was wandering in a trice,
Far from the grey and grimy heat
Of that intolerable street,
O'er sapphire berg and emerald floe,
Beneath the still, cold ruby glow
Of everlasting Polar night,
Bewildered by the queer half-light,   10
Until I stumbled, unawares,
Upon a creek where big white bears
Plunged headlong down with flourished heels,
And floundered after shining seals
Through shivering seas of blinding blue.
And as I watched them, ere I knew,
I'd stripped, and I was swimming, too,
Among the seal-pack, young and hale,
And thrusting on with threshing tail,
With twist and twirl and sudden leap   20
Through cracking ice and salty deep –
Diving and doubling with my kind,
Until, at last, we left behind
Those big white, blundering bulks of death,
And lay, at length, with panting breath
Upon a far untravelled floe,
Beneath a gentle drift of snow –
Snow drifting gently, fine and white,
Out of the endless Polar night,
Falling and falling evermore   30
Upon that far untravelled shore,

Till I was buried fathoms deep
Beneath that cold, white drifting sleep –
Sleep drifting deep,
Deep drifting sleep. . . .

The carter cracked a sudden whip:
I clutched my stool with startled grip,
Awakening to the grimy heat
Of that intolerable street.

Wilfrid Wilson Gibson

SEA-FEVER

I must go down to the seas again, to the lonely sea and the sky,
And all I ask is a tall ship, and a star to steer her by,
And the wheel's kick and the wind's song and the white sail's
     shaking,
And a grey mist on the sea's face and a grey dawn breaking.

I must go down to the seas again, for the call of the running tide
Is a wild call and a clear call that may not be denied;
And all I ask is a windy day with the white clouds flying,
And the flung spray and the blown spume, and the seagulls crying.

I must go down to the seas again, to the vagrant gypsy life,
To the gull's way and the whale's way where the wind's like a   10
     whetted knife;
And all I ask is a merry yarn from a laughing fellow-rover,
And quiet sleep and a sweet dream when the long trick's over.

John Masefield

SUNDAY MORNING

Outside the sunlight, outside the summer wind revelled.
Revelled and called to them, where behind dust-
     covered windows
They chanted
Their evening hymn.
Though it was morning,
Their thoughts were an evening hymn.

Then sudden – I heard it, I swear to you,
Sheer through the well restrained bassos –
Sheer through the delicate
Modestly mantled sopranos,   10
A naked voice, joyously naked,
Responsive to sunlight and summer wind suddenly
    thrilled.
Even so it is rumoured that once at a Sunday-school
    picnic
In a well-restrained gaiety nicely arranged by a river
Broke suddenly out of the forest
A naked faun.
Paused for a moment
With wonder-arched eyebrows,
Then, over the summer grass tripping
On delicate hooves,   20
Vanished again in the forest.

Seumas O'Sullivan

WHAT TOMAS SAID IN A PUB

I saw God! Do you doubt it?
Do you dare to doubt it?
I saw the Almighty Man! His hand
Was resting on a mountain! And
He looked upon the World, and all about it:
I saw Him plainer than you see me now
– You mustn't doubt it!

He was not satisfied!
His look was all dissatisfied!
His beard swung on a wind, far out of sight   10
Behind the world's curve! And there was light
Most fearful from His forehead! And He sighed –
– That star went always wrong, and from the start
I was dissatisfied! –

He lifted up His hand!
I say He heaved a dreadful hand
Over the spinning earth! Then I said, – Stay,
You must not strike it, God! I'm in the way!
And I will never move from where I stand! –
He said, – Dear child, I feared that you were dead, –   20
. . . And stayed His hand!

James Stephens

THE ROAD

Because our lives are cowardly and sly,
Because we do not dare to take or give,
Because we scowl and pass each other by,
We do not live; we do not dare to live.

We dive, each man, into his secret house,
And bolt the door, and listen in affright,
Each timid man beside a timid spouse,
With timid children huddled out of sight.

Kissing in secret, fighting secretly!
We crawl and hide like vermin in a hole,   10
Under the bravery of sun and sky,
We flash our meannesses of face and soul.

Let us go out and walk upon the road,
And quit for evermore the brick-built den,
And lock and key, the hidden, shy abode
That separates us from our fellow-men.

And by contagion of the sun we may,
Catch at a spark from that primeval fire,
And learn that we are better than our clay,
And equal to the peaks of our desire.   20

James Stephens

DREAMERS

Soldiers are citizens of death's grey land,
   Drawing no dividend from time's to-morrows.
In the great hour of destiny they stand,
   Each with his feuds, and jealousies, and sorrows.
Soldiers are sworn to action; they must win
   Some flaming, fatal climax with their lives.
Soldiers are dreamers; when the guns begin,
   They think of firelit homes, clean beds, and wives.
I see them in foul dug-outs, gnawed by rats,
   And in the ruined trenches, lashed with rain,   10
Dreaming of things they did with balls and bats,
   And mocked by hopeless longing to regain
Bank holidays, and picture shows, and spats,
   And going to the office in the train.

Siegfried Sassoon

PRELUDES (I)

The winter evening settles down
With smells of steaks in passageways.
Six o'clock.
The burnt-out ends of smoky days.
And now a gusty shower wraps
The grimy scraps
Of withered leaves about your feet
And newspapers from vacant lots;
The showers beat
On broken blinds and chimney-pots,   10
And at the corner of the street
A lonely cab-horse steams and stamps.
And then the lighting of the lamps.

T. S. Eliot

FUTILITY

Move him into the sun –
Gently its touch awoke him once,
At home, whispering of fields unsown.
Always it woke him, even in France,
Until this morning and this snow.
If anything might rouse him now
The kind old sun will know.

Think how it wakes the seeds –
Woke, once, the clays of a cold star.
Are limbs so dear-achieved, are sides   10
Full-nerved, – still warm, – too hard to stir?
Was it for this the clay grew tall?
– O what made fatuous sunbeams toil
To break earth's sleep at all?

Wilfred Owen

IN WESTMINSTER ABBEY

Let me take this other glove off
   As the *vox humana* swells,
And the beauteous fields of Eden
   Bask beneath the Abbey bells.
Here, where England's statesmen lie,
Listen to a lady's cry.

Gracious Lord, oh bomb the Germans.
   Spare their women for Thy Sake,
And if that is not too easy
   We will pardon Thy Mistake.
But, gracious Lord, whate'er shall be,
Don't let anyone bomb me.

Keep our Empire undismembered
   Guide our Forces by Thy Hand,
Gallant blacks from far Jamaica,
   Honduras and Togoland;
Protect them Lord in all their fights,
And, even more, protect the whites.

Think of what our Nation stands for,
   Books from Boots and country lanes
Free speech, free passes, class distinction,
   Democracy and proper drains.
Lord, put beneath Thy special care
One-eighty-nine Cadogan Square.

Although dear Lord I am a sinner,
   I have done no major crime;
Now I'll come to Evening Service
   Whensoever I have time.
So, Lord, reserve for me a crown,
And do not let my shares go down.

I will labour for Thy Kingdom,
   Help our lads to win the war,
Send white feathers to the cowards
   Join the Women's Army Corps,
Then wash the Steps around Thy Throne
In the Eternal Safety Zone.

Now I feel a little better,
      What a treat to hear Thy Word,
Where the bones of leading statesmen,
      Have so often been interred.
And now, dear Lord, I cannot wait
Because I have a luncheon date.

John Betjeman

THE AVERAGE

His peasant parents killed themselves with toil
To let their darling leave a stingy soil
For any of those smart professions which
Encourage shallow breathing, and grow rich.

The pressure of their fond ambition made
Their shy and country-loving child afraid
No sensible career was good enough,
Only a hero could deserve such love.

So here he was without maps or supplies,
A hundred miles from any decent town;   10
The desert glared into his blood-shot eyes;

The silence roared displeasure: looking down,
He saw the shadow of an Average Man
Attempting the exceptional, and ran.

W. H. Auden

REFUGEE BLUES

Say this city has ten million souls,
Some are living in mansions, some are living in holes;
Yet there's no place for us, my dear, yet there's no place for us.

Once we had a country and we thought it fair,
Look in the atlas and you'll find it there;
We cannot go there now, my dear, we cannot go there now.

In the village churchyard there grows an old yew,
Every spring it blossoms anew;
Old passports can't do that, my dear, old passports can't do that.

The consul banged the table and said;   10
"If you've no passport, you're officially dead":
But we are still alive, my dear, but we are still alive.

Went to a committee; they offered me a chair;
Asked me politely to return next year:
But where shall we go today, my dear, but where shall we go today?

Came to a public meeting; the speaker got up and said:
"If we let them in, they will steal our daily bread";
He was talking of you and me, my dear, he was talking of you
    and me.

Thought I heard the thunder rumbling in the sky,
It was Hitler over Europe, saying: "They must die";   20
O we were in his mind, my dear, O we were in his mind.

Saw a poodle in a jacket fastened with a pin,
Saw a door open and a cat let in:
But they weren't German Jews, my dear, but they weren't German
    Jews.

Went down the harbour and stood upon the quay,
Saw the fish swimming as if they were free:
Only ten feet away, my dear, only ten feet away.

Walked through a wood, saw the birds in the trees;
They had no politicians and sang at their ease:
They weren't the human race, my dear, they weren't the human
    race.   30

Dreamt I saw a building with a thousand floors,
A thousand windows and a thousand doors;
Not one of them was ours, my dear, not one of them was ours.

Stood on a great plain in the falling snow;
Ten thousand soldiers marched to and fro:
Looking for you and me, my dear, looking for you and me.

                                        W. H. Auden

DO NOT GO GENTLE INTO THAT GOOD NIGHT

Do not go gentle into that good night,
Old age should burn and rave at close of day;
Rage, rage against the dying of the light.

Though wise men at their end know dark is right,
Because their words had forked no lightning they
Do not go gentle into that good night.

Good men, the last wave by, crying how bright
Their frail deeds might have danced in a green bay,
Rage, rage against the dying of the light.

Wild men who caught and sang the sun in flight,   10
And learn, too late, they grieved it on its way,
Do not go gentle into that good night.

Grave men, near death, who see with blinding sight
Blind eyes could blaze like meteors and be gay,
Rage, rage against the dying of the light.

And you, my father, there on the sad height,
Curse, bless, me now with your fierce tears, I pray.
Do not go gentle into that good night.
Rage, rage against the dying of the light.

Dylan Thomas

THE INARTICULATE

His name was never mentioned in despatches,
nor was he hero of the desperate stand.
His death obscured no headlines, roused no snatches
of sympathy or personal sense of loss
even in comrade hearts. Under strict command
of parent, schoolmaster, and caustic boss,
his mind and limbs were harnessed to the clock;
and all his hours were blossoms for others to tread.
He gathered experience from the books he read,
and clambered mountains with a dreamer's alpenstock.   10
From attic windows he watched the white rains falling
but lacked the sounding-thought to fathom flood.
Hid was the voice of the lonely seagull calling
over the roof-tops to winds and an empty sky.
He sought no revelation in unfolding bud;
nor claimed a nobler cause for which to die
than the accidental bursting of a gun:
so little song or colour to warrant his remaining –
yet one there was for whom his life held meaning,
and with his passing, grief walled up the sun.   20

Howard Sergeant

WHEN I HEARD THE LEARN'D ASTRONOMER

When I heard the learn'd astronomer,
When the proofs, the figures, were ranged in columns before
    me,
When I was shown the charts and diagrams, to add, divide, and
    measure them,
When I sitting heard the astronomer where he lectured with
    much applause in the lecture-room,
How soon unaccountable I became tired and sick,
Till rising and gliding out I wander'd off by myself,
In the mystical moist night-air, and from time to time,
Look'd up in perfect silence at the stars.

Walt Whitman

A THUNDERSTORM

The wind begun to rock the grass
With threatening tunes and low, –
He flung a menace at the earth,
A menace at the sky.

The leaves unhooked themselves from trees
And started all abroad;
The dust did scoop itself like hands
And throw away the road.

The wagons quickened on the streets,
The thunder hurried slow;
The lightning showed a yellow beak,
And then a livid claw.

10

The birds put up the bars to nests,
The cattle fled to barns;
There came one drop of giant rain,
And then, as if the hands

That held the dams had parted hold,
The waters wrecked the sky,
But overlooked my father's house,
Just quartering a tree.   20

Emily Dickinson

AN OLD STORY

Strange that I did not know him then,
    That friend of mine.
I did not even show him then
    One friendly sign;

But cursed him for the ways he had
    To make me see
My envy of the praise he had
    For praising me.

I would have rid the earth of him
    Once, in my pride.   10
I never knew the worth of him
    Until he died.

Edwin Arlington Robinson

THE HOUSE ON THE HILL

They are all gone away,
    The House is shut and still,
There is nothing more to say.

Through broken walls and gray
    The winds blow bleak and shrill;
They are all gone away.

Nor is there one today
    To speak them good or ill:
There is nothing more to say.

Why is it then we stray   10
    Around that sunken sill?
They are all gone away,

137

And our poor fancy-play
   For them is wasted skill:
There is nothing more to say.

There is ruin and decay
   In the House on the Hill:
They are all gone away,
There is nothing more to say.

              Edwin Arlington Robinson

MEETING-HOUSE HILL

I must be mad, or very tired
When the curve of a blue bay beyond a railroad track
Is shrill and sweet to me like the sudden springing of a
      tune,
And the sight of a white church above thin trees in a city
      square
Amazes my eyes as though it were the Parthenon.
Clear, reticent, superbly final,
With the pillars of its portico refined to a cautious elegance,
It dominates the weak trees,
And the shot of its spire
Is cool and candid,   10
Rising into an unresisting sky.

Strange meeting-house
Pausing a moment upon a squalid hill-top.
I watch the spire sweeping the sky,
I am dizzy with the movement of the sky;

I might be watching a mast
With its royals set full
Straining before a two-reef breeze,
I might be sighting a tea-clipper,
Tacking into the blue bay,   20
Just back from Canton
With her hold full of green and blue porcelain
And a Chinese coolie leaning over the rail
Gazing at the white spire
With dull, sea-spent eyes.

                    Amy Lowell

AFTER APPLE-PICKING

My long two-pointed ladder's sticking through a tree
Toward heaven still,
And there's a barrel that I didn't fill
Beside it, and there may be two or three
Apples I didn't pick upon some bough.
But I am done with apple-picking now.
Essence of winter sleep is on the night,
The scent of apples: I am drowsing off.
I cannot rub the strangeness from my sight
I got from looking through a pane of glass   10
I skimmed this morning from the drinking trough
And held against the world of hoary grass.
It melted, and I let it fall and break.
But I was well
Upon my way to sleep before it fell,
And I could tell
What form my dreaming was about to take.
Magnified apples appear and disappear,
Stem end and blossom end,
And every fleck of russet showing clear.   20
My instep arch not only keeps the ache,
It keeps the pressure of a ladder-round.
I feel the ladder sway as the boughs bend.
And I keep hearing from the cellar bin
The rumbling sound
Of load on load of apples coming in.
For I have had too much
Of apple-picking: I am overtired
Of the great harvest I myself desired.
There were ten thousand fruit to touch,   30
Cherish in hand, lift down, and not let fall.
For all
That struck the earth,
No matter if not bruised or spiked with stubble,
Went surely to the cider-apple heap
As of no worth.
One can see what will trouble
This sleep of mine, whatever sleep it is.
Were he not gone,
The woodchuck could say whether it's like his   40
Long sleep, as I describe its coming on,
Or just some human sleep.

Robert Frost

THE LAST WORDS OF
MY ENGLISH GRANDMOTHER

1920

There were some dirty plates
and a glass of milk
beside her on a small table
near the rank, disheveled bed—

Wrinkled and nearly blind
she lay and snored
rousing with anger in her tones
to cry for food,

Gimme something to eat—
They're starving me–
I'm all right—I won't go
to the hospital. No, no, no

    10

Give me something to eat!
Let me take you
to the hospital, I said
and after you are well

you can do as you please.
She smiled, Yes
you do what you please first
then I can do what I please–

    20

Oh, oh, oh! she cried
as the ambulance men lifted
her to the stretcher—
Is this what you call

making me comfortable?
By now her mind was clear—
Oh you think you're smart
you young people,

she said, but I'll tell you
you don't know anything.
Then we started.
On the way

    30

we passed a long row
of elms, she looked at them
awhile out of
the ambulance window and said,

What are all those
fuzzy looking things out there?
Trees? Well, I'm tired
of them and rolled her head away.   40

William Carlos Williams

THE GARDEN

En robe de parade.—SAMAIN

Like a skein of loose silk blown against a wall
She walks by the railing of a path in Kensington Gardens,
And she is dying piece-meal
        of a sort of emotional anaemia.

And round about there is a rabble
Of the filthy, sturdy, unkillable infants of the very poor.
They shall inherit the earth.

In her is the end of breeding.
Her boredom is exquisite and excessive.
She would like some one to speak to her,   10
And is almost afraid that I
        will commit that indiscretion.

Ezra Pound

THE FALCONER OF GOD

I flung my soul to the air like a falcon flying.
I said, "Wait on, wait on, while I ride below!
    I shall start a heron soon
    In the marsh beneath the moon—
A strange white heron rising with silver on its wings,
        Rising and crying
    Wordless, wondrous things;
The secret of the stars, of the world's heart-strings
    The answer to their woe.
Then stoop thou upon him, and grip and hold him so!"   10

141

My wild soul waited on as falcons hover.
I beat the reedy fens as I trampled past.
 I heard the mournful loon
 In the marsh beneath the moon.
And then, with feathery thunder, the bird of my desire
 Broke from the cover
 Flashing silver fire.
 High up among the stars I saw his pinions spire.
 The pale clouds gazed aghast
As my falcon stooped upon him, and gript and held him fast. 20

My soul dropped through the air – with heavenly plunder? –
Gripping the dazzling bird my dreaming knew?
 Nay! but a piteous freight,
 A dark and heavy weight
Despoiled of silver plumage, its voice forever stilled –
 All of the wonder
 Gone that ever filled
 Its guise with glory. O bird that I have killed,
 How brilliantly you flew
Across my rapturous vision when first I dreamed of you!   30

Yet I fling my soul on high with new endeavour,
And I ride the world below with a joyful mind.
 I shall start a heron soon
 In the marsh beneath the moon –
A wondrous silver heron its inner darkness fledges!
 I beat forever
 The fens and the sedges.
 The pledge is still the same – for all disastrous pledges,
 All hopes resigned!
My soul still flies above me for the quarry it shall find.   40

William Rose Benét

THE STUDENT

 "In America," began
the lecturer, "everyone must have a
degree. The French do not think that
all can have it, they don't say everyone
 must go to college." We
do incline to feel
 that although it may be unnecessary
142

to know fifteen languages,
one degree is not too much. With us, a
school – like the singing tree of which   10
the leaves were mouths singing in concert – is
      both a tree of knowledge
and of liberty, –
      seen in the unanimity of college

mottoes, *lux et veritas,*
Christo et ecclesiae, sapiet
felici. It may be that we
have not knowledge, just opinions, that we
      are undergraduates,
not students; we know   20
      we have been told with smiles, by expatriates

of whom we had asked "When will
your experiment be finished?" "Science
is never finished." Secluded
from domestic strife, Jack Bookworm led a
      college life, says Goldsmith;
and here also as
      in France or Oxford, study is beset with

dangers, — with bookworms, mildews,
and complaisancies. But someone in New   30
England has known enough to say
the student is patience personified,
      is a variety
of hero, "patient
      of neglect and of reproach," – who can "hold by

himself." You can't beat hens to
make them lay. Wolf's wool is the best of wool,
but it cannot be sheared because
the wolf will not comply. With knowledge as
      with the wolf's surliness,
the student studies
      voluntarily, refusing to be less

than individual. He
"gives his opinion and then rests on it;"
he renders service when there is
no reward, and is too reclusive for
            some things to seem to touch
him, not because he
            has no feeling but because he has so much.

Marianne Moore

DEAD BOY

The little cousin is dead, by foul subtraction,
A green bough from Virginia's aged tree,
And none of the county kin like the transaction,
Nor some of the world of outer dark, like me.

A boy not beautiful, nor good, nor clever,
A black cloud full of storms too hot for keeping,
A sword beneath his mother's heart – yet never
Woman bewept her babe as this is weeping.

A pig with a pasty face, so I had said,
Squealing for cookies, kinned by poor pretense   10
With a noble house. But the little man quite dead,
I see the forebears' antique lineaments.

The elder men have strode by the box of death
To the wide flag porch, and muttering low send round
The bruit of the day. O friendly waste of breath!
Their hearts are hurt with a deep dynastic wound.

He was pale and little, the foolish neighbours say;
The first-fruits, saith the Preacher, the Lord hath taken;
But this was the old tree's late branch wrenched away,
Grieving the sapless limbs, the shorn and shaken.   20

John Crowe Ransom

LOVE IS NOT ALL

Love is not all: it is not meat nor drink
Nor slumber nor a roof against the rain;
Nor yet a floating spar to men that sink
And rise and sink and rise and sink again;
Love can not fill the thickened lung with breath,
Nor clean the blood, nor set the fractured bone;
Yet many a man is making friends with death
Even as I speak, for lack of love alone.
It well may be that in a difficult hour,
Pinned down by pain and moaning for release,   10
Or nagged by want past resolution's power,
I might be driven to sell your love for peace,
Or trade the memory of this night for food.
It well may be. I do not think I would.

Edna St. Vincent Millay

when god lets my body be

when god lets my body be

From each brave eye shall sprout a tree
fruit that dangles therefrom

the purpled world will dance upon
Between my lips which did sing

a rose shall beget the spring
that maidens whom passion wastes

will lay between their little breasts
My strong fingers beneath the snow

Into strenuous birds shall go   10
my love walking in the grass

their wings will touch with her face
and all the while shall my heart be

With the bulge and nuzzle of the sea.

E. E. Cummings

WOMEN

Women have no wilderness in them,
They are provident instead,
Content in the tight hot cell of their hearts
To eat dusty bread.

They do not see cattle cropping red winter grass,
They do not hear
Snow water going down under culverts
Shallow and clear.

They wait, when they should turn to journeys,
They stiffen, when they should bend.   10

They use against themselves that benevolence
To which no man is friend.

They cannot think of so many crops to a field
Or of clean wood cleft by an ax.
Their love is an eager meaninglessness
Too tense, or too lax.

They hear in every whisper that speaks to them
A shout and a cry.
As like as not, when they take life over their door-sills
They should let it go by.   20

Louise Bogan

AUTUMN

Autumn is filling his harvest-bins
    With red and yellow grain,
Fire begins and frost begins
    And the floors are cold again.

Summer went when the crop was sold,
    Summer is piled away,
Dry as a faded marigold
    In the dry, long-gathered hay.

It is time to walk to the cider-mill
    Through air like apple wine   10
And watch the moon rise over the hill,
    Stinging and hard and fine.

It is time to cover your seed-pods deep
    And let them wait and be warm,
It is time to sleep the heavy sleep
    That does not wake for the storm.

Winter walks from the green, streaked West
    With a bag of Northern Spies,
The skins are red as a robin's breast,
    The honey chill as the skies.   20

                              Stephen Vincent Benét

DEATH OF LITTLE BOYS

When little boys grown patient at last, weary,
Surrender their eyes immeasurably to the night,
The event will rage terrific as the sea;
Their bodies fill a crumbling room with light.

Then you will touch at the bedside, torn in two,
Gold curls now deftly intricate with gray
As the windowpane extends a fear to you
From one peeled aster drenched with the wind all day.

And over his chest the covers, in an ultimate dream,
Will mount to the teeth, ascend the eyes, press back   10
The locks – while round his sturdy belly gleam
The suspended breaths, white spars above the wreck:

Till all the guests, come in to look, turn down
Their palms, and delirium assails the cliff
Of Norway where you ponder, and your little town
Reels like a sailor drunk in his rotten skiff. . . .

The bleak sunshine shrieks its chipped music then
Out to the milkweed amid the fields of wheat.
There is a calm for you where men and women
Unroll the chill precision of moving feet.   20

                              Allen Tate

AUTO WRECK

Its quick soft silver bell beating, beating
And down the dark, one ruby flare
Pulsing out red light like an artery,
The ambulance at top speed floating down
Past beacons and illuminated clocks
Wings in a heavy curve, dips down,
And brakes speed, entering the crowd.
The doors leap open, emptying light;
Stretchers are laid out, the mangled lifted
And stowed into the little hospital.   10

Then the bell, breaking the hush, tolls once,
And the ambulance with its terrible cargo
Rocking, slightly rocking, moves away,
As the doors, an afterthought, are closed.

We are deranged, walking among the cops
Who sweep glass and are large and composed.
One is still making notes under the light.
One with a bucket douches ponds of blood
Into the street and gutter.
One hangs lanterns on the wrecks that cling,   20
Empty husks of locusts, to iron poles.

Our throats were tight as tourniquets,
Our feet were bound with splints, but now
Like convalescents intimate and gauche,
We speak through sickly smiles and warn
With the stubborn saw of common sense,
The grim joke and the banal resolution.
The traffic moves around with care,
But we remain, touching a wound
That opens to our richest horror.   30

Already old, the question Who shall die?
Becomes unspoken Who is innocent?
For death in war is done by hands;
Suicide has cause; and stillbirth, logic.
But this invites the occult mind,
Cancels our physics with a sneer,
And spatters all we know of dénouement
Across the expedient and wicked stones.

Karl Shapiro

THE WOMAN AT THE
WASHINGTON ZOO

The saris go by me from the embassies.

Cloth from the moon. Cloth from another planet.
They look back at the leopard like the leopard.

And I. . . .
 this print of mine, that has kept its colour
Alive through so many cleanings; this dull null
Navy I wear to work, and wear from work, and so
To my bed, so to my grave, with no
Complaints, no comment: neither from my chief,
The Deputy Chief Assistant, nor his chief –   10
Only I complain. . . . this serviceable
Body that no sunlight dyes, no hand suffuses
But, dome-shadowed, withering among columns,
Wavy beneath fountains – small, far-off, shining
In the eyes of animals, these beings trapped
As I am trapped but not, themselves, the trap,
Aging, but without knowledge of their age,
Kept safe here, knowing not of death, for death –
Oh, bars of my own body, open, open!

The world goes by my cage and never sees me.   20
And there come not to me, as come to these,
The wild beasts, sparrows pecking the llamas' grain,
Pigeons settling on the bears' bread, buzzards
Tearing the meat the flies have clouded. . . .
 Vulture,
When you come for the white rat that the foxes left,
Take off the red helmet of your head, the black
Wings that have shadowed me, and step to me as man:
The wild brother at whose feet the white wolves fawn,
To whose hand of power the great lioness   30
Stalks, purring. . . .
 You know what I was,
You see what I am: change me, change me!

Randall Jarrell

DEATH FROM CANCER

This Easter, Arthur Winslow, less than dead,
Your people set you up in Phillips' House
To settle off your wrestling with the crab –
The claws drop flesh upon your yachting blouse
Until longshoreman Charon come and stab
Through your adjusted bed
And crush the crab. On Boston Basin, shells
Hit water by the Union Boat Club wharf:
You ponder why the coxes' squeakings dwarf
The *resurrexit dominus* of all the bells.   10

Grandfather Winslow, look, the swanboats coast
That island in the Public Gardens, where
The bread-stuffed ducks are brooding, where with tub
And strainer the mid-Sunday Irish scare
The sun-struck shallows for the dusky chub
This Easter, and the ghost
Of risen Jesus walks the waves to run
Arthur upon a trumpeting black swan
Beyond Charles River to the Acheron
Where the wide waters and their voyager are one.   20

Robert Lowell

ADVICE TO A PROPHET

When you come, as you soon must, to the streets of our city,
Mad-eyed from stating the obvious,
Not proclaiming our fall but begging us
In God's name to have self-pity,

Spare us all word of the weapons, their force and range,
The long numbers that rocket the mind;
Our slow, unreckoning hearts will be left behind,
Unable to fear what is too strange.

Nor shall you scare us with talk of the death of the race.
How should we dream of this place without us? –   10
The sun mere fire, the leaves untroubled about us,
A stone look on the stone's face?

Speak of the world's own change. Though we cannot conceive
Of an undreamt thing, we know to our cost
How the dreamt cloud crumbles, the vines are blackened by frost,
How the view alters. We could believe,

If you told us so, that the white-tailed deer will slip
Into perfect shade, grown perfectly shy,
The lark avoid the reaches of our eye,
The jack-pine lose its knuckled grip   20

On the cold ledge, and every torrent burn
As Xanthus once, its gliding trout
Stunned in a twinkling. What should we be without
The dolphin's arc, the dove's return,

These things in which we have seen ourselves and spoken?
Ask us, prophet, how we shall call
Our natures forth when that live tongue is all
Dispelled, that glass obscured or broken

In which we have said the rose of our love and the clean
Horse of our courage, in which beheld   30
The singing locust of the soul unshelled,
And all we mean or wish to mean.

Ask us, ask us whether with the worldless rose
Our hearts shall fail us; come demanding
Whether there shall be lofty or long standing
When the bronze annals of the oak-tree close.

Richard Wilbur

HOW ONE WINTER CAME IN THE LAKE REGION

For weeks and weeks the autumn world stood still,
    Clothed in the shadow of a smoky haze;
The fields were dead, the wind had lost its will,
And all the lands were hushed by wood and hill,
    In those grey, withered days.

Behind a mist the blear sun rose and set,
    At night the moon would nestle in a cloud;
The fisherman, a ghost, did cast his net;
The lake its shores forgot to chafe and fret,
    And hushed its caverns loud.   10

Far in the smoky woods the birds were mute,
    Save that from blackened tree a jay would scream,
Or far in swamps the lizard's lonesome lute
Would pipe in thirst, or by some gnarlèd root
    The tree-toad trilled his dream.

From day to day still hushed the season's mood,
    The streams stayed in their runnels shrunk and dry;
Suns rose aghast by wave and shore and wood,
And all the world, with ominous silence, stood
    In weird expectancy: 20

When one strange night the sun like blood went down,
    Flooding the heavens in a ruddy hue;
Red grew the lake, the sere fields parched and brown,
Red grew the marshes where the creeks stole down,
    But never a wind-breath blew.

That night I felt the winter in my veins,
    A joyous tremor of the icy glow;
And woke to hear the north's wild vibrant strains,
While far and wide, by withered woods and plains,
    Fast fell the driving snow.   30

Wilfred Campbell

THE PASSING OF SPRING

No longer in the meadow coigns shall blow
The creamy blood-root in her suit of gray,
But all the first strange flowers have passed away,
Gone with the childlike dreams that touched us so;
April is spent, and summer soon shall go,
Swift as a shadow o'er the heads of men,
And autumn with the painted leaves; and then,
When fires are set, and windows blind with snow,
We shall remember, with a yearning pang,
How in the poplars the first robins sang,   10
The wind-flowers risen from their leafy cots,
When life was gay and spring was at the helm,
The maple full of little crimson knots,
And all that delicate blossoming of the elm.

Archibald Lampman

LATE NOVEMBER

The hills and leafless forests slowly yield
To the thick-driving snow. A little while
And night shall darken down. In shouting file
The woodmen's carts go by me homeward-wheeled,
Past the thin fading stubbles, half concealed,
Now golden-gray, sowed softly through with snow,
Where the last ploughman follows still his row,
Turning black furrows through the whitening field.
Far off the village lamps begin to gleam,
Fast drives the snow, and no man comes this way; 10
The hills grow wintry white, and bleak winds moan
About the naked uplands. I alone
Am neither sad, nor shelterless, nor gray,
Wrapped round with thought, content to watch
  and dream.

Archibald Lampman

LOW TIDE ON GRAND PRÉ

The sun goes down, and over all
    These barren reaches by the tide
Such unelusive glories fall,
    I almost dream they yet will bide
    Until the coming of the tide.

And yet I know that not for us,
    By any ecstasy of dream,
He lingers to keep luminous
    A little while the grievous stream,
    Which frets, uncomforted of dream; –   10

A grievous stream, that to and fro,
    Athrough the fields of Acadie
Goes wandering, as if to know
    Why one belovèd face should be
    So long from home and Acadie.

Was it a year or lives ago
    We took the grasses on our hands,
And caught the summer flying low
    Over the waving meadow lands,
    And held it there between our hands?   20

The while the river at our feet –
    A drowsy inland meadow stream –
At set of sun the after-heat
    Made running gold, and in the gleam
    We freed our birch upon the stream.

There down along the elms at dusk
    We lifted dripping blade to drift,
Through twilight scented fine like musk,
    Where night and gloom awhile uplift,
    Nor sunder soul and soul adrift.   30

And that we took into our hands
    Spirit of life or subtler thing –
Breathed on us there, and loosed the bands
    Of death, and taught us, whispering,
    The secrets of some wonder-thing.

Then all your face grew light, and seemed
  To hold the shadow of the sun;
The evening faltered, and I deemed
  That time was ripe, and years had done
  Their wheeling underneath the sun.   40

So all desire and all regret,
  And fear and memory, were naught;
One to remember or forget
  The keen delight our hands had caught;
  Morrow and yesterday were naught.

The night has fallen, and the tide. . .
  Now and again comes drifting home,
Across these aching barrens wide,
  A sigh like driven wind or foam:
  In grief the flood is bursting home.   50

                                        Bliss Carman

AT THE CEDARS

You had two girls – Baptiste –
One is Virginie –
Hold hard – Baptiste!
Listen to me.

The whole drive was jammed
In that bend at the Cedars;
The rapids were dammed
With the logs tight rammed
And crammed; you might know
The Devil had clinched them below.   10

We worked three days – not a budge,
"She's as tight as a wedge, on the ledge,"
Says our foreman;
"Mon Dieu! boys, look here,
We must get this thing clear."

155

He cursed at the men
And we went for it then;
With our cant-dogs arow,
We just gave he-yo-ho;
When she gave a big shove   20
From above.

The gang yelled and tore
For the shore,
The logs gave a grind
Like a wolf's jaws behind,
And as quick as a flash,
With a shove and a crash,
They were down in a mash,
But I and ten more,
All but Isaac Dufour,   30
Were ashore.

He leaped on a log in the front of the rush,
And shot out from the bind
While the jam roared behind;
As he floated along
He balanced his pole
And tossed us a song.
But just as we cheered,
Up darted a log from the bottom,
Leaped thirty feet square and fair,   40
And came down on his own.

He went up like a block
With the shock,
And when he was there
In the air,
Kissed his hand to the land;
When he dropped
My heart stopped,
For the first logs had caught him
And crushed him;   50
When he rose in his place
There was blood on his face.

There were some girls, Baptiste,
Picking berries on the hillside,
Where the river curls, Baptiste,
You know – on the still side.

One was down by the water,
She saw Isaac
Fall back.

She did not scream, Baptiste,   60
She launched her canoe;
It did seem, Baptiste,
That she wanted to die too,
For before you could think
The birch cracked like a shell
In that rush of hell,
And I saw them both sink –

Baptiste! –
He had two girls,
One is Virginie,   70
What God calls the other
Is not known to me.

Duncan Campbell Scott

IN FLANDERS FIELDS

In Flanders fields the poppies blow
Between the crosses, row on row,
    That mark our place; and in the sky
    The larks, still bravely singing, fly
Scarce heard amid the guns below.

We are the Dead. Short days ago
We lived, felt dawn, saw sunset glow,
    Loved and were loved, and now we lie
    In Flanders fields.

Take up our quarrel with the foe: 10
To you from failing hands we throw
    The torch; be yours to hold it high.
    If ye break faith with us who die
We shall not sleep, though poppies grow
    In Flanders fields.

John McCrae

THE SONG OF THE SKI

Norse am I when the first snow falls;
Norse am I till the ice departs.
The fare for which my spirit calls
Is blood from a hundred viking-hearts.
The curved wind wraps me like a cloak;
The pines blow out their ghostly smoke.
I'm high on the hill and ready to go –
A wingless bird in a world of snow:
Yet I'll ride the air
With a dauntless dare   10
That only a child of the north can know.

The bravest ski has a cautious heart
And moves like a tortoise at the start,
But when it tastes the tang of the air
It leaps away like a frightened hare.
The day is gloomy, the curtains half-drawn,
And light is stunted as at the dawn:
But my foot is sure and my arm is brawn.

I poise on the hill and I wave adieu:
(My curving skis are firm and true)   20
The slim wood quickens, the air takes fire
And sings to me like a gypsy's lyre.
Swifter and swifter grows my flight:
The dark pines ease the unending white.
The lean, cold birches, as I go by,
Are like blurred etchings against the sky.

One am I for a moment's joy
With the falling star and the plunging bird.
The world is swift as an Arab boy;
The world is sweet as a woman's word.   30
Never came such a pure delight
To a bacchanal or a sybarite:
Swifter and swifter grows my flight,
And glad am I, as I near the leap,
That the snow is fresh and the banks are deep.

Swifter and swifter on I fare,
And soon I'll float with the birds on air,
The speed is blinding; I'm over the ridge,
Spanning space on a phantom bridge.

The drifts await me: I float, I fall: 40
The world leaps up like a lunging carp.
I land erect and the tired winds drawl
A lazy rune on a broken harp.

Child of the roofless world am I;
Not of those hibernating drones
Who fear the grey of a wintry sky
And the shrieking wind's ironic tones,
Who shuffle cards in a cloud of smoke
Or crawl like frozen flies at chess,
Or gossip all day with meddling folk   50
In collar of starch and a choking dress.
Come, ye maids of the vanity-box,
Come, ye men of the stifling air;
The white wind waits at your door and knocks;
The white snow calls you everywhere.
Come, ye lads of the lounge and chair,
And gird your feet with the valiant skis
And mount the steed of the winter air
And hold the reins of the winter breeze.

Lord of the mountains dark with pine!   60
Lord of the fields of smoking snow!
Grant to this vagrant heart of mine
A path of wood where my feet may go,
And a roofless world to my journey's end,
And a cask of wind for my cup of wine,
And yellow gold of the sun to spend,
And at night the stars in endless line,
And, after it all, the hand of a friend –
The hand of a trusted friend in mine.

Wilson MacDonald

THE LITTLE SISTER OF THE PROPHET

I have left a basket of dates
In the cool dark room that is under the vine,
Some curds set out in two little crimson plates
And a flask of the amber wine,
And cakes most cunningly beaten
Of savoury herbs, and spice, and the delicate wheaten
Flour that is best,
And all to lighten his spirit and sweeten his rest.

159

That morning he cried, "Awake,
And see what the wonderful grace of the Lord hath revealed!" 10
And we ran for his sake,
But 'twas only the dawn outspread o'er our father's field,
And the house of the potter white in the valley below
But his hands were upraised to the east and he cried to us, "So
Ye may ponder and read
The strength and the beauty of God outrolled in a fiery screed!"

Then the little brown mother smiled,
As one does on the words of a well-loved child,
And, "Son," she replied, "have the oxen been watered and fed?
For work is to do, though the skies be never so red,   20
And already the first sweet hours of the day are spent."
And he sighed and went.

Will he come from the byre
With his head all misty with dreams, and his eyes on fire,
Shaking us all with the weight of the words of his passion?
I will give him raisins instead of dates,
And wreathe young leaves on the little red plates.

I will put on my new head-tyre,
And braid my hair in a comelier fashion.
Will he note? Will he mind?   30
Will he touch my cheek as he used to, and laugh and be kind?

Marjorie Pickthall

THE SHARK

He seemed to know the harbour,
So leisurely he swam;
His fin,
Like a piece of sheet-iron,
Three-cornered,
And with knife-edge,
Stirred not a bubble
As it moved
With its base-line on the water.

His body was tubular   10
And tapered,
And smoke-blue,
And as he passed the wharf
He turned,
And snapped at a flat-fish
That was dead and floating.
And I saw the flash of a white throat,
And a double row of white teeth,
And eyes of metallic grey,
Hard and narrow and slit.   20

Then out of the harbour,
With that three-cornered fin
Shearing without a bubble the water
Lithely,
Leisurely,
He swam –
That strange fish,
Tubular, tapered, smoke-blue,
Part vulture, part wolf,
Part neither – for his blood was cold.   30

E. J. Pratt

IN ABSENTIA

Erect and motionless he stood,
   His face a hieroglyph of stone,
Stopped was his pulse, chilled was his blood,
   And stiff each sinew, nerve and bone.

The spell an instant held him, when
   His veins were swept by tidal power,
And then life's threescore years and ten
   Were measured by a single hour.

The world lay there beneath his eye;
   The sun had left the heavens to float   10
A hand-breadth from him, and the sky
   Was but an anchor for his boat.

Fled was the class-room's puny space –
    His eye saw but a whirling disk;
His old and language-weathered face
    Shone like a glowing asterisk!

What chance had he now to remember
    The year held months so saturnine
As ill-starred May and blank September,
    With that brute tugging at his line?   20

E. J. Pratt

THE MULLEINS

Here are the mulleins, steadfast at their posts;
A lost battalion, sere and grim and tall,
They hold the line where ran the old stone wall
Between the meadows. On its rampart coasts
Once beat the waves of timothy, the hosts
Of busbied clover. Time has felled them all
Save the lank mulleins standing sentinel
Above the snowdrifts. These are Summer's ghosts.

Rigid they rise where oft the bobolink
Swung the sweet censer of his ecstasy,   10
Or, hovering, swayed their dizzy spikes around.

Like them I shiver with the wind; and think
Of bobolinks that nested in the hay
And how June's passion slumbers underground.

Robert W. Cumberland

WINTER

Stern and strong, great lord of the Arctic spaces,
Fierce yet fair-faced, ruler of snowy tundras,
I salute thee, hail thee as benefactor,
    Kind to my country!

Noble nights, nights lit with the streaming glories
Cast abroad, bright-haired, by the Northern Dawnlight –
These enfold thee, these are thy royal mantle,
      Monarch most mighty!

Sultry south-lands, sick with the suns of summer,
Swoon to death, deep-smitten with fenny fevers,   10
Stung by fly-foes, seized by colossal vipers
      Lurking in jungles –

Ah, but here, here Canada's fragrant forests
Breathe out health, breathe peace from the south's
    infection.
Purged by thee, O Winter, our plains and mountains
      Heal us and hold us.

Ay, and more! Thy boisterous woods have made us
Brave and man-souled, eager to wrestle danger,
Laughing loud, exultant amid thy blizzards,
      Fronting thy frenzy.   20

See our youth, hot-hearted, assail thy snow-fields!
See them, steel-shod, tramp on thy frozen torrents!
See them fly, men-eagles, about our Arctic,
      Crowning our rights there!

These proclaim thee, Winter, as friend and father,
Thanking thee, great king of the strong and daring.
Thee our land exalts, through the stalwart ages,
      Sire of our greatness!

                      Watson Kirkconnell

COMRÀDE

Of course I am a friend of yours, within
The limits of expediency. My motto
Is expediency before principle. It ought to
Be yours, no doubt is, if not, soon will then.

And if I ever seem to double-cross you
Don't let it get you down. Get the same leaning.
Double-crossing has no derogatory meaning
If one succeeds. Not that I want to boss you

But we're a pair of animals, economic
Animals under the law of the jungle, 10
Cheek by jowl, and it doesn't do to bungle.
You won't if fit. There's nothing the fit can't stomach

Except that talk of yours about ultimate value,
Keep that up and I won't know what to call you.

Robert Finch

ATLANTIC DOOR

Through or over the deathless feud
of the cobra sea and the mongoose wind
you must fare to reach us,
through hiss and throttle
where the great ships are scattered twigs on a green
     commotion
and the plane is a fugitive mote
in the stare of the sun.
Come, by a limbo of motion humbled,
under cliffs of cloud
and over the vaulting whalehalls. 10
In this lymph's abyss a billion
years of spawning and dying have passed and will pass
without ministration of man.
And for all the red infusions of sailors,
the veins of vikings drained and of lascars,
blood of Gilbert's jollies and Jellicoe's,
for all haemoglobin seeping from corvette and sealer,
from the sodden hulls of Hood and Titanic –
still do these waves when the gale snaps them
fracture white as the narwhal's tusk. 20
Come then trailing your pattern of gain or solace
and think no more than you must
of the simple unhuman truth of this ocean,
that down deep below the lowest pulsing of primal cell
tar-dark and still
lie the bleak and forever capacious tombs of the sea.

Earle Birney

ELLESMERELAND

Explorers say that harebells rise
from the cracks of Ellesmereland
and cod swim fat beneath the ice
that grinds its meagre sands
No man is settled on that coast
The harebells are alone
Nor is there talk of making man
from ice cod bell or stone

Earle Birney

TAKE BEAUTY

Take Beauty for your bread;
   Beauty's not far to seek;
   When the soul is weak
For want of being fed,

Find it the manna given
   In lovely solitude:
   Find it the precious food
Daily dropped from heaven.

Gather your strength and go
   Where there is none to guard,   10
   Through meadows many-starred
With whiter flowers than snow.

Look to the sea's ellipse
   On whose celestial glass
   Pass and again repass
The slant sails of the ships.

Walk where the hare has trod,
   Taste where the moth has fed:
   Take Beauty for your bread
From the stretched hand of God.   20

Audrey Alexandra Brown

FOR ALL WHO REMEMBER

Cold as the North, along this western run
The white stuff comes aboard like streaming snow –
A job to finish, and a job begun;
Warm-blooded flesh must go where convoys go.

Shadows move on the hayfield; uplands dream
in the sun.

Shudder of wind and sweep of gusty rain,
And gas-caped columns moving up the line;
Up to the rubble and the guns again,
The shrapnel and the mortar and the mine.

Laughing crowds in the drugstore, corner of
Bridge and Main.   10

Twelve hundred deadly feet . . . and flaming grey,
The sky afire with flak from field and town;
"Steady now skipper . . . now the stuff's away . . ."
The multi-coloured parachutes go down.

Frozen ruts in a woodroad; southwest wind
on the bay.

Charles Bruce

SIMEON TAKES HINTS FROM HIS ENVIRONS

Heaven is God's grimace at us on high.
This land is a cathedral; speech, its sermon.
The moon is a rude gargoyle in the sky.

The leaves rustle. Come, who will now determine
Whether this be the wind, or priestly robes.
The frogs croak out ecclesiastic German,

Whereby our slavish ears have punctured lobes.
The stars are mass-lamps on a lofty altar;
Even the angels are Judaeophobes.

There is one path; in it I shall not falter.   10
Let me rush to the bosom of the state
And church, grasp lawyer-code and monkish psalter,

And being Christianus Simeon, late
Of Jewry, have much comfort and salvation –
Salvation in this life, at any rate.

A. M. Klein

TIME IN A PUBLIC WARD

As life goes on to worse and worse
The bed beside me calls the nurse
And says, It's getting worse, I guess.
She makes the worse a little less
By needle. Soon along the wall
Another bed puts in a call.

After pills the lights go down;
The walls turn gray and pink and brown.
Time passes. All at once a jet
Of orange lights a cigarette   10
Within whose glow a caverned eye
Watches the cinder burn and die.

The walls go back to gray and pink
And brown again. One hears a sink
And low voices, rustling feet;
There's music somewhere, late and sweet.
Clocks in the town put by the night
Hour by hour, ticked and right.

George Johnston

CANTERBURY

Here is no peace. Though swallows thread the towers
That soar themselves like swallows, like the lark,
And in the sunlight swims the holy ark
Billowed on fields of hops and garden flowers,
That droop and wait for evening. Though there is cool
Within the welling crypt; the chant comes down
In runnels, sliding on the well-worn stone
To fall in water-drops upon the pool.

167

Yet brings no peace. Martyrdom staining the steps,
Pain prisoned in the pillars; no chant can hide.   10
And underneath a greater act that seeps
Below the masonry, of One who died
In throb and sweat, Whose bloody kindness flows
Through arch and apse and buttress of this Rose.

Douglas Le Pan

CANOE-TRIP

What of this fabulous country
Now that we have it reduced to a few hot hours
And sun-burn on our backs?
On this south side the countless archipelagoes,
The slipway where titans sent splashing the last great
    glaciers;
And then up to the foot of the blue pole star
A wilderness,
The pinelands whose limits seem distant as Thule,
The millions of lakes once cached and forgotten,
The clearings enamelled with blueberries, rank silence
    about them;   10
And skies that roll all day with cloud-chimeras
To baffle the eye with portents and unwritten myths,
The flames of sunset, the lions of gold and gules.
Into this reservoir we dipped and pulled out lakes and
    rivers,
We strung them together and made our circuit.
Now what shall be our word as we return,
What word of this curious country?

It is good,
It is a good stock to own though it seldom pays dividends.
There are holes here and there for a gold-mine or a
    hydro-plant.   20
But the tartan of river and rock spreads undisturbed,
The plaid of a land with little desire to buy or sell.
The dawning light skirls out its independence;
At noon the brazen trumpets slash the air;
Night falls, the gulls scream sharp defiance;
Let whoever comes to tame this land, beware!
Can you put a bit to the lunging wind?

Can you hold wild horses by the hair?
Then have no hope to harness the energy here,
It gallops along the wind away.   30
But here are crooked nerves made straight,
The fracture cured no doctor could correct.
The hand and mind, reknit, stand whole for work;
The fable proves no cul-de-sac.
Now from the maze we circle back;
The map suggested a wealth of cloudy escapes;
That was a dream, we have converted the dream to act.
And what we now expect is not simplicity,
No steady breeze, or any surprise,
Orchids along the portage, white water, crimson leaves.   40
Content, we face again the complex task.

And yet the marvels we have seen remain.
We think of the eagles, of the fawns at the river bend,
The storms, the sudden sun, the clouds sheered
          downwards.
O so to move! With such immaculate decision!
O proudly as waterfalls curling like cumulus!

Douglas Le Pan

THE MAN WHO FINDS THAT
HIS SON HAS BECOME A THIEF

Coming into the store at first angry
At the accusation, believing in
The word of his boy who has told him:
I didn't steal anything, honest.

Then becoming calmer, seeing that anger
Will not help in the business, listening painfully
As the other's evidence unfolds, so painfully slow.

Then seeing gradually that evidence
Almost as if tighten slowly around the neck
Of his son, at first vaguely circumstantial, then
          gathering damage,   10
Until there is present the unmistakable odour of guilt
Which seeps now into the mind and lays its poison.

169

Suddenly feeling sick and alone and afraid,
As if an unseen hand had slapped him in the face
For no reason whatsoever: wanting to get out
Into the street, the night, the darkness, anywhere to hide
The pain that must show in the face to these strangers,
     the fear.

It must be like this.
It could hardly be otherwise.

Raymond Souster

TO THE AVON RIVER
ABOVE STRATFORD, CANADA

What did the Indians call you?
For you do not flow
With English accents.
I hardly know
What I should call you
     Because before
I drank coffee or tea
     I drank you
     With my cupped hands
And you did not taste English to me   10
     And you do not sound
     Like Avon
     Or swans & bards
But rather like the sad wild fowl
     In prints drawn
     By Audubon
And like dear bad poets
     Who wrote
     Early in Canada
And never were of note.   20
You are the first river
     I crossed
And like the first whirlwind
     The first rainbow
     First snow, first
     Falling star I saw,
You, for other rivers are my law.
     These other rivers:

The Red & the Thames
Are never so sweet   30
To skate upon, swim in
    Or for baptism of sin.
    Silver and light
The sentence of your voice,
    With a soprano
Continuous cry you shall
    Always flow
    Through my heart.
The rain and the snow of my mind
Shall supply the spring of that river   40
    Forever.
Though not your name
Your coat of arms I know
    And motto:
A shield of reeds and cresses
    Sedges, crayfishes
The hermaphroditic leech
Minnows, muskrats and farmers' geese
And printed above this shield
One of my earliest wishes   50
"To flow like you."

James Reaney

WARREN PRYOR

When every pencil meant a sacrifice
his parents boarded him at school in town,
slaving to free him from the stony fields,
the meagre acreage that bore them down.

They blushed with pride when, at his graduation,
they watched him picking up the slender scroll,
his passport from the years of brutal toil
and lonely patience in a barren hole.

When he went in the Bank their cups ran over.
They marvelled how he wore a milk-white shirt   10
work days and jeans on Sundays. He was saved
from their thistle-strewn farm and its red dirt.

And he said nothing. Hard and serious
like a young bear inside his teller's cage,
his axe-hewn hands upon the paper bills
aching with empty strength and throttled rage.

Alden Nowlan

STORY

She tells me a child built her house
one Spring afternoon,
but that the child was killed
crossing the street.

She says she read it in the newspaper,
that at the corner of this and that avenue
a child was run down by an automobile.

Of course I do not believe her.
She has built the house herself,
hung the oranges and coloured beads in the doorways,   10
crayoned flowers on the walls.

She has made the paper things for the wind,
collected crooked stones for their shadows in the sun,
fastened yellow and dark balloons to the ceiling.

Each time I visit her
she repeats the story of the child to me.
I never question her. It is important
to understand one's part in a legend.

I take my place
among the paper fish and make-believe clocks,   20
naming the flowers she has drawn,
smiling while she paints my head on large clay coins,
and making a sort of courtly love to her
when she contemplates her own traffic death.

Leonard Cohen

PART THREE

BINNORIE

There were twa sisters sat in a bour,
  Binnorie, O Binnorie!
There cam a knight to be their wooer,
  By the bonnie milldams o' Binnorie.

He courted the eldest with glove and ring,
But he lo'ed the youngest abune a' thing.

The eldest she was vexèd sair,
And sair envièd her sister fair.

Upon a morning fair and clear,
She cried upon her sister dear: 10

"O sister, sister, tak my hand,
And let's go down to the river-strand."

She's ta'en her by the lily hand,
And led her down to the river-strand.

The youngest stood upon a stane,
The eldest cam and push'd her in.

"O sister, sister, reach your hand!
And ye sall be heir o' half my land:

"O sister, reach me but your glove!
And sweet William sall be your love."   20

Sometimes she sank, sometimes she swam,
Until she cam to the miller's dam.

Out then cam the miller's son,
And saw the fair maid soummin' in.

"O father, father, draw your dam!
There's either a mermaid or a milk-white swan."

The miller hasted and drew his dam,
And there he found a drown'd womàn.

You couldna see her middle sma',
Her gowden girdle was sae braw.   30

You couldna see her lily feet,
Her gowden fringes were sae deep.

All amang her yellow hair
A string o' pearls was twisted rare.

You couldna see her fingers sma',
Wi' diamond rings they were cover'd a'.

And by there cam a harper fine,
That harpit to the king at dine.

And when he look'd that lady on,
He sigh'd and made a heavy moan.   40

He's made a harp of her breast-bane,
Whose sound wad melt a heart of stane.

He's ta'en three locks o' her yellow hair,
And wi' them strung his harp sae rare.

He went into her father's hall,
And there was the court assembled all.

He laid his harp upon a stane,
And straight it began to play by lane.

"O yonder sits my father, the King,
And yonder sits my mother, the Queen;   50

"And yonder stands my brother Hugh,
And by him my William, sweet and true."

But the last tune that the harp play'd then –
  Binnorie, O Binnorie!
Was, "Woe to my sister, false Helèn!"
  By the bonnie milldams o' Binnorie.

Anonymous

176

THE BRAES OF YARROW

Late at e'en, drinking the wine,
　　And ere they paid the lawing,
They set a combat them between,
　　To fight it in the dawing.

"What though ye be my sister's lord,
　　We'll cross our swords to-morrow."
"What though my wife your sister be,
　　I'll meet ye then on Yarrow."

"O stay at hame, my ain gude lord!
　　O stay my ain dear marrow!　　　　　　10
My cruel brither will you betray
　　On the dowie banks o' Yarrow."

"O fare thee weel, my lady dear!
　　And put aside your sorrow;
For if I gae, I'll sune return
　　Frae the bonnie banks o' Yarrow."

She kiss'd his cheek, she kaim'd his hair,
　　As oft she'd done before, O;
She belted him wi' his gude brand,
　　And he's awa' to Yarrow.　　　　　　　20

When he gaed up the Tennies bank,
　　As he gaed many a morrow,
Nine armed men lay in a den,
　　On the dowie braes o' Yarrow.

"O come ye here to hunt or hawk
　　The bonnie Forest thorough?
Or come ye here to wield your brand
　　Upon the banks o' Yarrow?"

"I come not here to hunt or hawk,
　　As oft I've dune before, O,　　　　　　30
But I come here to wield my brand
　　Upon the banks o' Yarrow.

"If ye attack me nine to ane,
　　That God may send ye sorrow! –
Yet will I fight while stand I may,
　　On the bonnie banks o' Yarrow."

Two has he hurt, and three has slain,
    On the bloody braes o' Yarrow;
But the stubborn knight crept in behind,
    And pierced his body thorough.   40

"Gae hame, gae hame, you brither John,
    And tell your sister sorrow, –
To come and lift her leafu' lord
    On the dowie banks o' Yarrow."

Her brither John gaed ower yon hill,
    As oft he'd dune before, O;
There he met his sister dear,
    Cam' rinnin' fast to Yarrow.

"I dreamt a dream last night," she says,
    "I wish it binna sorrow;   50
I dreamt I pu'd the heather green
    Wi' my true love on Yarrow."

"I'll read your dream, sister," he says,
    "I'll read it into sorrow;
Ye're bidden go take up your love,
    He's sleeping sound on Yarrow."

She's torn the ribbons frae her head,
    That were baith braid and narrow;
She's kilted up her lang claithing,
    And she's awa' to Yarrow.   60

She's ta'en him in her arms twa,
    And gi'en him kisses thorough;
She sought to bind his mony wounds,
    But he lay dead on Yarrow.

"O haud your tongue," her father says,
    "And let be a' your sorrow;
I'll wed you to a better lord
    Than him ye lost on Yarrow."

"O haud your tongue, father," she says,
    Far warse ye mak' my sorrow;   70
A better lord could never be
    Than him that lies on Yarrow."

She kiss'd his lips, she kaim'd his hair,
As aft she had dune before, O;
And there wi' grief her heart did break,
Upon the banks o' Yarrow.

Anonymous

THE CANTERBURY TALES

The General Prologue
(Prioress)

Ther was also a nonne, a PRIORESSÉ,

unpretentious   That of hir smylyng was ful symple* and
shy or demure   coy.*

Hir gretteste ooth was but by Sainté Loy; 120

called   And she was clepéd* Madame Eglentyné.

sang   Ful wel she soong* the servycé dyvyné,
Intoned properly   Entunéd* in hir nose ful semély,*
elegantly   And Frenssh she spak ful faire and fetisly*

After the scole of Stratford-atté-Bowé,

For Frenssh of Parys was to hire unknowé.

At meté wel y-taught was she with-allé;

let   She leet* no morsel from hir lippés fallé,

Ne wette hir fyngrés in hir saucé depé;

Wel kould she carie a morsel, and wel
take care   kepé*   130

fell   That no drope ne fille* upon hir brest.

much pleasure   In curteisie was set ful muchel* hir lest.*

Hir over-lippé wypéd she so clené

cup particle   That in hir coppe* ther was no ferthyng* sené

Of grecé whan she dronken hadde hir
draughté.

reached   Ful semély after hir mete she raughté,*

certainly good humour   And sikerly* she was of greet desport,*

bearing   And ful plesaunt and amyable of port,*

strove imitate fashions   And peynéd hire* to countrefeté cheeré*

dignified   Of court, and been estatlich* of maneré, 140

considered worthy   And to ben holden digne* of reverencé.

sympathetic nature   But for to speken of hir consciencé,*

full of pity   She was so charitable and so pitous,*

She woldé wepe if that she sawe a mous

Caught in a trappe, if it were deed or bleddé.

lap dogs   Of smalé houndés* hadde she that she feddé

white wheat, fine flour	With rosted flessh, or mylk and wastel* breed;
	But soore wepte she if oon of hem were deed,
someone stick severely	Or if men* smoot it with a yerdė smertė.*
	And al was conscience and tendrė hertė. 150
neatly head-dress *pleated*	Ful semyly* hir wympel pynchėd* was,
shapely eyes	Hir nose tretys,* hir eyen* greye as glas,
	Hir mouth ful smal, and therto softe and reed,
certainly	But sikerly* she hadde a fair forheed;
believe	It was almoost a spannė brood, I trowė,*
assuredly	For hardily* she was nat undergrowė.
graceful aware	Ful fetys* was hir cloke, as I was war;*
carried	Of smal coral aboute hir arm she bar*
string	A peyre* of bedės, gauded al with grenė,
	And theron heng a brooch of gold ful
bright	shenė,* 160
	On which ther was first write a crownėd A,
Love conquers all.	And after *Amor vincit omnia.**

Geoffrey Chaucer

I WILL LIFT UP MINE EYES

I will lift up mine eyes unto the hills,
From whence cometh my help.
My help cometh from the LORD,
Which made heaven and earth.

He will not suffer thy foot to be moved:
He that keepeth thee will not slumber.
Behold, he that keepeth Israel
Shall neither slumber nor sleep.

The LORD is thy keeper:
The LORD is thy shade upon thy right hand.   10
The sun shall not smite thee by day,
Nor the moon by night.

The LORD shall preserve thee from all evil;
He shall preserve thy soul.
The LORD shall preserve thy going out and thy coming in,
From this time forth, and even for evermore.

Psalm 121

REMEMBER NOW THY CREATOR

Remember now thy Creator in the days of thy youth,
While the evil days come not, nor the years draw nigh,
When thou shalt say, I have no pleasure in them;
While the sun, or the light, or the moon, or the stars, be not
    darkened,
Nor the clouds return after the rain:
In the day when the keepers of the house shall tremble,
And the strong men shall bow themselves,
And the grinders cease because they are few,
And those that look out of the windows be darkened,
And the doors shall be shut in the streets,   10
When the sound of the grinding is low,
And he shall rise up at the voice of the bird,
And all the daughters of musick shall be brought low:
Also when they shall be afraid of that which is high,
And fears shall be in the way,
And the almond tree shall flourish,
And the grasshopper shall be a burden,
And desire shall fail:
Because man goeth to his long home,
And the mourners go about the streets: 20
Or ever the silver cord be loosed,
Or the golden bowl be broken,
Or the pitcher be broken at the fountain,
Or the wheel broken at the cistern.
Then shall the dust return to the earth as it was:
And the spirit shall return unto God who gave it.

Ecclesiastes 12: 1-7

WHEN ICICLES HANG BY THE WALL

When icicles hang by the wall,
    And Dick the shepherd blows his nail,
And Tom bears logs into the hall,
    And milk comes frozen home in pail;
When blood is nipped, and ways be foul,
Then nightly sings the staring owl,
                    Tu-who;
Tu-whit, tu-who – a merry note,
While greasy Joan doth keel the pot.

When all aloud the wind doth blow,   10
        And coughing drowns the parson's saw,
And birds sit brooding in the snow,
        And Marian's nose looks red and raw;
When roasted crabs hiss in the bowl,
Then nightly sings the staring owl,
                                Tu-who;
Tu-whit, tu-who – a merry note,
While greasy Joan doth keel the pot.

William Shakespeare

SONNET CVI

When in the chronicle of wasted time
I see descriptions of the fairest wights,
And beauty making beautiful old rhyme
In praise of ladies dead and lovely knights,
Then, in the blazon of sweet beauty's best,
Of hand, of foot, of lip, of eye, of brow,
I see their antique pen would have expressed
Even such a beauty as you master now.
So all their praises are but prophecies
Of this our time, all you prefiguring;   10
And, for they looked but with divining eyes,
They had not skill enough your worth to sing:
        For we, which now behold these present days,
        Have eyes to wonder, but lack tongues to praise.

William Shakespeare

SONNET CVII

Not mine own fears, nor the prophetic soul
Of the wide world, dreaming on things to come,
Can yet the lease of my true love control,
Supposed as forfeit to a confined doom.
The mortal moon hath her eclipse endured,
And the sad augurs mock their own presage;
Incertainties now crown themselves assured,
And peace proclaims olives of endless age.
Now with the drops of this most balmy time
My love looks fresh, and Death to me subscribes,   10
Since, spite of him, I'll live in this poor rhyme,
While he insults o'er dull and speechless tribes.
        And thou in this shalt find thy monument.
        When tyrants' crests and tombs of brass are spent.

William Shakespeare

SONNET CXLVI

Poor soul, the centre of my sinful earth,
Fooled by these rebel powers that thee array,
Why dost thou pine within and suffer dearth,
Painting thy outward walls so costly gay?
Why so large cost, having so short a lease,
Dost thou upon thy fading mansion spend?
Shall worms, inheritors of this excess,
Eat up thy charge? Is this thy body's end?
Then, soul, live thou upon thy servant's loss,
And let that pine to aggravate thy store;   10
Buy terms divine in selling hours of dross;
Within be fed, without be rich no more:
  So shalt thou feed on Death, that feeds on men,
  And Death once dead, there's no more dying then.

William Shakespeare

THE PARTING

Since there's no help, come let us kiss and part —
Nay, I have done, you get no more of me;
And I am glad, yea, glad with all my heart,
That thus so cleanly, I myself can free.
Shake hands for ever, cancel all our vows,
And when we meet at any time again,
Be it not seen in either of our brows
That we one jot of former love retain.
Now at the last gasp of Love's latest breath,
When, his pulse failing, Passion speechless lies,   10
When Faith is kneeling by his bed of Death,
And Innocence is closing up his eyes —
  Now, if thou would'st, when all have given him over,
  From Death to Life thou might'st him yet recover.

Michael Drayton

DEATH THE LEVELLER

The glories of our blood and state
   Are shadows, not substantial things;
There is no armour against Fate;
   Death lays his icy hand on kings:
      Sceptre and Crown
      Must tumble down,
And in the dust be equal made
With the poor crooked scythe and spade.

Some men with swords may reap the field,
   And plant fresh laurels where they kill: 10
But their strong nerves at last must yield:
   They tame but one another still:
      Early or late
      They stoop to fate,
And must give up their murmuring breath
When they, pale captives, creep to death.

The garlands wither on your brow;
   Then boast no more your mighty deeds;
Upon Death's purple altar now
   See, where the victor-victim bleeds.   20
      Your heads must come
      To the cold tomb:
Only the actions of the just
Smell sweet, and blossom in the dust.

James Shirley

A THANKSGIVING TO GOD FOR HIS HOUSE

Lord, Thou hast given me a cell
      Wherein to dwell,
A little house, whose humble roof
      Is weather-proof;
Under the spars of which I lie
      Both soft and dry;
Where Thou, my chamber for to ward,
      Hast set a guard
Of harmless thoughts, to watch and keep
      Me while I sleep.   10

Low is my porch, as is my fate,
     Both void of state;
And yet the threshold of my door
     Is worn by the poor,
Who thither come and freely get
     Good words or meat.
Like as my parlour so my hall
     And kitchen's small;
A little buttery, and therein
     A little bin,   20
Which keeps my little loaf of bread
     Unchipped, unflead;
Some little sticks of thorn or briar
     Make me a fire,
Close by whose living coal I sit,
     And glow like it.
Lord, I confess too, when I dine,
     The pulse is Thine,
And all those other bits that be
     There placed by Thee;   30
The worts, the purslane, and the mess
     Of water-cress,
Which of Thy kindness Thou has sent;
     And my content
Makes those, and my beloved beet,
     To be more sweet.
'Tis Thou that crown'st my glittering hearth
     With guiltless mirth,
And giv'st me wassail-bowls to drink,
     Spiced to the brink.   40
Lord, 'tis Thy plenty-dropping hand
     That soils my land,
And giv'st me, for my bushel sown,
     Twice ten for one;
Thou mak'st my teeming hen to lay
     Her egg each day;
Besides my healthful ewes to bear
     Me twins each year;
The while the conduits of my kine
     Run cream, for wine,   50
All these, and better Thou dost send
     Me, to this end,
That I should render, for my part,

A thankful heart,
Which, fired with incense, I resign,
As wholly Thine;
But the acceptance, that must be,
My Christ, by Thee.

Robert Herrick

ON SHAKESPEARE, 1630

What needs my Shakespeare for his honoured bones,
The labour of an age in pilèd stones,
Or that his hallowed relics should be hid
Under a stary pointing pyramid?
Dear son of memory, great heir of Fame,
What need'st thou such weak witness of thy name?
Thou in our wonder and astonishment
Hast built thyself a lifelong monument.
For whilst to the shame of slow-endeavouring art,
Thy easy numbers flow, and that each heart   10
Hath from the leaves of thy unvalued book,
Those Delphic lines with deep impression took,
Then thou our fancy of itself bereaving,
Dost make us marble with too much conceiving;
And so sepulchred in such pomp dost lie,
That kings for such a tomb would wish to die.

John Milton

I DID BUT PROMPT

I did but prompt the age to quit their clogs
    By the known rules of ancient liberty,
      When straight a barbarous noise environs me
    Of owls and cuckoos, asses, apes, and dogs;
As when those hinds that were transformed to frogs
    Railed at Latona's twin-born progeny,
    Which after held the Sun and Moon in fee.
    But this is got by casting pearls to hogs,
That bawl for freedom in their senseless mood,
    And still revolt when Truth would set them free.   10

Licence they mean when they cry Liberty;
For who loves that, must first be wise and good;
But from that mark how far they rove we see,
For all this waste of wealth, and loss of blood.

John Milton

TO ALTHEA, FROM PRISON

When Love with unconfinèd wings
    Hovers within my gates,
And my divine Althea brings
    To whisper at the grates:
When I lie tangled in her hair,
    And fetter'd to her eye,
The birds that wanton in the air
    Know no such liberty.

When flowing cups run swiftly round
    With no allaying Thames,   10
Our careless heads with roses bound,
    Our hearts with loyal flames;
When thirsty grief in wine we steep,
    When healths and draughts go free –
Fishes that tipple in the deep,
    Know no such liberty.

When, like committed linnets, I
    With shriller throat shall sing
The sweetness, mercy, majesty,
    And glories of my King;   20
When I shall voice aloud how good
    He is, how great should be,
Enlargèd winds, that curl the flood,
    Know no such liberty.

Stone walls do not a prison make,
    Nor iron bars a cage;
Minds innocent and quiet take
    That for an hermitage;
If I have freedom in my love
    And in my soul am free,   30
Angels alone, that soar above,
    Enjoy such liberty.

Richard Lovelace

187

SONG OF THE EMIGRANTS
IN THE BERMUDAS

Where the remote Bermudas ride
In the ocean's bosom unespied,
From a small boat that rowed along
The listening winds received this song:

"What should we do but sing His praise
That led us through the watery maze
Unto an isle so long unknown,
And yet far kinder than our own?
Where He the huge sea-monsters wracks,
That lift the deep upon their backs.   10
He lands us on a grassy stage,
Safe from the storms, and prelates' rage:
He gave us this eternal spring
Which here enamels everything,
And sends the fowls to us in care
On daily visits through the air.
He hangs in shades the orange bright
Like golden lamps in a green night,
And does in the pomegranates close
Jewels more rich than Ormuz shows: 20
He makes the figs our mouths to meet,
And throws the melons at our feet;
But apples, plants of such a price,
No tree could ever bear them twice.
With cedars chosen by His hand
From Lebanon He stores the land;
And makes the hollow seas that roar
Proclaim the ambergris on shore.
He cast (of which we rather boast)
The Gospel's pearl upon our coast;   30
And in these rocks for us did frame
A temple where to sound His name.
O, let our voice His praise exalt
Till it arrive at Heaven's vault,
Which thence (perhaps) rebounding may
Echo beyond the Mexique bay!"

– Thus sung they in the English boat
A holy and a cheerful note:
And all the way, to guide their chime,
With falling oars they kept the time.   40

Andrew Marvell

THE HARE WITH MANY FRIENDS

Friendship, like love, is but a name,
Unless to one you stint the flame.
The child, whom many fathers share,
Hath seldom known a father's care.
'Tis thus in friendships; who depend
On many, rarely find a friend.
   A Hare who in a civil way,
Complied with every thing, like Gay,
Was known by all the bestial train,
Who haunt the wood, or graze the plain.   10
Her care was never to offend,
And every creature was her friend.
   As forth she went at early dawn
To taste the dew-besprinkled lawn,
Behind she hears the hunter's cries,
And from the deep-mouthed thunder flies.
She starts, she stops, she pants for breath;
She hears the near advance of death;
She doubles to mislead the hound,
And measures back her mazy round;   20
Till, fainting in the public way,
Half-dead with fear, she gasping lay.
   What transport in her bosom grew,
When first the Horse appeared in view!
"Let me," says she, "your back ascend,
And owe my safety to a friend.
You know my feet betray my flight;
To friendship every burden's light."
The Horse replied: "Poor honest Puss,
It grieves my heart to see thee thus;   30
Be comforted, relief is near;
For all your friends are in the rear."
   She next the stately Bull implored,
And thus replied the mighty Lord:
"Since every beast alive can tell
That I sincerely wish you well,
I may without offence pretend
To take the freedom of a friend.
Love calls me hence; a favourite cow
Expects me near yon barley-mow;   40
And when a lady's in the case,
You know, all other things give place.

To leave you thus might seem unkind,
But see, the Goat is just behind."
    The Goat remarked her pulse was high,
Her languid head, her heavy eye:
"My back," says he, "may do you harm;
The Sheep's at hand, and wool is warm."
    The Sheep was feeble, and complained
His sides a load of wool sustained;   50
Said he was slow, confessed his fears;
For hounds eat Sheep as well as Hares!
    She now the trotting Calf addressed;
To save from death a friend distressed:
"Shall I," says he, "of tender age,
In this important care engage?
Older and abler passed you by;
How strong are those! how weak am I!
Should I presume to bear you hence,
Those friends of mine may take offence.   60
Excuse me, then. You know my heart;
But dearest friends, alas! must part;
How shall we all lament! Adieu,
For see the hounds are just in view."

John Gay

'TIS HARD TO SAY

From *An Essay on Criticism*

'Tis hard to say, if greater want of skill
Appear in writing or in judging ill;
But, of the two, less dangerous is th' offence
To tire our patience, than mislead our sense.
Some few in that, but numbers err in this
Ten censure wrong for one who writes amiss;
A fool might once himself alone expose,
Now one in verse makes many more in prose.
    'Tis with our judgments as our watches, none
Go just alike, yet each believes his own.   10
In poets as true genius is but rare,
True taste as seldom is the critic's share;

Both must alike from Heaven derive their light,
These born to judge, as well as those to write
Let such teach others who themselves excel,
And censure freely who have written well,
Authors are partial to their wit, 'tis true,
But are not critics to their judgment too?

THE TIGER

Tiger, tiger, burning bright,
In the forests of the night,
What immortal hand or eye
Could frame thy fearful symmetry?

In what distant deeps or skies
Burnt the fire of thine eyes?
On what wings dare he aspire?
What the hand dare seize the fire?

And what shoulder and what art
Could twist the sinews of thy heart?   10
And, when thy heart began to beat,
What dread hand and what dread feet?

What the hammer? What the chain?
In what furnace was thy brain?
What the anvil? What dread grasp
Dare its deadly terrors clasp?

When the stars threw down their spears,
And watered heaven with their tears,
Did He smile His work to see?
Did He who made the lamb make thee?   20

Tiger, tiger, burning bright,
In the forests of the night,
What immortal hand or eye
Dare frame thy fearful symmetry?

William Blake

I LOVE MY JEAN

Of a' the airts the wind can blaw
    I dearly like the West,
For there the bonnie lassie lives,
    The lassie I lo'e best:
There wild woods grow, and rivers row,
    And mony a hill between;
But day and night my fancy's flight
    Is ever wi' my Jean.

I see her in the dewy flowers,
    I see her sweet and fair: 10
I hear her in the tunefu' birds,
    I hear her charm the air:
There's not a bonnie flower that springs
    By fountain, shaw, or green,
There's not a bonnie bird that sings
    But minds me o' my Jean.

O blaw ye westlin winds, blaw saft
    Amang the leafy trees;
Wi' balmy gale, frae hill and dale
    Bring hame the laden bees;   20
And bring the lassie back to me
    That's aye sae neat and clean;
Ae smile o' her wad banish care,
    Sae charming is my Jean.

What sighs and vows amang the knowes
    Hae pass'd atween us twa!
How fond to meet, how wae to part
    That night she gaed awa!
The Powers aboon can only ken
    To whom the heart is seen,   30
That nane can be sae dear to me
    As my sweet lovely Jean!

Robert Burns

HIGHLAND MARY

Ye banks, and braes, and streams around
    The castle o' Montgomery,
Green be your woods and fair your flowers,
    Your waters never drumlie!
There simmer first unfauld her robes,
    And there the langest tarry;
For there I took the last fareweel,
    O' my sweet Highland Mary.

How sweetly bloom'd the gay green birk,
    How rich the hawthorn's blossom,   10
As underneath their fragrant shade
    I clasp'd her to my bosom!
The golden hours, on angel wings,
    Flew o'er me and my dearie;
For dear to me as light and life,
    Was my sweet Highland Mary.

Wi' monie a vow and lock'd embrace
    Our parting was fu' tender:
And, pledging aft to meet again,
    We tore oursels asunder;   20
But Oh! fell death's untimely frost,
    That nipt my flower sae early!
Now green's the sod, and cauld's the clay,
    That wraps my Highland Mary!

O pale, pale now, those rosy lips,
    I aft hae kiss'd sae fondly!
And closed for aye the sparkling glance,
    That dwelt on me sae kindly!
And mold'ring now in silent dust,
    That heart that lo'ed me dearly!
But still within my bosom's core
    Shall live my Highland Mary.

Robert Burns

Three years she grew in sun and shower,
Then Nature said, "A lovelier flower
   On earth was never sown;
This Child I to myself will take;
She shall be mine, and I will make
   A Lady of my own.

"Myself will to my darling be
Both law and impulse: and with me
   The Girl, in rock and plain,
In earth and heaven, in glade and bower,   10
Shall feel an overseeing power
   To kindle or restrain.

"She shall be sportive as the fawn
That wild with glee across the lawn
   Or up the mountain springs;
And hers shall be the breathing balm,
And hers the silence and the calm
   Of mute insensate things.

"The floating clouds their state shall lend
To her; for her the willow bend;   20
   Nor shall she fail to see
Even in the motions of the Storm
Grace that shall mould the Maiden's form
   By silent sympathy.

"The stars of midnight shall be dear
To her; and she shall lean her ear
   In many a secret place
Where rivulets dance their wayward round,
And beauty born of murmuring sound
   Shall pass into her face.   30

"And vital feelings of delight
Shall rear her form to stately height,
   Her virgin bosom swell;
Such thoughts to Lucy I will give
While she and I together live
   Here in this happy dell."

Thus Nature spake – The work was done –
How soon my Lucy's race was run!
    She died, and left to me
This heath, this calm, and quiet scene;   40
The memory of what has been,
    And never more will be.

William Wordsworth

LONDON, 1802

Milton! thou shouldst be living at this hour:
England hath need of thee: she is a fen
Of stagnant waters: altar, sword, and pen,
Fireside, the heroic wealth of hall and bower,
Have forfeited their ancient English dower
Of inward happiness. We are selfish men:
Oh! raise us up, return to us again;
And give us manners, virtue, freedom, power.
Thy soul was like a star, and dwelt apart;
Thou hadst a voice whose sound was like the sea: 10
Pure as the naked heavens, majestic, free,
So didst thou travel on life's common way,
In cheerful godliness; and yet thy heart
The lowliest duties on herself did lay.

William Wordsworth

THE WORLD IS TOO MUCH WITH US

The world is too much with us; late and soon,
Getting and spending, we lay waste our powers:
Little we see in Nature that is ours;
We have given our hearts away, a sordid boon!
This Sea that bares her bosom to the moon;
The winds that will be howling at all hours,
And are up-gathered now like sleeping flowers;
For this, for everything, we are out of tune;
It moves us not. – Great God! I'd rather be
A Pagan suckled in a creed outworn;   10

So might I, standing on this pleasant lea,
Have glimpses that would make me less forlorn;
Have sight of Proteus rising from the sea;
Or hear old Triton blow his wreathèd horn.

William Wordsworth

KUBLA KHAN
OR, A VISION IN A DREAM

In Xanadu did Kubla Khan
A stately pleasure-dome decree:
Where Alph, the sacred river, ran
Through caverns measureless to man
   Down to a sunless sea.
So twice five miles of fertile ground
With walls and towers were girdled round:
And there were gardens bright with sinuous rills
Where blossomed many an incense-bearing tree;
And here were forests ancient as the hills,   10
Enfolding sunny spots of greenery.

But oh, that deep romantic chasm which slanted
Down the green hill athwart a cedarn cover!
A savage place! as holy and enchanted
As e'er beneath a waning moon was haunted
By woman wailing for her demon-lover!
And from this chasm, with ceaseless turmoil seething,
As if this earth in fast thick pants were breathing,
A mighty fountain momently was forced;
Amid whose swift half-intermitted burst   20
Huge fragments vaulted like rebounding hail,
Or chaffy grain beneath the thresher's flail:
And 'mid these dancing rocks at once and ever
It flung up momently the sacred river.
Five miles meandering with a mazy motion
Through wood and dale the sacred river ran,
Then reached the caverns measureless to man,
And sank in tumult to a lifeless ocean:
And 'mid this tumult Kubla heard from far
Ancestral voices prophesying war!   30

The shadow of the dome of pleasure
Floated midway on the waves;
Where was heard the mingled measure
From the fountain and the caves.
It was a miracle of rare device,
A sunny pleasure-dome with caves of ice!
A damsel with a dulcimer
In a vision once I saw:
It was an Abyssinian maid
And on her dulcimer she played,   40
Singing of Mount Abora.
Could I revive within me
Her symphony and song,
To such a deep delight 'twould win me,
That with music loud and long
I would build that dome in air,
That sunny dome! those caves of ice!
And all who heard should see them there,
And all should cry, Beware! Beware!
His flashing eyes, his floating hair!   50
Weave a circle round him thrice,
And close your eyes with holy dread,
For he on honey-dew hath fed,
And drunk the milk of Paradise.

Samuel Taylor Coleridge

BONNIE DUNDEE

To the Lords of Convention 'twas Claver'se who spoke,
"Ere the King's crown shall fall there are crowns to be broke;
So let each Cavalier who loves honour and me,
Come follow the bonnet of Bonnie Dundee.

 "Come fill up my cup, come fill up my can,
 Come saddle your horses, and call up your men;
 Come open the West Port, and let me gang free,
 And it's room for the bonnets of Bonnie Dundee!"

Dundee he is mounted, he rides up the street,
The bells are rung backward, the drums they are beat: 10
But the Provost, douce man, said, "Just e'en let him be,
The Gude Town is weel quit of that Deil of Dundee."

As he rode down the sanctified bends of the Bow,
Ilk carline was flyting and shaking her pow;
But the young plants of grace they looked couthie and slee,
Thinking, luck to thy bonnet, thou Bonnie Dundee!

With sour-featured Whigs the Grassmarket was crammed,
As if half the West had set tryst to be hanged;
There was spite in each look, there was fear in each e'e,
As they watched for the bonnets of Bonnie Dundee.   20

These cowls of Kilmarnock had spits and had spears,
And lang-hafted gullies to kill Cavaliers;
But they shrunk to close-heads, and the causeway was free,
At the toss of the bonnet of Bonnie Dundee.

He spurred to the foot of the proud Castle rock,
And with the gay Gordon he gallantly spoke;
"Let Mons Meg and her marrows speak twa words or three
For the love of the bonnet of Bonnie Dundee."

The Gordon demands of him which way he goes:
"Where'er shall direct me the shade of Montrose!   30
Your Grace in short space shall hear tidings of me,
Or that low lies the bonnet of Bonnie Dundee.

"There are hills beyond Pentland, and lands beyond Forth,
If there's lords in the Lowlands, there's chiefs in the North;
There are wild Duniewassals three thousand times three,
Will cry *hoigh!* for the bonnet of Bonnie Dundee.

"There's brass on the target of barkened bullhide;
There's steel in the scabbard that dangles beside;
The brass shall be burnished, the steel shall flash free
At a toss of the bonnet of Bonnie Dundee.   40

"Away to the hills, to the caves, to the rocks,
Ere I own an usurper, I'll couch with the fox;
And tremble, false Whigs, in the midst of your glee,
You have not seen the last of my bonnet and me!"

He waved his proud hand, and the trumpets were blown,
The kettle-drums clashed, and the horsemen rode on,
Till on Ravelston's cliffs and on Clermiston's lee
Died away the wild war-notes of Bonnie Dundee.

Come fill up my cup, come fill up my can,
Come saddle the horses and call up the men,   50
Come open your gates, and let me gae free,
For it's up with the bonnèts of Bonnie Dundee!

Sir Walter Scott

CHILLON

Eternal Spirit of the chainless Mind!
    Brightest in dungeons, Liberty! thou art,
    For there thy habitation is the heart –
The heart which love of thee alone can bind;
And when thy sons to fetters are consigned –
    To fetters, and the damp vault's dayless gloom,
    Their country conquers with their martyrdom,
And Freedom's fame finds wing on every wind.
Chillon! thy prison is a holy place,
    And thy sad floor an altar – for 'twas trod,   10
Until his very steps have left a trace
    Worn, as if thy cold pavement were a sod,
By Bonnivard! – May none those marks efface!
    For they appeal from tyranny to God.

George Gordon, Lord Byron

WHEN I HAVE FEARS

When I have fears that I may cease to be
Before my pen has glean'd my teeming brain,
Before high pilèd books, in charact'ry,
Hold like rich garners the full-ripen'd grain;
When I behold, upon the night's starr'd face,
Huge cloudy symbols of a high romance,
And think that I may never live to trace
Their shadows, with the magic hand of chance;
And when I feel, fair creature of an hour!
That I shall never look upon thee more,   10
Never have relish in the faery power
Of unreflecting love! – then on the shore
    Of the wide world I stand alone, and think
    Till Love and Fame to nothingness do sink.

John Keats

199

BRIGHT STAR

Bright Star, would I were steadfast as thou art –
Not in lone splendour hung aloft the night,
And watching, with eternal lids apart,
Like Nature's patient, sleepless Eremite,
The moving waters at their priestlike task
Of pure ablution round earth's human shores,
Or gazing on the new soft-fallen mask
Of snow upon the mountains and the moors –
No – yet still steadfast, still unchangeable,
Pillow'd upon my fair Love's ripening breast,   10
To feel for ever its soft fall and swell,
Awake for ever in a sweet unrest,
     Still, still to hear her tender-taken breath,
     And so live ever, – or else swoon to death.

John Keats

ODE ON A GRECIAN URN

Thou still unravished bride of quietness,
     Thou foster-child of silence and slow time,
Sylvan historian, who canst thus express
     A flowery tale more sweetly than our rime:
What leaf-fringed legend haunts about thy shape
     Of deities or mortals, or of both,
In Tempe or the dales of Arcady?
     What men or gods are these? What maidens loath?
What mad pursuit? What struggle to escape?
     What pipes and timbrels? What wild ecstasy?   10

Heard melodies are sweet, but those unheard
     Are sweeter; therefore, ye soft pipes, play on;
Not to the sensual ear, but, more endeared,
     Pipe to the spirit ditties of no tone:
Fair youth, beneath the trees, thou canst not leave
     Thy song, nor ever can those trees be bare;
     Bold Lover, never, never canst thou kiss,
Though winning near the goal – yet, do not grieve;
     She cannot fade, though thou hast not thy bliss,
     For ever wilt thou love, and she be fair!   20

Ah, happy, happy boughs! that cannot shed
  Your leaves, nor ever bid the Spring adieu;
And, happy melodist, unwearied,
  For ever piping songs for ever new;
More happy love! more happy, happy love!
  For ever warm and still to be enjoy'd,
    For ever panting and for ever young;
All breathing human passion far above,
  That leaves a heart high-sorrowful and cloy'd,
    A burning forehead, and a parching tongue.   30

Who are these coming to the sacrifice?
  To what green altar, O mysterious priest,
Lead'st thou that heifer lowing at the skies,
  And all her silken flanks with garlands drest?
What little town by river or sea-shore,
  Or mountain-built with peaceful citadel,
    Is emptied of its folk, this pious morn?
And, little town, thy streets for evermore
  Will silent be; and not a soul to tell
    Why thou art desolate can e'er return.   40

O Attic shape! Fair attitude! with brede
  Or marble men and maidens overwrought,
With forest branches and the trodden weed;
  Thou, silent form, dost tease us out of thought
As doth eternity: Cold Pastoral!
  When old age shall this generation waste,
    Thou shalt remain, in midst of other woe
Than ours, a friend to man, to whom thou say'st,
"Beauty is truth, truth beauty!" – that is all
    Ye know on earth, and all ye need to know.   50

John Keats

HOW DO I LOVE THEE?

How do I love thee? Let me count the ways.
  I love thee to the depth and breadth and height
  My soul can reach, when feeling out of sight
For the ends of Being and ideal Grace.
I love thee to the level of every day's
  Most quiet need, by sun and candlelight.

I love thee freely, as men strive for Right;
I love thee purely as they turn from Praise.
I love thee with the passion put to use
    In my old griefs, and with my childhood's faith.   10
I love thee with a love I seemed to lose
    With my lost saints, – I love thee with the breath,
Smiles, tears, of all my life! – and, if God choose,
    I shall but love thee better after death.

Elizabeth Barrett Browning

IN MEMORIAM
XXVII

I envy not in any moods
    The captive void of noble rage,
    The linnet born within the cage,
That never knew the summer woods:

I envy not the beast that takes
    His licence in the field of time,
    Unfettered by the sense of crime,
To whom a conscience never wakes:

Nor, what may count itself as blest,
    The heart that never plighted troth   10
    But stagnates in the weeds of sloth;
Nor any want-begotten rest.

I hold it true, whate'er befall;
    I feel it, when I sorrow most;
    'Tis better to have loved and lost
Than never to have loved at all.

Alfred, Lord Tennyson

IN MEMORIAM
CI

Unwatch'd, the garden bough shall sway,
    The tender blossom flutter down,
    Unloved, that beech will gather brown,
This maple burn itself away;

Unloved, the sun-flower, shining fair
    Ray round with flames her disk of seed,
    And many a rose-carnation feed
With summer spice the humming air;

Unloved, by many a sandy bar,
    The brook shall babble down the plain,   10
    At noon or when the lesser wain
Is twisting round the polar star;

Uncared for, gird the windy grove,
    And flood the haunts of hern and crake;
    Or into silver arrows break
The sailing moon in creek and cove;

Till from the garden and the wild
    A fresh association blow,
    And year by year the landscape grow
Familiar to the stranger's child;   20

As year by year the labourer tills
    His wonted glebe, or lops the glades;
    And year by year our memory fades
From all the circle of the hills.

                    Alfred, Lord Tennyson

HOME-THOUGHTS, FROM ABROAD

Oh, to be in England
Now that April's there,
And whoever wakes in England
Sees, some morning, unaware,
That the lowest boughs and the brush-wood sheaf
Round the elm-tree bole are in tiny leaf,
While the chaffinch sings on the orchard bough
In England – now!

And after April, when May follows,
And the whitethroat builds, and all the swallows!   10
Hark, where by blossomed pear-tree in the hedge
Leans to the field and scatters on the clover

Blossoms and dewdrops – at the bent spray's edge –
That's the wise thrush; he sings each song twice over,
Lest you should think he never could recapture
The first fine careless rapture!
And though the fields look rough with hoary dew,
All will be gay when noontide wakes anew
The buttercups, the little children's dower
– Far brighter than this gaudy melon-flower!   20

Robert Browning

SHAKESPEARE

Others abide our question. Thou art free.
We ask and ask: Thou smilest and art still,
Out-topping knowledge. For the loftiest hill
That to the stars uncrowns his majesty,
Planting his steadfast footsteps in the sea,
Making the heaven of heavens his dwelling-place,
Spares but the cloudy border of his base
To the foil'd searching of mortality:
And thou, who didst the stars and sunbeams know,
Self-schooled, self-scanned, self-honoured, self-secure, 10
Didst tread on earth unguess'd at. Better so!
All pains the immortal spirit must endure,
    All weakness that imparts, all griefs that bow,
    Find their sole voice in that victorious brow.

Matthew Arnold

PEACE

A Study

He stood, a worn-out City clerk –
    Who'd toil'd and seen no holiday,
For forty years from dawn to dark –
    Alone beside Caermarthen Bay.

He felt the salt spray on his lips;
    Heard children's voices on the sands;
Up the sun's path he saw the ships
    Sail on and on to other lands;

And laugh'd aloud. Each sight and sound
 To him was joy too deep for tears;   10
He sat him on the beach, and bound
 A blue bandana round his ears,

And thought how, posted near his door,
 His own green door on Camden Hill,
Two bands at least, most likely more,
 Were mingling at their own sweet will

Verdi with Vance. And at the thought
 He laugh'd again, and softly drew
That morning Herald that he'd bought
 Forth from his breast, and read it through.   20

Charles Calverley

IN TIME OF "THE BREAKING OF NATIONS"
Jeremiah 51:20

I
Only a man harrowing clods
 In a slow silent walk
With an old horse that stumbles and nods
 Half asleep as they stalk.

II
Only thin smoke without flame
 From the heaps of couch-grass;
Yet this will go onward the same
 Though Dynasties pass.

III
Yonder a maid and her wight
 Come whispering by:
War's annals will cloud into night
 Ere their story die.

Thomas Hardy

NATURE'S QUESTIONING

When I look forth at dawning, pool,
    Field, flock, and lonely tree,
    All seem to gaze at me
Like chastened children sitting silent in a school;

    Their faces dulled, constrained, and worn,
    As though the master's ways
    Through the long teaching days
Had cowed them till their early zest was overborne.

    Upon them stirs in lippings mere
    (As if once clear in call,   10
    But now scarce breathed at all) –
"We wonder, ever wonder, why we find us here!

    "Has some Vast Imbecility,
    Mighty to build and blend,
    But impotent to tend,
Framed us in jest, and let us now to hazardry?

    "Or come we of an Automaton
    Unconscious of our pains? . . .
    Or are we live remains
Of Godhead dying downwards, brain and eye now gone? 20

    "Or is it that some high Plan betides,
    As yet not understood,
    Of Evil stormed by Good,
We the Forlorn Hope over which Achievement strides?"

    Thus things around. No answerer I . . .
    Meanwhile the winds, and rains,
    And Earth's old glooms and pains
Are still the same, and Life and Death are neighbours
    nigh.

Thomas Hardy

GOD'S GRANDEUR

The world is charged with the grandeur of God.
  It will flame out, like shining from shook foil;
  It gathers to a greatness, like the ooze of oil
Crushed. Why do men then now not reck his rod?
Generations have trod, have trod, have trod;
  And all is seared with trade; bleared, smeared with toil;
  And wears man's smudge and shares man's smell: the soil
Is bare now, nor can foot feel, being shod.

And for all this, nature is never spent;
  There lives the dearest freshness deep down things;   10
And though the last lights off the black West went
  Oh, morning, at the brown brink eastward, springs –
Because the Holy Ghost over the bent
  World broods with warm breast and with ah! bright wings.

Gerard Manley Hopkins

SMOOTH BETWEEN
SEA AND LAND

Smooth between sea and land
Is laid the yellow sand,
And here through summer days
The seed of Adam plays.

Here, the child comes to found
His unremaining mound,
And the grown lad to score
Two names upon the shore.

Here, on the level sand,
Between the sea and land,   10
What shall I build or write
Against the fall of night?

Tell me of runes to grave
That hold the bursting wave,
Or bastions to design
For longer date than mine.

Shall it be Troy or Rome
I fence against the foam,
Or my own name, to stay
When I depart for aye?   20

Nothing: too near at hand,
Planing the figured sand,
Effacing clean and fast
Cities not built to last
And charms devised in vain,
Pours the confounding main.

A. E. Housman

L'ENVOI

When Earth's last picture is painted and the tubes are twisted
    and dried,
When the oldest colours have faded, and the youngest critic
    has died,
We shall rest, and, faith, we shall need it – lie down for an
    æon or two,
Till the Master of All Good Workmen shall put us to work
    anew!

And those that were good shall be happy; they shall sit in a
    golden chair;
They shall splash at a ten-league canvas with brushes of
    comets' hair;
They shall find real saints to draw from – Magdalene, Peter,
    and Paul;
They shall work for an age at a sitting and never be tired
    at all!

And only the Master shall praise us, and only the Master
    shall blame;
And no one shall work for money, and no one shall work
    for fame,   10
But each for the joy of the working, and each in his separate
    star,
Shall draw the Thing as he sees It for the God of Things as
    They Are!

Rudyard Kipling

BEFORE THE WORLD WAS MADE

If I make the lashes dark
And the eyes more bright
And the lips more scarlet,
Or ask if all be right
From mirror after mirror,
No vanity's displayed:
I'm looking for the face I had
Before the world was made.

What if I look upon a man
As though on my beloved,   10
And my blood be cold the while
And my heart unmoved?
Why should he think me cruel
Or that he is betrayed?
I'd have him love the thing that was
Before the world was made.

William Butler Yeats

AN IRISH AIRMAN
FORESEES HIS DEATH

I know that I shall meet my fate
Somewhere among the clouds above;
Those that I fight I do not hate,
Those that I guard I do not love;
My country is Kiltartan Cross,
My countrymen Kiltartan's poor,
No likely end could bring them loss
Or leave them happier than before.
Nor law, nor duty bade me fight,
Nor public men, nor cheering crowds,   10
A lonely impulse of delight
Drove to this tumult in the clouds;
I balanced all, brought all to mind,
The years to come seemed waste of breath,
A waste of breath the years behind
In balance with this life, this death.

William Butler Yeats

THE GIPSY GIRL

"Come, try your skill, kind gentlemen,
A penny for three tries!"
Some threw and lost, some threw and won
A ten-a-penny prize.

She was a tawny gipsy girl,
A girl of twenty years,
I liked her for the lumps of gold
That jingled from her ears;

I liked the flaring yellow scarf
Bound loose about her throat,   10
I liked her showy purple gown
And flashy velvet coat.

A man came up, too loose of tongue,
And said no good to her;
She did not blush as Saxons do,
Or turn upon the cur;

She fawned and whined, "Sweet gentleman,
A penny for three tries!"
– But, oh, the den of wild things in
The darkness of her eyes!   20

Ralph Hodgson

THE LISTENERS

"Is there anybody there?" said the Traveller,
    Knocking on the moonlit door;
And his horse in the silence champed the grasses
    Of the forest's ferny floor:
And a bird flew up out of the turret,
    Above the Traveller's head:
And he smote upon the door again a second time;
    "Is there anybody there?" he said.
But no one descended to the Traveller;
    No head from the leaf-fringed sill   10
Leaned over and looked into his grey eyes,
    Where he stood perplexed and still.

But only a host of phantom listeners
    That dwelt in the lone house then
Stood listening in the quiet of the moonlight
    To that voice from the world of men:
Stood thronging the faint moon-beams on the dark
        stair,
    That goes down to the empty hall,
Hearkening in an air stirred and shaken
    By the lone Traveller's call.   20

And he felt in his heart their strangeness,
    Their stillness answering his cry,
While his horse moved, cropping the dark turf,
    'Neath the starred and leafy sky;
For he suddenly smote on the door, even
    Louder, and lifted his head: –
"Tell them I came, and no one answered,
    That I kept my word," he said.
Never the least stir made the listeners,
    Though every word he spake   30
Fell echoing through the shadowiness of the still house
    From the one man left awake:
Ay, they heard his foot upon the stirrup,
    And the sound of iron on stone
And how the silence surged softly backward
    When the plunging hoofs were gone.

Walter de la Mare

TEWKESBURY ROAD

It is good to be out on the road, and going one knows not where,
    Going through meadow and village, one knows not whither
        nor why;
Through the gray light drift of the dust, in the keen cool rush of
    the air,
    Under the flying white clouds, and the broad blue lift of
        the sky.

And to halt at the chattering brook, in the tall green fern at the
    brink
    Where the harebell grows, and the gorse, and the foxgloves
        purple and white;

Where the shy-eyed delicate deer come down in a troop to drink
 When the stars are mellow and large at the coming on of
  the night.

O, to feel the beat of the rain, and the homely smell of the earth,
 Is a tune for the blood to jig to, a joy past power of words; 10
And the blessed green comely meadows are all a-ripple with
  mirth
 At the noise of the lambs at play and the dear wild cry of
  the birds.

John Masefield

CAVALIER

All the merry kettle-drums are thudding into rhyme,
 Dust is swimming dizzily down the village street,
The scabbards are clattering, the feathers nodding time,
 To a clink of many horses' shoes, a tramp of many feet.

Seven score of Cavaliers fighting for the King,
 Trolling lusty stirrup-songs, clamouring for wine,
Riding with a loose rein, marching with a swing,
 Beneath the blue bannerol of Rupert of the Rhine.

Hey the merry company; – the loud fifes playing –
 Blue scarves and bright steel and blossom of the may, 10
Roses in the feathered hats, the long plumes swaying,
 A king's son ahead of them showing them the way.

John Masefield

HATE

My enemy came nigh;
And I
Stared fiercely in his face.
My lips went writhing back in a grimace,
And stern I watched him with a narrow eye.
Then, as I turned away, my enemy,
That bitter heart and savage said to me:
"Some day, when this is past,
When all the arrows that we have are cast,
We may ask one another why we hate, 10
And fail to find a story to relate.

212

It may seem to us then a mystery
That we could hate each other."

Thus said he,
And did not turn away,
Waiting to hear what I might have to say;
But I fled quickly, fearing if I stayed
I might have kissed him as I would a maid.

James Stephens

THE SHELL

And then I pressed the shell
Close to my ear
And listened well.
And straightway, like a bell,
Came low and clear
The slow, sad murmur of far distant seas
Whipped by an icy breeze
Upon a shore
Wind-swept and desolate.
It was a sunless strand that never bore   10
The footprint of a man,
Nor felt the weight
Since time began
Of any human quality or stir,
Save what the dreary winds and waves incur.

And in the hush of waters was the sound
Of pebbles, rolling round;
For ever rolling, with a hollow sound:
And bubbling sea-weeds, as the waters go,
Swish to and fro   20
Their long cold tentacles of slimy grey:
There was no day;
Nor ever came a night
Setting the stars alight
To wonder at the moon:
'Twas twilight only, and the frightened croon,
Smitten to whimpers, of the dreary wind
And waves that journeyed blind. . . .
And then I loosed my ear – Oh, it was sweet
To hear a cart go jolting down the street.   30

James Stephens

IN THE COOL OF THE EVENING

I thought I heard Him calling! Did you hear
A sound? a little sound!
My curious ear
Is dinned with flying noises; and the tree
Goes – whisper, whisper, whisper, silently,
Till all its whispers spread into the sound
Of a dull roar. . . .

– Lie closer to the ground:
The shade is deep, and He may pass us by,
We are so very small, and His great eye,   10
Customed to starry majesties, may gaze
Too wide to spy us hiding in the maze:

– Ah, misery! The sun has not yet gone,
And we are naked! He will look upon
Our crouching shame! May make us stand upright,
Burning in terror – O that it were night – !
He may not come . . . What! Listen! Listen now–
He's here! Lie closer . . . *Adam, where art thou?*

James Stephens

TO A POET A THOUSAND YEARS HENCE

I who am dead a thousand years,
   And wrote this sweet archaic song,
Send you my words for messengers
   The way I shall not pass along.
I care not if you bridge the seas,
   Or ride secure the cruel sky,
Or build consummate palaces
   Of metal or of masonry.

But have you wine and music still,
   And statues and a bright-eyed love,   10
And foolish thoughts of good or ill,
   And prayers to them who sit above?

How shall we conquer? Like a wind
    That falls at eve our fancies blow,
And old Mæonides the blind
    Said it three thousand years ago.

O friend unseen, unborn, unknown,
    Student of our sweet English tongue,
Read out my words at night, alone:
    I was a poet, I was young.   20

Since I can never see your face,
    And never shake you by the hand,
I send my soul through time and space
    To greet you. You will understand.

James Elroy Flecker

SNAKE

A snake came to my water-trough
On a hot, hot day, and I in pyjamas for the heat,
To drink there.

In the deep, strange-scented shade of the great dark carob-tree
I came down the steps with my pitcher
And must wait, must stand and wait, for there he was at the
    trough before me.

He reached down from a fissure in the earth-wall in the gloom
And trailed his yellow-brown slackness soft-bellied down, over
    the edge of the stone trough
And rested his throat upon the stone bottom,
And where the water had dripped from the tap, in a small
    clearness,   10
He sipped with his straight mouth,
Softly drank through his straight gums, into his slack long body,
Silently.

Someone was before me at my water-trough,
And I, like a second comer, waiting.

He lifted his head from his drinking, as cattle do,
And looked at me vaguely, as drinking cattle do,
And flickered his two-forked tongue from his lips, and mused a
  moment,
And stooped and drank a little more,
Being earth-brown, earth-golden from the burning bowels of the
  earth   20
On the day of Sicilian July, with Etna smoking.

The voice of my education said to me
He must be killed,
For in Sicily the black, black snakes are innocent, the gold are
  venomous.

And voices in me said, If you were a man
You would take a stick and break him now, and finish him off.

But must I confess how I liked him,
How glad I was he had come like a guest in quiet, to drink at my
  water-trough
And depart peaceful, pacified, and thankless,
Into the burning bowels of this earth!   30

Was it cowardice, that I dared not kill him?
Was it perversity, that I longed to talk to him?
Was it humility, to feel honoured?
I felt so honoured.

And yet those voices:
If you were not afraid, you would kill him!

And truly I was afraid, I was most afraid,
But even so, honoured still more
That he should seek my hospitality
From out the dark door of the secret earth.   40

He drank enough
And lifted his head, dreamily, as one who has drunken,
And flickered his tongue like a forked night on the air, so black,
Seeming to lick his lips,
And looked around like a god, unseeing, into the air,
And slowly turned his head,
And slowly, very slowly, as if thrice adream,
Proceeded to draw his slow length curving round
And climb again the broken bank of my wall-face.

And as he put his head into that dreadful hole, 50
And as he slowly drew up, snake-easing his shoulders, and
    entered farther,
A sort of horror, a sort of protest against his withdrawing into
    that horrid black hole,
Deliberately going into the blackness, and slowly drawing himself
    after,
Overcame me now his back was turned.

I looked round, I put down my pitcher,
I picked up a clumsy log,
And threw it at the water-trough with a clatter.

I think it did not hit him,
But suddenly that part of him that was left behind convulsed in
    undignified haste,
Writhed like lightning, and was gone 60
Into the black hole, the earth-lipped fissure in the wall-front,
    At which, in the intense still noon, I stared with fascination.

And immediately I regretted it.
I thought how paltry, how vulgar, what a mean act!
I despised myself and the voices of my accursèd human education.

And I thought of the albatross,
And I wished he would come back, my snake.

For he seemed to me again like a king,
Like a king in exile, uncrowned in the underworld,
Now due to be crowned again. 70

And so, I missed my chance with one of the lords
Of life.
And I have something to expiate;
A pettiness.

D. H. Lawrence

GRANDEUR OF GHOSTS

When I have heard small talk about great men
I climb to bed; light my two candles; then
Consider what was said; and put aside
What Such-a-one remarked and Someone-else replied.

They have spoken lightly of my deathless friends
(Lamps for my gloom, hands guiding where I stumble),
Quoting, for shallow conversational ends,
What Shelley shrilled, what Blake once wildly muttered. . . .

How can they use such names and be not humble?
I have sat silent; angry at what they uttered.　　　　　10
The dead bequeathed them life; the dead have said
What these can only memorize and mumble.

Siegfried Sassoon

THE DEAD

These hearts were woven of human joys and cares,
　　Washed marvellously with sorrow, swift to mirth.
The years had given them kindness. Dawn was theirs,
　　And sunset, and the colours of the earth.
These had seen movement, and heard music; known
　　Slumber and waking; loved, gone proudly friended;
Felt the quick stir of wonder; sat alone;
　　Touched flowers and furs, and cheeks. All this is ended.
There are waters blown by changing winds to laughter
And lit by the rich skies, all day. And after,　　　　　10
　　Frost, with a gesture, stays the waves that dance
And wandering loveliness. He leaves a white
　　Unbroken glory, a gathered radiance,
A width, a shining peace, under the night.

Rupert Brooke

SUBURBAN DREAM

Walking the suburbs in the afternoon
In summer when the idle doors stand open
　　And the air flows through the rooms
　　Fanning the curtain hems,

You wander through a cool elysium
Of women, schoolgirls, children, garden talks,
　　With a schoolboy here and there
　　Conning his history book.

The men are all away in offices,
Committee-rooms, laboratories, banks,   10
    Or pushing cotton goods
    In wick or Ilfracombe.

The massed unanimous absence liberates
The light keys of the piano and sets free
    Chopin and everlasting youth
    Now, with the masters gone.

And all things turn to images of peace,
The boy curled over his book, the young girl poised
    On the path as if beguiled
    By the silence of a wood.   20

It is a child's dream of a grown-up world.
But soon the brazen evening clocks will bring
    The tramp of feet and brisk
    Fanfare of motor horns
    And the masters come.

Edwin Muir

JOURNEY OF THE MAGI

"A cold coming we had of it,
Just the worst time of the year
For a journey, and such a long journey:
The ways deep and the weather sharp,
The very dead of winter."
And the camels galled, sore-footed, refractory,
Lying down in the melting snow.
There were times we regretted
The summer palaces on slopes, the terraces,
And the silken girls bringing sherbet.   10
Then the camel men cursing and grumbling
And running away, and wanting their liquor and women,
And the night-fires going out, and the lack of shelters,
And the cities hostile and the towns unfriendly
And the villages dirty and charging high prices:
A hard time we had of it.

At the end we preferred to travel all night,
Sleeping in snatches,
With the voices singing in our ears, saying
That this was all folly.   20

Then at dawn we came down to a temperate valley,
Wet, below the snow line, smelling of vegetation;
With a running stream and a water-mill beating the darkness,
And three trees on the low sky,
And an old white horse galloped away in the meadow.
Then we came to a tavern with vine-leaves over the lintel,
Six hands at an open door dicing for pieces of silver,
And feet kicking the empty wine-skins.
But there was no information, and so we continued
And arrived at evening, not a moment too soon   30
Finding the place; it was (you may say) satisfactory.

All this was a long time ago, I remember,
And I would do it again, but set down
This set down
This: were we led all that way for
Birth or Death? There was a Birth, certainly,
We had evidence and no doubt. I had seen birth and death,
But had thought they were different; this Birth was
Hard and bitter agony for us, like Death, our **death**.
We returned to our places, these Kingdoms,   40
But no longer at ease here, in the old dispensation,
With an alien people clutching their gods.
I should be glad of another death.

T. S. Eliot

ARMS AND THE BOY

Let the boy try along this bayonet-blade
How cold steel is, and keen with hunger of blood;
Blue with all malice, like a madman's flash;
And thinly drawn with famishing for flesh.

Lend him to stroke these blind, blunt bullet-heads
Which long to nuzzle in the hearts of lads,
Or give him cartridges of fine zinc teeth,
Sharp with the sharpness of grief and death.

For his teeth seem for laughing round an apple.
There lurk no claws behind his fingers supple;   10
And God will grow no talons at his heels,
Nor antlers through the thickness of his curls.

Wilfred Owen

ON ANOTHER THEME
FROM NICOLAS OF CUSA

When soul and body feed, one sees
Their differing physiologies.
Firmness of apple, fluted shape
Of celery, or the bloom of grape
I grind and mangle as I eat,
Then in dark, salt, internal heat
Obliterates their natures by
The mastering art that makes them I.

But when the soul partakes of good
Or truth, which are her savoury food,
By a far subtler chemistry
It is not they that change but she,
Who lets them enter with the state
Of conquerors her surrendered gate,
Or mirror-like digests their ray
By turning luminous as they.

C. S. Lewis

ON A PORTRAIT OF A DEAF MAN

The kind old face, the egg-shaped head,
    The tie, discreetly loud,
The loosely fitting shooting clothes,
    A closely fitting shroud.

He liked old City dining-rooms,
    Potatoes in their skin,
But now his mouth is wide to let
    The London clay come in.

He took me on long silent walks
  In country lanes when young,   10
He knew the name of ev'ry bird
  But not the song it sung.

And when he could not hear me speak
  He smiled and looked so wise
That now I do not like to think
  Of maggots in his eyes.

He liked the rain-washed Cornish air
  And smell of ploughed-up soil,
He liked a landscape big and bare
  And painted it in oil.   20

But least of all he liked that place
  Which hangs on Highgate Hill
Of soaked Carrara-covered earth
  For Londoners to fill.

He would have liked to say good-bye,
  Shake hands with many friends,
In Highgate now his finger-bones
  Stick through his finger-ends.

You, God, who treat him thus and thus,
  Say "Save his soul and pray."   30
You ask me to believe You and
  I only see decay.

John Betjeman

BALLAD

O what is that sound which so thrills the ear
  Down in the valley drumming, drumming?
Only the scarlet soldiers, dear,
  The soldiers coming.

O what is that light I see flashing so clear
  Over the distance brightly, brightly?
Only the sun on their weapons, dear,
  As they step lightly.

O what are they doing with all that gear;
   What are they doing this morning, this morning?   10
Only the usual manœuvres, dear,
   Or perhaps a warning.

O why have they left the road down there;
   Why are they suddenly wheeling, wheeling?
Perhaps a change in the orders, dear;
   Why are you kneeling?

O haven't they stopped for the doctor's care;
   Haven't they reined their horses, their horses?
Why, they are none of them wounded, dear,
   None of these forces.   20

O is it the parson they want, with white hair;
   Is it the parson, is it, is it?
No, they are passing his gateway, dear,
   Without a visit.

O it must be the farmer who lives so near,
   It must be the farmer, so cunning, cunning;
They have passed the farm already, dear,
   And now they are running.

O where are you going? Stay with me here.
   Were the vows you swore me deceiving, deceiving?   30
No, I promised to love you, dear,
   But I must be leaving.

O it's broken the lock and splintered the door,
   O it's the gate where they're turning, turning;
Their feet are heavy on the floor
   And their eyes are burning.

W. H. Auden

THE SUNLIGHT ON THE GARDEN

The sunlight on the garden
Hardens and grows cold,
We cannot cage the minute
Within its nets of gold;
When all is told
We cannot beg for pardon.

Our freedom as free lances
Advances towards its end;
The earth compels, upon it
Sonnets and birds descend;   10
And soon, my friend,
We shall have no time for dances.

The sky was good for flying
Defying the church bells
And every evil iron
Siren and what it tells:
The earth compels,
We are dying, Egypt, dying

And not expecting pardon,
Hardened in heart anew,   20
But glad to have sat under
Thunder and rain with you,
And grateful too
For sunlight on the garden.

Louis MacNeice

FERN HILL

Now as I was young and easy under the apple boughs
About the lilting house and happy as the grass was green,
   The night above the dingle starry,
     Time let me hail and climb
   Golden in the heydays of his eyes,
And honoured among wagons I was prince of the apple towns
And once below a time I lordly had the trees and leaves
     Trail with daisies and barley
   Down the rivers of the windfall light.

And as I was green and carefree, famous among the barns   10
About the happy yard and singing as the farm was home,
    In the sun that is young once only,
     Time let me play and be
   Golden in the mercy of his means,
And green and golden I was huntsman and herdsman, the calves
Sang to my horn, the foxes on the hills barked clear and cold,
    And the sabbath rang slowly
   In the pebbles of the holy streams.

All the sun long it was running, it was lovely, the hay
Fields high as the house, the tunes from the chimneys, it was air 20
    And playing, lovely and watery
        And fire green as grass.
    And nightly under the simple stars
As I rode to sleep the owls were bearing the farm away,
All the moon long I heard, blessed among stables, the nightjars
    Flying with the ricks, and the horses
        Flashing into the dark.

And then to awake, and the farm, like a wanderer white
With the dew, come back, the cock on his shoulder: it was all
    Shining, it was Adam and maiden,   30
        The sky gathered again
    And the sun grew round that very day.
So it must have been after the birth of the simple light
In the first, spinning place, the spellbound horses walking warm
    Out of the whinnying green stable
        On to the fields of praise.

And honoured among foxes and pheasants by the gay house
Under the new made clouds and happy as the heart was long,
    In the sun born over and over,
        I ran my heedless ways,   40
    My wishes raced through the house high hay
And nothing I cared, at my sky blue trades, that time allows
In all his tuneful turning so few and such morning songs
    Before the children green and golden
        Follow him out of grace.

Nothing I cared, in the lamb white days, that time would take me
Up to the swallow thronged loft by the shadow of my hand,
    In the moon that is always rising,
        Nor that riding to sleep
    I should hear him fly with the high fields   50
And wake to the farm forever fled from the childless land.
Oh as I was young and easy in the mercy of his means,
        Time held me green and dying
    Though I sang in my chains like the sea.

Dylan Thomas

NAMING OF PARTS

To-day we have naming of parts. Yesterday,
We had daily cleaning. And to-morrow morning,
We shall have what to do after firing. But to-day,
To-day we have naming of parts. Japonica
Glistens like coral in all of the neighbouring gardens,
     And to-day we have naming of parts.

This is the lower sling swivel. And this
Is the upper sling swivel, whose use you will see,
When you are given your slings. And this is the piling swivel,
Which in your case you have not got. The branches   10
Hold in the gardens their silent, eloquent gestures,
     Which in our case we have not got.

This is the safety-catch, which is always released
With an easy flick of the thumb. And please do not let me
See anyone using his finger. You can do it quite easy
If you have any strength in your thumb. The blossoms
Are fragile and motionless, never letting anyone see
     Any of them using their finger.

And this you can see is the bolt. The purpose of this
Is to open the breech, as you see. We can slide it
Rapidly backwards and forwards: we call this
Easing the spring. And rapidly backwards and forwards
The early bees are assaulting and fumbling the flowers:
     They call it easing the Spring.

They call it easing the Spring: it is perfectly easy
If you have any strength in your thumb: like the bolt,
And the breech, and the cocking-piece, and the point of balance,
Which in our case we have not got; and the almond-blossom
Silent in all of the gardens and the bees going backwards and
      forwards,
     For to-day we have naming of parts.   30

Henry Reed

VERSES AT NIGHT

Sleepless, by the windowpane I stare –
    black aeroplanes disturb the air.
    The ticking moon glares down aghast.
        The seven branched tree is bare.

Oh how much like Europe's gothic Past!
    This scene my nightmare's metaphrast:
    glow of the radioactive worm,
        the preterites of the Blast.

Unreal? East and West fat Neros yearn
    for other fiddled Romes to burn,   10
    and so dogma cancels dogma
        and heretics in their turn.

By my wife now I lie quiet as a
    thought of how moon and stars might blur,
    and miles of smoke squirm overhead
        rising to Man's arbiter;

the grey skin shrivelling from the head,
    our two skulls in the double bed,
    leukaemia in the soul of all
        flowing through the blood instead.   20

"No," I shout, as by her side I sprawl,
    "No," again, as I hear my small
    dear daughter whimper in her cot
        and across the darkness call.

Danny Abse

AMERICAN POETS

DAREST THOU NOW O SOUL

Darest thou now O soul,
Walk out with me toward the unknown region,
Where neither ground is for the feet nor any path to follow?

No map there, nor guide,
Nor voice sounding, nor touch of human hand,
Nor face with blooming flesh, nor lips, nor eyes, are in that land.

I know it not O soul,
Nor dost thou, all is a blank before us,
All waits undream'd of in that region, that inaccessible land.

Till when the ties loosen,   10
All but the ties eternal, Time and Space,
Nor darkness, gravitation, sense, nor any bounds bounding us.

Then we burst forth, we float,
In Time and Space O Soul, prepared for them,
Equal, equipped at last, (O joy! O fruit of all!) them to fulfil O soul.

Walt Whitman

INDIAN SUMMER

These are the days when the birds come back,
A very few, a bird or two,
To take a backward look.

These are the days when skies put on
The old, old sophistries of June, –
A blue and gold mistake.

Oh, fraud that cannot cheat the bee,
Almost thy plausibility
Induces my belief,

Till ranks of seeds their witness bear,   10
And softly through the altered air
Hurries a timid leaf!

Oh, sacrament of summer days,
Oh, last communion in the haze,
Permit a child to join,

Thy sacred emblems to partake,
Thy consecrated bread to break,
Taste thine immortal wine!

Emily Dickinson

THE RAILWAY TRAIN

I like to see it lap the miles,
And lick the valleys up,
And stop to feed itself at tanks;
And then, prodigious, step

Around a pile of mountains,
And, supercilious, peer
In shanties by the sides of roads;
And then a quarry pare

To fit its sides, and crawl between,
Complaining all the while   10
In horrid, hooting stanza:
Then chase itself downhill

And neigh like Boanerges;
Then, punctual as a star,
Stop – docile and omnipotent –
At its own stable door.

Emily Dickinson

WITH YOU A PART OF ME

With you a part of me hath passed away;
For in the peopled forest of my mind
A tree made leafless by this wintry wind
Shall never don again its green array.
Chapel and fireside, country road and bay,
Have something of their friendliness resigned;
Another, if I would, I could not find,
And I am grown much older in a day.
But yet I treasure in my memory
Your gift of charity, and young heart's ease,   10
And the dear honour of your amity;
For thee once mine, my life is rich with these.
And I scarce know which part may greater be –
What I keep of you, or you rob from me.

George Santayana

O WORLD

O world, thou choosest not the better part!
It is not wisdom to be only wise,
And on the inward vision close the eyes,
But it is wisdom to believe the heart.
Columbus found a world, and had no chart,
Save one that faith deciphered in the skies;
To trust the soul's invincible surmise
Was all his science and his only art.
Our knowledge is a torch of smoky pine
That lights the pathway but one step ahead   10
Across a void of mystery and dread.
Bid, then, the tender light of faith to shine
By which alone the mortal heart is led
Unto the thinking of the thought divine.

George Santayana

CALVARY

Friendless and faint, with martyred steps and slow,
Faint for the flesh, but for the spirit free,
Stung by the mob that came to see the show,
The Master toiled along to Calvary;
We gibed him, as he went, with houndish glee,
Till his dimmed eyes for us did overflow;
We cursed his vengeless hands thrice wretchedly, –
And this was nineteen hundred years ago.
But after nineteen hundred years the shame
Still clings, and we have not made good the loss   10
That outraged faith has entered in his name.
Ah, when shall come love's courage to be strong!
Tell me, O Lord – tell me, O Lord, how long
Are we to keep Christ writhing on the cross!

Edwin Arlington Robinson

STOPPING BY WOODS
ON A SNOWY EVENING

Whose woods these are I think I know.
His house is in the village though;
He will not see me stopping here
To watch his woods fill up with snow.

My little horse must think it queer
To stop without a farmhouse near
Between the woods and frozen lake
The darkest evening of the year.

He gives his harness bells a shake
To ask if there is some mistake.   10
The only other sound's the sweep
Of easy wind and downy flake.

The woods are lovely, dark and deep,
But I have promises to keep,
And miles to go before I sleep,
And miles to go before I sleep.

Robert Frost

CHICAGO

Hog Butcher for the World,
Tool Maker, Stacker of Wheat,
Player with Railroads and the Nation's Freight Handler;
Stormy, husky, brawling,
City of the Big Shoulders:
They tell me you are wicked and I believe them, for I have seen your
    painted women under the gas lamps luring the farm boys.
And they tell me you are crooked and I answer: Yes, it is true I have
    seen the gunman kill and go free to kill again.
And they tell we you are brutal and my reply is: On the faces of
    women and children I have seen the marks of wanton hunger.
And having answered so, I turn once more to those who sneer at this
    my city, and I give them back the sneer and say to them:
Come and show me another city with lifted head singing so proud
    to be alive and coarse and strong and cunning.   10
Flinging magnetic curses amid the toil of piling job on job, here is a
    tall bold slugger set vivid against the little soft cities;
Fierce as a dog with tongue lapping for action, cunning as a savage
    pitted against the wilderness,
    Bareheaded,
    Shoveling,
    Wrecking,
    Planning,
    Building, breaking, rebuilding,
Under the smoke, dust all over his mouth, laughing with white teeth,
Under the terrible burden of destiny laughing as a young man laughs,
Laughing even as an ignorant fighter laughs who has never lost a
    battle.
Bragging and laughing that under his wrist is the pulse, and under his
    ribs the heart of the people,
                 Laughing!
Laughing the stormy, husky, brawling laughter of Youth, half-naked,
    sweating, proud to be Hog Butcher, Tool Maker, Stacker of
    Wheat, Player with Railroads and Freight Handler to the Nation.

Carl Sandburg

BURNING THE CHRISTMAS GREENS

Their time past, pulled down
cracked and flung to the fire
—go up in a roar

All recognition lost, burnt clean
clean in the flame, the green
dispersed, a living red,
flame red, red as blood wakes
on the ash—

and ebbs to a steady burning
the rekindled bed became   10
a landscape of flame

At the winter's midnight
we went to the trees, the coarse
holly, the balsam and
the hemlock for their green

At the thick of the dark
the moment of the cold's
deepest plunge we brought branches
cut from the green trees

to fill our need, and over   20
doorways, about paper Christmas
bells covered with tinfoil
and fastened by red ribbons

we stuck the green prongs,
in the windows hung
woven wreaths and about pictures
the living green. On the

mantle we built a green forest
and among those hemlock
sprays put a herd of small   30
white deer as if they

were walking there. All this!
and it seemed gentle and good
to us. Their time past,
relief! The room bare. We

stuffed the dead grate
with them upon the half burnt-out
log's smouldering eye, opening
red and closing under them

and we stood there looking down.   40
Green is a solace
a promise of peace, a fort
against the cold (though we

did not say so) a challenge
above the snow's
hard shell. Green (we might
have said) that, where

small birds hide and dodge
and lift their plaintive
rallying cries, blocks for them   50
and knocks down

the unseeing bullets of
the storm. Green spruce boughs
pulled down by a weight of
snow—Transformed!

Violence leaped and appeared.
Recreant! roared to life
as the flames rose through and
our eyes recoiled from it.

In the jagged flames green   60
to red, instant and alive. Green!
those sure abutments . . . . Gone!
lost to mind

and quick in the contracting
tunnel of the grate
appeared a world! Black
mountains, black and red—as

yet uncoloured—and ash white,
an infant landscape of shimmering
ash and flame and we, in   70
that instant, lost

breathless to be witnesses,
as if we stood
ourselves refreshed among
the shining fauna of that fire.

William Carlos Williams

TO THE STONE-CUTTERS

Stone-cutters fighting time with marble, you foredefeated
Challengers of oblivion,
Eat cynical earnings, knowing rock splits, records fall down,
The square-limbed Roman letters
Scale in the thaws, wear in the rain. The poet as well
Builds his monument mockingly;
For man will be blotted out, the blithe earth die, the brave sun
Die blind, his heart blackening:
Yet stones have stood for a thousand years, and pained thoughts
found
The honey of peace in old poems.   10

Robinson Jeffers

PIAZZA PIECE

– I am a gentleman in a dustcoat trying
To make you hear. Your ears are soft and small
And listen to an old man not at all;
They want the young men's whispering and sighing.
But see the roses on your trellis dying
And hear the spectral singing of the moon –
For I must have my lovely lady soon,
I am a gentleman in a dustcoat trying.

– I am a lady young in beauty waiting
Until my truelove comes, and then we kiss.   10
But what grey man among the vines is this
Whose words are dry and faint as in a dream?
Back from my trellis, Sir, before I scream!
I am a lady young in beauty waiting.

John Crowe Ransom

235

BELLS FOR JOHN WHITESIDE'S DAUGHTER

There was such speed in her little body,
And such lightness in her footfall,
It is no wonder her brown study
Astonishes us all.

Her wars were bruited in our high window.
We looked among orchard trees and beyond,
Where she took arms against her shadow,
Or harried unto the pond

The lazy geese, like a snow cloud
Dripping their snow on the green grass,   10
Tricking and stopping, sleepy and proud,
Who cried in goose, Alas,

For the tireless heart within the little
Lady with rod that made them rise
From their noon apple-dreams and scuttle
Goose-fashion under the skies!

But now go the bells, and we are ready,
In one house we are sternly stopped
To say we are vexed at her brown study,
Lying so primly propped.   20

John Crowe Ransom

anyone lived in a pretty how town

anyone lived in a pretty how town
(with up so floating many bells down)
spring summer autumn winter
he sang his didn't he danced his did.

Women and men (both little and small)
cared for anyone not at all
they sowed their isn't they reaped their same
sun moon stars rain

children guessed (but only a few
and down they forgot as up they grew   10
autumn winter spring summer)
that noone loved him more by more

when by now and tree by leaf
she laughed his joy she cried his grief
bird by snow and stir by still
anyone's any was all to her

someones married their everyones
laughed their cryings and did their dance
(sleep wake hope and then) they
said their nevers they slept their dream 20

stars rain sun moon
(and only the snow can begin to explain
how children are apt to forget to remember
with up so floating many bells down)

one day anyone died i guess
(and noone stooped to kiss his face)
busy folk buried them side by side
little by little and was by was

all by all and deep by deep
and more by more they dream their sleep 30
noone and anyone earth by april
wish by spirit and if by yes.

Women and men (both dong and ding)
summer autumn winter spring
reaped their sowing and went their came
sun moon stars rain

E. E. Cummings

IMMORTAL

The last thin acre of stalks that stood
    Was never the end of the wheat.
Always something fled to the wood
    As if the field had feet.

In front of the sickle something rose –
    Mouse, or weasel, or hare;
We struck and struck, but our worst blows
    Dangled in the air.

othing could touch the little soul
    Of the grain. It ran to cover,   10
And nobody knew in what warm hole
    It slept till the winter was over,

And early seeds lay cold in the ground.
    Then – but nobody saw –
It burrowed back with never a sound,
    And awoke the thaw.

Mark Van Doren

EVENING IN THE SANITARIUM

The free evening fades, outside the windows fastened with decorative
    iron grilles.
The lamps are lighted; the shades drawn; the nurses are watching a
    little.
It is the hour of the complicated knitting on the safe bone needles;
    of the games of anagrams and bridge;
The deadly game of chess; the book held up like a mask.

The period of the wildest weeping, the fiercest delusion, is over.
The women rest their tired half-healed hearts; they are almost well.
Some of them will stay almost well always: the blunt-faced woman
    whose thinking dissolved
Under academic discipline; the manic-depressive girl
Now leveling off; one paranoiac afflicted with jealousy,
Another with persecution. Some alleviation has been possible.   10

O fortunate bride, who never again will become elated after
    childbirth!
O lucky older wife, who has been cured of feeling unwanted!
To the suburban railway station you will return, return,
To meet forever Jim home on the 5:35.
You will be again as normal and selfish and heartless as anybody else.

There is life left: the piano says it with its octave smile.
The soft carpets pad the thump and splinter of the suicide to be.
Everything will be splendid: the grandmother will not drink
    habitually.
The fruit salad will bloom on the plate like a bouquet
And the garden produce the blue-ribbon aquilegia.   20

The cats will be glad; the fathers feel justified; the mothers
    relieved.
The sons and husbands will no longer need to pay the bills.
Childhoods will be put away, the obscene nightmare abated.

At the ends of the corridors the baths are running.
Mrs. C. again feels the shadow of the obsessive idea.
Miss R. looks at the mantel-piece, which must mean something.

Louise Bogan

LETTER TO N.Y.

In your next letter I wish you'd say
where you are going and what you are doing;
how are the plays, and after the plays
what other pleasures you're pursuing:

taking cabs in the middle of the night,
driving as if to save your soul
where the road goes round and round the park
and the meter glares like a moral owl,

and the trees look so queer and green
standing alone in big black caves   10
and suddenly you're in a different place
where everything seems to happen in waves,

and most of the jokes you just can't catch,
like dirty words rubbed off a slate,
and the songs are loud but somehow dim
and it gets so terribly late,

and coming out of the brownstone house
to the gray sidewalk, the watered street,
one side of the buildings rises with the sun
like a glistening field of wheat.   20

— Wheat, not oats, dear. I'm afraid
if it's wheat it's none of your sowing,
nevertheless I'd like to know
what you are doing and where you are going.

Elizabeth Bishop

A CAMP IN THE PRUSSIAN FOREST

I walk beside the prisoners to the road.
Load on puffed load,
Their corpses, stacked like sodden wood,
Lie barred or galled with blood

By the charred warehouse. No one comes today
In the old way
To knock the fillings from their teeth;
The dark, coned, common wreath

Is plaited for their grave – a kind of grief.
The living leaf   10
Clings to the planted profitable
Pine if it is able;

The boughs sigh, mile on green, calm, breathing mile,
From this dead file
The planners ruled for them. . . . One year
They sent a million here:

Here men were drunk like water, burnt like wood.
The fat of good
And evil, the breast's star of hope
Were rendered into soap.   20

I paint the star I sawed from yellow pine –
And plant the sign
In soil that does not yet refuse
Its usual Jews

Their first asylum. But the white, dwarfed star –
This dead white star –
Hides nothing, pays for nothing; smoke
Fouls it, a yellow joke,

The needles of the wreath are chalked with ash,
A filmy trash   30
Litters the black woods with the death
Of men; and one last breath

Curls from the monstrous chimney. . . . I laugh aloud
Again and again;
The star laughs from its rotting shroud
Of flesh. O star of men!

Randall Jarrell

240

AS A PLANE TREE BY THE WATER

Darkness has called to darkness, and disgrace
Elbows about our windows in this planned
Babel of Boston where our money talks
And multiplies the darkness of a land
Of preparation where the Virgin walks
And roses spiral her enameled face
Or fall to splinters on unwatered streets.
Our Lady of Babylon, go by, go by,
I was once the apple of your eye;
Flies, flies are on the plane tree, on the streets.   10

The flies, the flies, the flies of Babylon
Buzz in my ear-drums while the devil's long
Dirge of the people detonates the hour
For floating cities where his golden tongue
Enchants the masons of the Babel Tower
To raise tomorrow's city to the sun
That never sets upon these hell-fire streets
Of Boston, where the sunlight is a sword
Striking at the withholder of the Lord:
Flies, flies are on the plane tree, on the streets.   20

Flies strike the miraculous waters of the iced
Atlantic and the eyes of Bernadette
Who saw Our Lady standing in the cave
At Massabielle, saw her so squarely that
Her vision put out reason's eyes. The grave
Is open-mouthed and swallowed up in Christ.
O walls of Jericho! And all the streets
To our Atlantic wall are singing: "Sing,
Sing for the resurrection of the King."
Flies, flies are on the plane tree, on the streets.   30

Robert Lowell

THE BEAUTIFUL CHANGES

One wading a Fall meadow finds on all sides
The Queen Anne's Lace lying like lilies
On water; it glides
So from the walker, it turns
Dry grass to a lake, as the slightest shade of you
Valleys my mind in fabulous blue Lucernes.

The beautiful changes as a forest is changed
By a chameleon's tuning his skin to it;
As a mantis, arranged
On a green leaf, grows   10
Into it, makes the leaf leafier, and proves
Any greenness is deeper than anyone knows.

Your hands hold roses always in a way that says
They are not only yours; the beautiful changes
In such kind ways,
Wishing ever to sunder
Things and things' selves for a second finding, to lose
For a moment all that it touches back to wonder.

Richard Wilbur

HIGH FLIGHT

Oh, I have slipped the surly bonds of earth
And danced the skies on laughter-silvered wings;
Sunward I've climbed and joined the tumbling mirth
Of sun-split clouds — and done a hundred things
You have not dreamed of—wheeled and soared and swung
High in the sunlit silence. Hov'ring there,
I've chased the shouting wind along and flung
My eager craft through footless halls of air.
Up, up the long delirious, burning blue
I've topped the wind-swept heights with easy grace,   10
Where never lark, or even eagle, flew;
And, while with silent, lifting mind I've trod
The high untrespassed sanctity of space,
Put out my hand and touched the face of God.

John Gillespie Magee

FIRST LESSON

Lie back, daughter, let your head
be tipped back in the cup of my hand.
Gently, and I will hold you. Spread
your arms wide, lie out on the stream
and look high at the gulls. A dead-
man's float is face down. You will dive
and swim soon enough where this tidewater
ebbs to the sea. Daughter, believe
me, when you tire on the long thrash
to your island, lie up, and survive.   10
As you float now, where I held you
and let go, remember when fear
cramps your heart what I told you:
lie gently and wide to the light-year
stars, lie back, and the sea will hold you.

Philip Booth

WE LIVE IN A RICKETY HOUSE

We live in a rickety house,
   In a dirty dismal street,
Where the naked hide from day,
   And thieves and drunkards meet.

And pious folks with their tracts,
   When our dens they enter in,
They point to our shirtless backs,
   As the fruits of beer and gin.

And they quote us texts to prove
   That our hearts are hard as stone,   10
And they feed us with the fact
   That the fault is all our own.

It will be long ere the poor
   Will learn their grog to shun
While it's raiment, food and fire,
   And religion all in one.

I wonder some pious folks
   Can look us straight in the face,
For our ignorance and crime
   Are the Church's shame and disgrace.   20

We live in a rickety house,
   In a dirty dismal street,
Where the naked hide from day,
   And thieves and drunkards meet.

Alexander McLachlan

THE FLIGHT OF THE GEESE

I hear the low wind wash the softening snow,
    The low tide loiters down the shore. The night,
    Full filled with April forecast, bore no light.
The salt wave on the sedge-flat pulses slow.

Through the hid furrows lisp in murmurous flow
    The thaw's shy ministers; and hark! the height
    Of heaven grows weird and loud with unseen flight
Of strong hosts prophesying as they go!

High through the drenched and hollow night their wings
    Beat northward hard on winter's trail. The sound   10
Of their confused and solemn voices borne
Athwart the dark to their long Arctic morn,
    Comes with a sanction and an awe profound,
A boding of unknown, foreshadowed things.

Charles G. D. Roberts

WINTER UPLANDS

The frost that stings like fire upon my cheek,
The loneliness of this forsaken ground,
The long white drift upon whose powdered peak
I sit in the great silence as one bound;
The rippled sheet of snow where the wind blew
Across the open fields for miles ahead;
The far-off city towered and roofed in blue
A tender line upon the western red;
The stars that singly, then in flocks appear,
Like jets of silver from the violet dome,   10
So wonderful, so many and so near,
And then the golden moon to light me home;
The crunching snowshoes and the stinging air,
And silence, frost and beauty everywhere.

Archibald Lampman

EVENING

From upland slopes I see the cows file by,
Lowing, great-chested, down the homeward trail,
By dusking fields and meadows shining pale
With moon-tipped dandelions. Flickering high,
A peevish night-hawk in the western sky
Beats up into the lucent solitudes,
Or drops with griding wing. The stilly woods
Grow dark and deep and gloom mysteriously.
Cool night winds creep, and whisper in mine ear.
The homely cricket gossips at my feet.   10
From far-off pools and wastes of reeds I hear,
Clear and soft-piped, the chanting frogs break sweet
In full Pandean chorus. One by one
Shine out the stars, and the great night comes on.

Archibald Lampman

INDIAN SUMMER

Along the line of smoky hills
    The crimson forest stands,
And all the day the blue-jay calls
    Throughout the autumn lands.

Now by the brook the maple leans
    With all his glory spread,
And all the sumachs on the hills
    Have turned their green to red.

Now by great marshes wrapt in mist,
    Or past some river's mouth,   10
Throughout the long, still autumn day
    Wild birds are flying south.

Wilfred Campbell

VESTIGIA

I took a day to search for God,
And found Him not. But as I trod
By rocky ledge, through woods untamed,
Just where one scarlet lily flamed,
I saw His footprint in the sod.

Then suddenly, all unaware,
Far off in the deep shadows, where
A solitary hermit thrush
Sang through the holy twilight hush —
I heard His voice upon the air.   10

And even as I marvelled how
God gives us Heaven here and now,
In a stir of wind that hardly shook
The poplar leaves beside the brook —
His hand was light upon my brow.

At last with evening as I turned
Homeward, and thought what I had learned
And all that there was still to probe —
I caught the glory of His robe
Where the last fires of sunset burned.   20

Back to the world with quickening start
I looked and longed for any part
In making saving Beauty be. . . .
And from that kindling ecstasy
I knew God dwelt within my heart.

Bliss Carman

THE HALF-BREED GIRL

She is free of the trap and the paddle,
    The portage and the trail,
But something behind her savage life
    Shines like a fragile veil.

Her dreams are undiscovered,
    Shadows trouble her breast,
When the time for resting cometh
    Then least is she at rest.

Oft in the morns of winter,
    When she visits the rabbit snares,
An appearance floats in the crystal air
    Beyond the balsam firs.

Oft in the summer mornings
    When she strips the nets of fish,
The smell of the dripping net-twine
    Gives to her heart a wish.

But she cannot learn the meaning
    Of the shadows in her soul,
The lights that break and gather,
    The clouds that part and roll,

The reek of rock-built cities,
    Where her fathers dwelt of yore,
The gleam of loch and shealing,
    The mist on the moor,

Frail traces of kindred kindness,
    Of feud by hill and strand,
The heritage of an age-long life
    In a legendary land.

She wakes in the stifling wigwam,
    Where the air is heavy and wild,
She fears for something or nothing
    With the heart of a frightened child.

She sees the stars turn slowly
    Past the tangle of the poles,
Through the smoke of the dying embers,
    Like the eyes of dead souls.

Her heart is shaken with longing
    For the strange, still years,
For what she knows and knows not,
    For the wells of ancient tears.

10

20

30

40

A voice calls from the rapids,
  Deep, careless and free,
A voice that is larger than her life
  Or than her death shall be.

She covers her face with her blanket,
  Her fierce soul hates her breath,
As it cries with a sudden passion
  For life or death.

Duncan Campbell Scott

THE FUNDAMENTALIST

You say it's this or that
  That nothing lies between:
Here is all black and foul;
  There is all white and clean.

Quick are your tongue's decrees;
  Your judgments swiftly given:
This unto outer darkness,
  That unto inner Heaven.

Hail to you, masters wise,
  Who can so well adjust   10
The problems of the skies
  With your amazing dust.

You say it's this or that,
  And measure by one rule
The pathway of the seer,
  The roadway of the fool.

And, while your holy host
  A faultless record makes,
The snail-like gods move on
  Through their divine mistakes.   20

Wilson MacDonald

THE LAMP OF POOR SOULS

*In many English churches before the Reformation there
was kept a little lamp continually burning, called the Lamp
of Poor Souls. People were reminded thereby to pray for
the souls of those dead whose kinsfolk were too poor to
pay for prayers and masses*

Above my head the shields are stained with rust,
The wind has taken his spoil, the moth his part,
Dust of dead men beneath my knees, and dust,
Lord, in my heart.

Lay Thou the hand of faith upon my fears;
The priest has prayed, the silver bell has rung,
But not for him. O unforgotten tears,
He was so young!

Shine, little lamp, nor let thy light grow dim.
Into what vast, dread dreams, what lonely lands,   10
Into what griefs hath death delivered him,
Far from my hands?

Cradled is he with half his prayers forgot.
I cannot learn the level way he goes.
He whom the harvest hath remembered not
Sleeps with the rose.

Shine, little lamp, fed with sweet oil of prayers.
Shine, little lamp, as God's own eyes may shine,
When he treads softly down his starry stairs
And whispers, "Thou art mine."   20

Shine, little lamp, for love hath fed thy gleam.
Sleep, little soul, by God's own hands set free.
Cling to his arms and sleep, and sleeping, dream,
And dreaming, look for me.

Marjorie Pickthall

FROST

The frost moved up the window-pane
Against the sun's advance,
In line and pattern weaving there
Rich scenes of old romance –
Armies on the Russian snows,
Cockade, sword, and lance.

It spun a web more magical,
Each moment creeping higher,
For marble cities crowned the hills
With turret, fane, and spire,   10
Till when it struck the flaming sash,
The Kremlin was on fire.

E. J. Pratt

SEA-GULLS

For one carved instant as they flew,
The language had no simile –
Silver, crystal, ivory
Were tarnished. Etched upon the horizon blue,
The frieze must go unchallenged, for the lift
And carriage of the wings would stain the drift
Of stars against a tropic indigo
Or dull the parable of snow.

Now settling one by one
Within green hollows or where curled   10
Crests caught the spectrum from the sun,
A thousand wings are furled.
No clay-born lilies of the world
Could blow as free
As those wild orchids of the sea.

E. J. Pratt

THE RETICENT PHRASE

Aptness shall come from whence, reticent phrase,
to tinge precisely your pellucid wave?
Not through the naked nonchalance of chance,
like lightning down an uncontradicted sky.

Aptness is folded underneath your candour,
pooled in the polish of a reflective glaze,
wavers, dawdles, expands, a marine flower
idling up fluid doldrums to the surface.

The phrase, beating its music, preening its crest
against a critical oar, draws at the secret   10
till the day the oar rests as the wave sunders
and the fastidious implication emerges

a flower to pelt, an excalibur to wield.

Robert Finch

CANADA

I have seen her in the quiet of the evening in the fields,
I have sensed her in the dusk-time that the star-decked prairie yields.
She has poised on purple mountains when my lonely step drew near,
And the North's green fires at midnight were her altar-lights austere.

Her voice is in the thunder of the raptured Falls of Bow,
In the memory of Daulac dying greatly long ago.
Her song is in the music of awakened April rills,
She whose spirit walked with Lampman on his silent wooded hills.

In the ancient lonely churchyards of the pioneers asleep.
She broods in voiceless twilight where eternal memories creep.   10
Where the dark heroic headlands stand the wintry ocean's roar,
She sits thinking of the seamen who will come to port no more.

On the red earth of the vinelands, through the orchards in the spring
She walks and feels in heart and hand her beauty's blossoming, —
And again she wanders weeping beneath an alien sky
Where her many sons are sleeping and her young lost legions lie.

She is one with all our laughter, with our wonder and our pain,
Living everywhere triumphant, in the heart and soul and brain.
She our mother, we who bore her, she the daughter yet to be
Who walks these mortal roads of death to immortality.   20

Indivisible and lovely, she the maiden of our thought,
Is an empress robed in beauty from our deepest dreaming wrought,
She whose centuries are storied, whose young banners far outborne
Are the heralds of a splendour in the ages yet unborn.

Nathaniel Benson

WINTER SATURDAY

Furred from the farmhouse
like caterpillars from wood
they emerge, the storm blown out,
and find in the Ford their cocoon.
Through hardening dusk and over
the cold void impelled, they move
to dreams of light and sound.
Over drifts like headlands they go,
drawn to the town's pink cloud,
gliding unamazed through snow   10
by the wind marbled and fluted.
With tentacle headlights now
they feel the watertank, grope
with Main Street, are blissfully caught.
Hatch from the car like trembling moths,
circle to faces, flutter to movie,
throb through the dance in a sultry swoon.
But lights fail, time is false,
the town was less than its glow.
Again in chrysalis folded   20
they must go lonely
drowsy back through ghosts
the wind starts from the waiting snow.

Earle Birney

THE NEGRESS

Dark as ebony,
   Darker than night –
With wine-red lips
   And teeth so white,
Teeth so bright
   They would tarnish pearl –
Down the street
   Went the tall black girl.

Round hips swaying
   And big eyes bright –   10
She moved as freely,
   She stepped as light
As though about her
   The jungle loomed
And the witch-bones clattered
   And the tomtoms boomed.

As she walked in her crimson
   Calico gown
Eyes peered from windows
   All across town;   20
Heads wagged, tongues clucked –
   The things they said!
But she was alive
   And they were dead.

Audrey Alexandra Brown

RESURRECTION IN OCTOBER

When Seigneur Death came riding through,
He graced the ranks that joined him here
With pride they earned, but never knew:
The stature of the cavalier.

The ghosts who bade reluctant mould
Take fire with life no spring could stay,
Are helmeted with shivering gold
Are booted high with dusty grey.

The dark earth knows the stir and start
When autumn on their sleep confers   10
The coloured cloak, the stubborn heart,
The thrust of rainy rapiers.

We shall not find achievement thus.
Though gold aspire and scarlet thrive,
There is no peace in these for us:
We are alive . . . we are alive.

Charles Bruce

SONG FOR NAOMI

Who is that in the tall grasses singing
By herself, near the water?
I can not see her
But can it be her
Than whom the grasses so tall
Are taller,
My daughter,
My lovely daughter?

Who is that in the tall grasses running
Beside her, near the water?   10
She can not see there
Time that pursued her
In the deep grasses so fast
And faster
And caught her,
My foolish daughter.

What is the wind in the fair grass saying
Like a verse, near the water?
Saviours that over
All things have power   20
Make Time himself grow kind
And kinder
That sought her,
My little daughter.

Who is that at the close of the summer
Near the deep lake? Who wrought her
Comely and slender?
Time but attends and befriends her
Than whom the grasses though tall
Are not taller,   30
My daughter,
My gentle daughter.

Irving Layton

PORTRAIT

Book-thin behind the desk
with fingers rigid as pencils she stamps
stacks returns, read or unread
she cares not.
Bloodless as paper she, and lifeless
as dead words on dull binding are her eyes,
looking not in nor out, only seeing
date-print on card and flyleaf;
and mute
as volumes never off the shelves her tongue –   10
the rubbered pencil used to point
the novel overdue the scanty fine.
O life – love – something – burst the resisting doors –
ignore the silence sign – vault the tall desk
and on her locked blank pages
write a living tale.

Anne Marriott

OCTOBER

Great bronze bells struck by the sun
    Are autumn trees,
Static – a dying civilization
    Or a frieze –
Unflawed by clamouring thoughts
    Of what's to come,
That tell their wealth, luxuriant,
    Chrysanthemum.

They sound the hour of memory
    But calmly, slowly.   10
The past on this late afternoon
    Converging wholly,
Folds summer weeks like starlings flying
    To thick brown leaves,
To bell-towers where a sundown city
    Last light receives.

Douglas Le Pan

ADOLESCENCE

In love they wore themselves in a green embrace.
A silken rain fell through the spring upon them.
In the park she fed the swans and he
whittled nervously with his strange hands.
And white was mixed with all their colours
as if they drew it from the flowering trees.

At night his two-finger whistle brought her down
the waterfall stairs to his shy smile
which, like an eddy, turned her round and round
lazily and slowly so her will   10
was nowhere – as in dreams things are and aren't.

Walking along the avenues in the dark
street lamps sang like sopranos in their heads
with a violence they never understood
and all their movements when they were together
had no conclusion.

Only leaning into the question had they motion;
after they parted were savage and swift as gulls.
Asking and asking the hostile emptiness
they were as sharp as partly sculptured stone   20
and all who watched, forgetting, were amazed
to see them form and fade before their eyes.

P. K. Page

THE EXECUTION

On the night of the execution
a man at the door
mistook me for the coroner.
"Press," I said.

But he didn't understand. He led me
into the wrong room
where the sheriff greeted me:
"You're late, Padre."

"You're wrong," I told him. "I'm Press."
"Yes, of course, Reverend Press."　　　　　　　　10
We went down a stairway.

"Ah, Mr. Ellis," said the Deputy.
"Press!" I shouted. But he shoved me
through a black curtain.
The lights were so bright
I couldn't see the faces
of the men sitting
opposite. But, thank God, I thought,
they can see me!

"Look!" I cried. "Look at my face!　　　　　　　20
Doesn't anybody know me?"

Then a hood covered my head.
"Don't make it harder for us," the hangman
　　　　　whispered.

Alden Nowlan

SOME LITERARY FORMS

Although the **ballad** originated in songs associated with dancing (*baller*, to dance), its story element was so prominent that whatever it possessed of song soon became a minstrel's chant. The impulse to create ballads was very strong in the fifteenth century, especially among the people who lived in the Border regions between Scotland and England. The times were turbulent. The mood in which Chaucer's leisurely descriptions were created had passed away. In this period of unrest, roughly from 1400 to 1550, people had little time for amusement, but they were eager to listen to stories that impressed upon them, without decorative detail, the violence they saw around them in nature, human and otherwise. Heroic exploits, tragic incidents, flashes of the supernatural, gleams of fairyland stirred their imaginations and aroused their basic emotions of love, hate, fear, revenge, and grief. Vivid actions and definite facts appealed to them, whether the source was a well-remembered battle or a popular superstition. At a time when newspapers, radio, and television were undreamed of, the chanting of ballads, either by a minstrel or by groups of people, kept alive in oral tradition the significant features of local history and culture. It is not surprising to find that many ballads appeared in several versions.

Whether the ancient popular ballads were the product of communal effort or the compositions of gifted individuals is not known, but there is a good deal of evidence in the ballads themselves to show that whoever created them had poetic insight and power. Strength and simplicity are combined in both the story and structure. The ballad plunges into the telling of a tale, and when it ends abruptly it does so because there is nothing more that artistically needs to be said. Its commonest form is a series of quatrains in which lines of four accented syllables alternate with lines of three accents, and in which the second and fourth lines usually rhyme. Our early "listening" ancestors loved vigorous dramatic action, strong rhythms, direct narration, repetitions, and refrains. In imagination they could jump from place to place in an instant and from joy to sorrow in a flash. They liked stories in a form that made them easy to remember and repeat. To the modern reader, an ancient popular ballad looks like a fragment of an epic.

The modern artistic ballad is an imitation of the old ballad. Although it retains the principal features of the form and spirit of the early ballad, the modern ballad is more polished in diction, phrasing, and rhythm. From the literary point of view, it is more refined. It contains more description and sentiment, and often attempts to create an atmosphere that will impress the reader and direct and shape the course of his imagination. The ancient popular ballad is largely objective in its treatment of its theme; the modern artistic ballad is often subjective. Scott's *The Minstrelsy of the Scottish Border* is a collection of old ballads, but it also contains some of his own imitations of their forms. Other titles of interest are *Lyrical Ballads* by Wordsworth and Coleridge; Kipling's *Barrack-Room Ballads*; Masefield's *Salt-Water Ballads*; Lomax's *Cowboy Songs and Other Frontier Ballads*; and Sandburg's *The American Songbag*. Some negro spirituals and the songs of river-drivers and sea-faring folk may be classified as modern ballads. The appeal of this old and simple poetic form is undying.

A **dramatic monologue** is a poem written in the words of a character invented by the writer. It is dramatic in that the speaker's words are addressed to and affected by one or more persons in his presence. It is usually written in blank verse, and it looks and sounds like a little play upon a stage. Browning's "My Last Duchess" is a good example of this form. A **dramatic lyric**, on the other hand, is a poem, lyric in form, that expresses the feelings of someone other than the writer. A good example is Tennyson's "Ulysses."

Free verse is poetry that follows no systematic metrical pattern. Although it is more rhythmical than ordinary prose, its rhythm is often based just upon the line or cadence. Usually free verse is unrhymed. Walt Whitman in *Leaves of Grass* (1855) used lines of varied lengths and loose rhythms that startled the literary world of his day. The modern exploitation of free verse which began in the 1920's led to many subtle individual innovations. See the poetry of Amy Lowell, William Carlos Williams, Marianne Moore, E. E. Cummings, and Raymond Souster.

Lyric poetry differs from narrative poetry and dramatic poetry in that it is personal and subjective. Its name suggests that it was once composed to be sung to the accompaniment of the music of the lyre. A lyric is usually brief and unique in its effect. It is an expression of a poet's temperament and emotional experience. **Songs** are particularly lyrics of mood, and their sentiment may be grave or gay.

An **ode** is a lyric poem that expresses exalted feeling in dignified form. Its subject may be either a person or an event of great importance. An **elegy** is also a lyric poem of great dignity and complex workmanship, but an elegy is a lament over the death of a person or persons, or the passing away of something revered. Keats's "Ode on a Grecian Urn" is an example of the former, and Tennyson's *In Memoriam* is an example of the latter.

A **rondeau** is a French poetic form that has been used occasionally by some poets writing in English. It is a poem of thirteen iambic tetrameter lines, divided into three stanzas, with a refrain, consisting of the first half of the first line, repeated at the end of the second and third stanzas. The rhyme scheme is *a a b b a, a a b, a a b b a*. The effect of the refrain is to bind the ideas into a neatly tied parcel of thought. "In Flanders Fields" is one of the most popular poems written in this form.

A **sonnet** is a poem of fourteen iambic pentameter lines with a rhyme scheme that is more or less fixed. The first eight lines, called the octave, are divided into two quatrains of four lines each. The last six lines, called the sestet, are divided into two tercets of three lines each. The first quatrain presents the theme and the second amplifies it. The first tercet draws forth some sentiment or reflection from the octave, and the second tercet releases the gathered force of the whole wave of emotion. The sonnet was born in Italy in the thirteenth century. It was originally a short love poem, and its form was perfected by an Italian poet, Petrarch, who established the rhyme scheme with which his name is still associated, *a b b a, a b b a, c d e, c d e*. In the middle of the sixteenth century, the sonnet was introduced into English by Sir Thomas Wyatt. Before the end of the century, leading poets such as Spenser and Shakespeare had adapted its form and rhyme scheme to the limitations of their native tongue. Shakespeare gave his name to a form that he immortalized, three quatrains followed by a couplet, rhyming *a b a b, c d c d, e f e f, g g*. Some variation of either the Petrarchan or the Shakespearean forms has prevailed in English ever since. In recent years there have been some innovations such as the substitution of assonance for rhyme. Milton and Wordsworth used the sonnet for the expression of some of their most profound reflections.

A **villanelle** is a complicated, French poetic form that originated, as its name suggests, among peasant folk long ago. Its unusual and emotional effects can be felt as soon as it is read aloud. It is a poem of six stanzas, the first five being tercets, and the last a quatrain. The rhyme scheme of the tercets is *a b a*, and of the quatrain *a b a a*. In the nineteen lines there are only two rhymes. Two refrains run through the poem. The first line is repeated in the sixth, twelfth, and eighteenth lines. The third line is repeated in the ninth, fifteenth, and nineteenth lines. In handling so intricate a form, the poet must guard against monotony of idea and of sound. Skilfully used, the villanelle has a charm that is irresistible.

An **iambus** (the adjective is "iambic") is a metrical foot in English verse that consists of two syllables, the second of which is stressed.

$$\overset{\times}{\text{In}}\;\overset{\prime}{\text{af}}|\overset{\times}{\text{ter}}\;\overset{\prime}{\text{days}}|\overset{\times}{\text{when}}\;\overset{\prime}{\text{grass}}|\overset{\times}{\text{es}}\;\overset{\prime}{\text{high}}$$

An **anapest** (anapestic) is a foot of three syllables with the stress upon the third.

$$\overset{\times}{\text{Ve}}\overset{\times}{\text{ry}}\;\overset{\prime}{\text{old}}|\overset{\times}{\text{are}}\;\overset{\times}{\text{the}}\;\overset{\prime}{\text{woods}}$$

A **trochee** (trochaic) is a foot of two syllables with the stress upon the first.

$$\overset{\prime}{\text{Trip}}\;\overset{\times}{\text{no}}|\overset{\prime}{\text{fur}}\overset{\times}{\text{ther}}|\overset{\prime}{\text{pret}}\overset{\times}{\text{ty}}|\overset{\prime}{\text{sweet}}\overset{\times}{\text{ing}}$$

A **dactyl** (dactylic) is a foot of three syllables with the stress upon the first.

$$\overset{\prime}{\text{Bird}}\;\overset{\times}{\text{of}}\;\overset{\times}{\text{the}}|\overset{\prime}{\text{wil}}\overset{\times}{\text{der}}\overset{\times}{\text{ness}}$$

An **amphibrach** (amphibrachic) is a foot of three syllables with the stress on the second or middle syllable.

$$\overset{\times}{\text{What}}\;\overset{\prime}{\text{heart}}\;\overset{\times}{\text{would}}|\overset{\times}{\text{have}}\;\overset{\prime}{\text{thought}}\;\overset{\times}{\text{you?}}$$

A **spondee** (spondaic) is a foot of two syllables both of which are stressed.

$$\overset{\times}{\text{The}}\;\overset{\prime}{\text{sedge}}|\overset{\times}{\text{is}}\;\overset{\prime}{\text{with}}|\overset{\times}{\text{ered}}\;\overset{\prime}{\text{from}}|\overset{\times}{\text{the}}\;\overset{\prime}{\text{lake}}$$
$$\overset{\times}{\text{And}}\;\overset{\prime}{\text{no}}|\overset{\prime}{\text{birds}}\;\overset{\prime}{\text{sing.}}$$

These are the principal metrical patterns. In order to achieve special rhythmic effects, a poet may substitute a foot other than the basic one in a line of poetry.

When a line of poetry consists of one foot it is called a **monometer;** of two, a **dimeter;** of three, a **trimeter;** of four, a **tetrameter;** of five, a **pentameter;** and of six, an **hexameter.** The metrical structure of a poem takes its name from the pattern that predominates. "Sir Patrick Spens" is a poem written in quatrains in which iambic tetrameter lines alternate with iambic trimeter lines. Other metres may be introduced occasionally for effect. When an extra syllable occurs at the end of a line of poetry, it produces a weak, or feminine ending.

$$\overset{\prime}{\text{Wee}}\;\overset{\prime}{\text{sleek}}|\overset{\times}{\text{it}}\;\overset{\prime}{\text{cow}}|\overset{\times}{\text{rin'}}\;\overset{\prime}{\text{tim'}}|\overset{\times}{\text{rous}}\;\overset{\prime}{\text{beast}}|\overset{\times}{\text{ie.}}$$

SOME LITERARY TERMS

ALLEGORY is the representation of one thing by another thing. Allegory is often in the form of a descriptive narrative, in which many or all of the elements represent specific events, situations, people, and places outside themselves.

ALLITERATION is a literary device. When two or more words in succession or at short intervals begin with the same letter or sound, the device is called alliteration.

> The fair *b*reeze *b*lew, the white *f*oam *f*lew,
> The *f*urrow *f*ollowed *f*ree.

ALLUSION is a reference to something outside the work of art. Allusions may evoke relevant associations that deepen the reader's appreciation of the work.

ANTITHESIS is a device that permits words or ideas to be brought into contrast by being balanced one against the other.

> 'Tis education forms the common mind,
> Just as the twig is bent, the tree's inclin'd.

ARCHETYPE comes from the Greek and means "the original pattern." According to Carl Jung, the Swiss psychologist, archetypes are unconscious memories, basic patterns of thought common to men throughout time and space. In literary terms, archetypes are mythical figures or themes that move through all of literature; for example, the Hero, the Terrible Mother, the Cinderella theme, the Death-Rebirth theme, the Wise Old Man. Literary critics who embrace Jung's hypothesis stress the importance of discerning these patterns as a means of apprehending the total significance of a literary work.

ASSONANCE is the agreement of vowel sounds in words in which the consonants differ. Assonance is sometimes used instead of rhyme in the poetry of Emily Dickinson, Wilfred Owen, and many modern writers.

BLANK VERSE is the name given to lines of iambic pentameter that do not rhyme. Blank verse is generally employed with dramatic poetry, such as Tennyson's "Ulysses" and the plays of Shakespeare.

CAESURA ("cutting") is the term applied to the principal pause that may, for rhetorical reasons, be made in a line of poetry.

> The mind is its own place, and in itself
> Can make a Heaven of Hell, a Hell of Heaven.

CLASSICISM is a term that describes the style, subject matter, tone, and structure of ancient Greek and Roman literature. The term emphasizes restraint, formal, orderly structure, and clear, simple style.

CLIMAX is the result of a series of words, phrases, or clauses being arranged in an ascending order of emphasis or expressiveness.

CONNOTATION means the implicit or associative meaning of a word, not the dictionary's definition. The opposite of denotation, connotation will likely vary from reader to reader.

CONTENT is the subject matter. The organization of the subject matter is the form.

CONVENTION is an unrealistic device, technique, or practice that the spectator or reader allows. Although rhymed speech, asides, and soliloquies are unrealistic, they are accepted as legitimate dramatic devices in a Shakespearean play.

DENOTATION, the opposite of connotation, is the explicit or basic meaning of a word. This meaning, which can be found in a dictionary, does not vary with the personalities or experiences of the reader or writer.

DICTION is the choice of words.

DIDACTIC is a term used to describe literature that is designed primarily to teach.

EMPATHY is the projection of one's feelings into the perceived object that aroused the feelings in the first place. Empathy is a sympathetic identification, usually more intellectual than emotional.

ENJAMBMENT is a French term that describes the continuation of a phrase or an idea beyond the end of one line of poetry and into the next. Wordsworth was fond of enjambment.

EPIGRAM means, literally, "writing upon." An epigram is a terse and pointed comment that expresses much meaning in few words: "Man never is, but always to be blest."

EXPRESSIONISM was a movement after World War I in which life was depicted, especially in painting and literature, not as it is but as the creator feels it to be. In literature, expressionism ignored the usual rules of style and structure and presented instead the writer's intellectual and emotional symbolism. The free expression of inner experience rather than the representation of appearance was the goal.

FIGURATIVE LANGUAGE is the fanciful use of words to imply more than the literal meaning of the phrases. Often figures of speech add significance, interest, and clarity.

FREE VERSE (or *vers libre*) is the term used to describe poetry that conforms to no regular metre, rhyme, line length, or stanzaic pattern. These conventions are discarded to let the length of lines reflect the meaning. Subtle variations are possible when verse is free from the necessity of a recurrent foot. Some of Amy Lowell's poetry is written in this form, and many modern poems are free in this sense.

HEROIC COUPLET consists of a pair of iambic pentameter lines held together by rhyme, wit, and sententiousness. Pope polished and popularized the heroic couplet.

HYPERBOLE (which means "over-shooting" in Greek) is a manner of expression that leaps the bounds of truth to achieve emphasis or provide humour. "Tons of money" is an exaggeration but no one is deceived by it. "Belinda smiled, and all the world was gay" is another example.

IMAGERY is the sensory content of a passage, what can actually be sensed. In recent criticism, however, imagery commonly signifies figurative language. Thus one speaks of "image-clusters" or recurrent groups of metaphors or similes.

IRONY (which means "dissimulation" in Greek) is the use of words to imply, in a humorous or mocking way, a meaning opposite to that literally stated. When Antony in *Julius Caesar* refers to the conspirators as "these honourable men," he is speaking ironically.

METAPHOR is an implied comparison, whereas a simile is an actual comparison between two things. In a metaphor, only one half of the comparison is actually identified; the rest is left to the imagination.

> Yet all experience is an arch wherethro'
> Gleams that untravell'd world.

A mixed metaphor may be amusing because of its absurdity. "The British lion will never pull in its horns."

METONYMY (meaning "change of name") is the term applied when the attribute of a thing is used in place of the thing itself. Instead of using the word "knife," Tennyson wrote: "The bright death quivered at the victim's throat."

MIDDLE ENGLISH is the form of the English language from approximately 1050 to 1475.

MODERN ENGLISH is the form of English from approximately 1475 to the present day.

MOTIF is the predominant idea in a work of art. The motif may be suggested by a recurring word, phrase, idea, object, or situation in a passage or in literature generally.

NATURALISM was a literary movement that aimed at the careful, objective, detailed representation of nature and life as they really are. It was a development of Realism and emphasized the application of scientific analysis and determinism to character and action. Frequently, unpleasant details were presented in a precise, frank manner.

NEOCLASSICISM is a term used to describe the revival of classical Greek and Roman styles in art and literature during the late seventeenth and eighteenth centuries. Neoclassical writers regarded art as an imitation of nature and emphasized order, reason, objectivity, and severity in their works. The Romantics, on the other hand, stressed spontaneity, feelings, subjectivity, and the individual.

OLD ENGLISH is the form of the English language from about 450 to 1050.

ONOMATOPOEIA (which is composed of two Greek words *onoma*, meaning "name," and *poieo*, meaning "make") is the term applied when the sound of a word echoes its sense.

> The moan of doves in immemorial elms,
> And murmur of innumerable bees.

OXYMORON means "sharp dull" or "pointedly foolish" in Greek. This term is used to describe the placing side by side of two words or two phrases that mean the opposite.

> His honour rooted in dishonour stood,
> And faith unfaithful kept him falsely true.

PARADOX (meaning "contrary to opinion") is the name given to a statement that appears to be absurd but which is really full of wisdom. For example, L. P. Smith wrote: "He who goes against the fashion is himself its slave."

PATHETIC FALLACY is the attribution of human feelings to nature. For example, "a sad day."

PATHOS is the quality in literature or art that arouses feelings of sorrow or pity or sympathy.

PERSONIFICATION is the attributing to abstract or inanimate objects qualities characteristic of persons. "Stern Daughter of the Voice of God!"

REALISM was a literary movement at the turn of the nineteenth century. Zola and de Maupassant, its leaders, sought to describe life as it is, not as people wish it were.

RENAISSANCE was the alleged rebirth of learning and art in Europe, influenced by the discovery of classical ideals and methods which emphasized the individual and this world. In Italy, the movement started in the fourteenth century and lasted through the sixteenth; in England, the Renaissance started later and reached its zenith in the Elizabethan period.

RESTORATION was the period from 1660, when Charles II was restored to the throne of England, to approximately 1700. It was a reaction against Puritanism. The period was marked by a witty licentiousness.

ROMANTICISM was a literary movement headed, in England, by Keats, Byron, Wordsworth, Shelley, Coleridge, Scott, and others. The romantic attitude emphasized the emotional, the picturesque, the imaginative, the subjective, and the rural.

SATIRE is a term that encompasses gentle, urbane mocking and bitter indignant attack. A satire is a literary work that ridicules vices, follies, and defects of human behaviour in order to arouse contempt in the reader for the weaknesses depicted.

SIMILE is a comparison introduced by "like," "as," or "so," which stresses the resemblance between two things.

> Then felt I like some watcher of the skies,
> When a new planet swims into his ken;

"His house is like a mansion" is a simile, but "his house is like ours" is not.

STANZA is a group of lines that form a regular metrical division in the formal pattern of a poem.

STRUCTURE is the organization or form of a literary work. It is the over-all design.

STYLE is the way of writing, the manner of expression. An author's style is individual and includes his choice of words, rhythms, tones, structures, and other effects peculiar to his writing.

SURREALISM was an artistic movement that during the 1920's and 1930's sought to present the world of the subconscious rather than the everyday world, the world of the logical mind. Surrealistic works emphasized feeling, sincerity, spontaneity, and irrationality.

SYMBOLISM is the use of symbols in art to suggest, rather than depict or transcribe. For example, a "rose" may suggest the immaterial concept of beauty with all its other associations. Symbols may arouse such deep feelings that it is difficult to explain their full significance.

SYNECDOCHE (meaning "understood among us") is making part of an object stand for the whole, or the whole for part. "All hands on deck" is an example of synecdoche, for "all hands" means all members of the crew. In "The town is without bread" the word "town" means the inhabitants and is an example of metonymy; the word "bread" means food in general and is an example of synecdoche.

TEXTURE. John Crowe Ransom analysed a poem as being composed of "logical structure" and "local texture." The former refers to the paraphrasable meaning, and the latter to the peculiarities of details and images that make the poem poetic and not prosaic. Usually, however, texture refers to the sensuous qualities or the density and pattern of the imagery.

THEMATIC DEVELOPMENT is the form or structure of a poem as related to the presentation of its theme.

THEME is the central idea of a work.

TONE is a term used to describe the writer's attitude to his subject and sometimes his attitude to the reader.

TRANSFERRED EPITHET is transferring an adjective or an adverb from the word with which it naturally goes to another with which it is associated. "Melissa shook her doubtful locks."

UNDERSTATEMENT is an assertion that purposely states less than it suggests, the opposite of exaggeration.

VICTORIAN is an adjective that describes the period of Queen Victoria's reign, from 1837 to 1901. During the early part of the nineteenth century, many poets continued in the Romantic tradition. Later, though, the poetry of the age reflected a growing concern for social problems and domestic life. In the last twenty years of the century, however, many new schools of poetry began in revolt against the excesses of the Victorian – their smug moralizing, pious sentimentality, and strained affectations.

PART ONE

P. 1   **The Twa Corbies:** (See the note on the ballad on page 259.)
Taken down from recitation and given to Walter Scott by a friend, this
old ballad first appeared in Scott's *The Minstrelsy of the Scottish Border*
in 1802. Its origin coincides perhaps with that of the ancient dirge "The
Three Ravens," but the two poems differ widely in the handling of the
details. In "The Three Ravens," the knight's body is faithfully attended
and buried. The ravens are done out of a meal, and the poem ends on a
moral and sentimental note. Although "The Twa Corbies" begins in the
first person, no hint is given concerning the speaker. It is sufficient to know
that the poem is someone's experience. What he relates is a grim, grue-
some, and cynical account of a raven's lament over the emptiness of its
own crop, and not over the death of a knight. The hawk, hound, and lady,
all associated with knighthood, might have been expected, in the traditional manner, to be faithful; by contrast they, like ravens, are callous and
self-interested. There is no sentimentalizing over the dead. Death is
regarded realistically. In form, as in theme, this old ballad is stark, simple,
and blunt – the composition of a genuine poet. Throughout this para-
bolical dialogue, with its undertones and implications, interest and tension
are never relaxed. The unfinished state in which the story is left increases
the reader's wonder at the fate of the knight. **Corbies,** ravens, a little
larger than the Canadian crow; **mane,** moan, complaint, lament; **t'other,
tither,** other; **yon** suggests the place is real, remote but well known to the
corbies; **auld fail dyke,** old turf wall; **kens,** knows; **hause-bane,** neck
bone, collar-bone; **gowden,** golden; **theek,** thatch.

P. 2   **Sir Patrick Spens:** (See the note on the ballad on page 259.)
Efforts to find a historical basis for the events here described have
proved fruitless. Sir Patrick Spens is unknown to history, but the character of the man, the intrigue at the court, and the effect of the tragedy are
all enshrined in this "grand old ballad," as Coleridge called it. The
reader's interest is in the poetry, not the history or the geography, and
perhaps half the story is better than the whole. Other versions exist that
are longer, but in the end just as fragmentary, if not more confusing. One
of these is given in Scott's *The Minstrelsy of the Scottish Border* along
with an account of political incidents that might be related to the story.
The version given here was taken down from recitation and first published
in Thomas Percy's *Reliques of Ancient English Poetry* in 1765. For
treachery and stark tragedy at sea, this version can hardly be improved
upon. Its composition probably dates from the early years of the fourteenth century. **Dumferling,** a town in Fifeshire, five miles inland from the
north shore of the Firth of Forth, a favourite seat of early Scottish Kings;

braid, open or patent, i.e., public in opposition to close rolls; **wi his hand,** with his personal seal; **on the strand,** on the seashore rather than at court; **lauch,** laugh; **this time o' the yeir,** a Scottish act of parliament forbade sailors to put to sea in the winter season; **yestreen,** yesterday evening; **laith,** loath; **cork-heild schoone,** cork-heeled shoes – a reference to the high rank of the men as well as to the style of the time; **But lang owre a' the play wer playd,** but long before the play was over; **swam aboone,** floated on the water; **kems,** combs; **haf owre to Aberdour,** halfway over to Aberdour, a small village on the Firth of Forth. It served Dumferling as a port and was the scene of many naval disasters. This suggests that the ship was wrecked while making a return voyage to its home port.

Pp. 3-4 The Canterbury Tales: Pilgrimages to the shrine of saints or other holy places were common in mediæval times, and Chaucer made use of just such an occasion to bring together a number of people who had tales to tell. On April 16, 1387 (the year has been variously set from 1382 to 1388 by different historians), twenty-nine travellers met at an inn in the south of London. Discovering that they were all going to the same destination, the shrine of St. Thomas at Canterbury, sixty miles away, they agreed to travel together. Then the genial innkeeper, the Host, decided to go along with them, making the total thirty. To pass the time on the journey, it was suggested that each pilgrim should tell two stories on the way and two on the way back, and that the teller of the best story, in the opinion of the Host, should be entertained at a feast at the expense of the rest. The plan served Chaucer well, but for reasons unknown, he was unable to carry out completely his original intention.

A long general prologue and twenty-four tales comprise the content of this descriptive-narrative poem. People are met from many occupations and stations in life. Rich or poor, urban or rural, religious or worldly, they appear as good companions and representatives of mediæval society in England – a cavalcade of happy, robust life. Each pilgrim is sharply distinguished by mannerisms, tricks of gesture, shade of complexion, dress, habits, or mood. Chaucer missed nothing that was typical or essential in a person's behaviour. In the light of his generously appraising eye, each person appeared comfortably at home. He built character out of traits, and bustling life out of spirited gestures. Virtues and vices he presented impartially and with quick wit and sly humour. He loved people and he loved life.

The selections given here are representative of the descriptive and narrative powers of the poet whom Tennyson called "that morning star of song." There is a perennial freshness about *The Canterbury Tales,* as there is an eternal spring in the opening lines of "The General Prologue." April showers, wooing breezes, stirring flowers, singing birds give promise of the renewal of life. Chaucer's poetry appeals directly to eye and ear, and through them it reaches into the emotions with phrases crisp and warm.

For the most part, *The Canterbury Tales* is written in ten-syllable verses that rhyme in couplets. In nearly six hundred years many changes have taken place in the spelling and pronunciation of English words. It is significant, however, that Chaucer chose to write in the vernacular of his day, rather than in French or Latin. Read aloud, these famous passages should cause little difficulty and afford much delight. Many final *e*'s, now lost or silent, were pronounced in Chaucer's day. For the sake of rhythm and euphony, and to bring out the full vigour of Chaucer's lines, they should be sounded; a dot has been placed above the *e*'s normally silent today, to indicate that they should be pronounced. The vowel *a* is usually broad in sound; *eth* is often the ending of the imperative plural. The verses are written in iambic pentameter, and if the meter is carefully emphasized in reading, the meaning should not be hard to understand. To see people through the clear, discerning eye of Chaucer is well worth the effort. To hear Chaucer, the most cheerful of poets, tell his tales with gusto, is a delight.

The General Prologue – Introduction: Ram, zodiacal sign; in April the sun runs partly in the Ram and partly in the Bull. It is now in the second half of its course, and the date suggested is probably April 16; **martir,** martyr, in this case Thomas à Becket, Archbishop of Canterbury, slain in 1170 and canonized in 1172; **Southwerk,** Southwark, a district in London south of the Thames; **Tabard,** name of an inn;

Knight: chivalrye, knighthood; **At Alisaundre,** Alexandria was captured from the pagans in 1365; in the service of his feudal lord the knight was a veteran of many wars and councils; **nevere . . . ne,** emphatic negative.

P. 5 **Benedicite:** This is sometimes called Benedictus, meaning, "blessing invoked." This passage can best be understood when the whole chapter of Luke has been read. A **horn of salvation** is a source of great healing, and the **dayspring from on high** is a beautiful way of referring to the sun to which God is compared. The antiphonal effect of the rhythm and the parallel structure is remarkable when this passage is read aloud.

P. 6 **A Sea Psalm:** The setting of this passage in stanza form is an attempt to accentuate its rhythm and meaning.

P. 7 **Easter:** (See the note on the sonnet on page 260.) **this day,** Easter Day; **thy,** Christ; **having harrowed Hell,** between his death and resurrection, Christ, according to apocryphal writings, went down into Hell and released the pre-Christian saints; **weighing worthily,** valuing fully; **that all lyke deare didst buy,** that by thy sacrifice paid the same high price for all mortals. In Elizabethan times poets made a fashion of sonnet sequences, and many sonneteers made love their theme. In "Easter," Spenser contemplates the source of love and gives to personal affection a broader and deeper meaning. As in the Petrarchan sonnet form so in the Spenserian, a pause in thought occurs between the octave and the sestet, but the rhyme schemes differ. The Petrarchan is *abba, abba, cde cde.* The Spenserian is usuallly *abab, bcbc, cdcd, ee,* the structure being three quatrains followed by a couplet. No matter how the rhyme scheme is varied, the sonnet form through the centuries has been identified by fourteen pentameter lines.

P. 7 **Sonnet XXIX** ("When in disgrace with fortune and men's eyes"): (See the note on the sonnet on page 260.) The form and rhyme schemes should be compared with those of Spenser's sonnet, and then with those used by Milton, Wordsworth, and later poets. **When in disgrace,** when in disfavour with circumstance and society; **bootless,** unprofitable, useless; **featur'd**, formed; **art**, skill, creative power; **scope**, freedom of fancy, range, and sweep of mind; **enjoy**, perceive, feel; **haply**, by chance; **state**, condition; **sullen**, dark. Clogged with consonants and long vowels, the opening lines move with slow rhythm and the heavy mood of hopelessness. When he thinks of his patron and friend, however, his mood suddenly changes and his spirit, like a lark ascending with short bursts of flight, rises swiftly through short vowels and light-footed rhythms. In the process of composition he forgets his youthful self-pity and envy; his mood changes from despair to hope.

P. 8   **Sonnet LXXVI** ("Why is my verse so barren of new pride"): (See the note on the sonnet on page 260.) This is one of the finest of all Shakespeare's sonnets. As in so much great art, sincerity is enhanced by the natural simplicity and ease of expression. **a noted weed**, a well-known or familiar garment, cloak, or manner of expression.

P. 8   **Sonnet CXVI** ("Let me not to the marriage of true minds"): (See the note on the sonnet on page 260.) This Shakespearean sonnet contrasts sharply with the Spenserian in rhyme scheme, thought-development from quatrain to quatrain, and the effect produced by the clinching rhymed couplet. **bends with the remover**, turns away as the loved one withdraws, leaves off loving when it is expedient to do so; **star**, a fixed mark by which a course may be set through a sea of changing circumstances; **height**, the star's place in the sky can be measured, but its real worth and influence cannot be calculated. True love is such a fixed star, and it is not subject to Time's vicissitudes; **fool**, plaything; **his** in lines 10 and 11 refers to Time, the reaper whose sickle cuts a wide swath; **bears it out**, persists unchanging to the end of time.

P. 9   **O Mistress Mine:** This delightful song from *Twelfth Night* expresses with genuine feeling a thought that other poets have entertained, sometimes as a truth observed, sometimes as a fancy. Horace wrote, *Carpe diem quam minime credula postero* (Seize upon today, trusting as little as possible in the morrow). And Herrick proclaimed:

> Gather ye rose-buds while ye may,
> Old Time is still a-flying.

Shakespeare wrote the best Elizabethan songs, and although most of them have been set to music they do not need such additions. Only to read them is to hear their music.

P. 9   **Fear No More:** In Shakespeare's *Cymbeline* (Act IV, Scene 2, lines 258-75), two brothers Guiderius and Arvirague, sing this dirge as they prepare to bury the body of Fidele, their enemy. But the body proves to be neither dead nor that of Fidele. It is the living body of their sister Imogen, in disguise. **sceptre**, symbol of sovereignty; **learning**, wisdom; **physic**, scientific knowledge; **thunder-stone**, thunderbolt; **Consign**, deliver themselves to death and dust.

P. 10   **Cherry Ripe:** A conceit is a fanciful, ingenious, or witty notion or expression, an affectation of thought or style. John Lyly, for example, calls love the "marrow of the mind," and George Herbert calls spring a "box where sweets compacted lie." Conceits abound in the hundreds of light lyrics that were written to music in the late sixteenth and early seventeenth centuries. The emotion of love usually underlies their themes, but the delicate humour of detachment often characterizes their sentiment or mood. Wherever the affectation is too clever to convince, the music invites connivance. "Cherry Ripe" is an excellent example of the poems that are sometimes called *vers de société*. This poem was composed about 1616. As late as 1648, Robert Herrick was still singing:

> Cherry-ripe, ripe, ripe, I cry,
> Full and fair ones; come and buy:
> If so be you ask me where
> They do grow? I answer, there,
> Where my Julia's lips do smile;
> There's the land, or cherry-isle,
> Whose plantations fully show
> All the year where cherries grow.

The rapid development of popular interest in vocal and instrumental music stimulated the art of song-writing, and the tripping meters and ingenious images of Carolean verse still delight the reader.

P. 10   Death, Be Not Proud: (See the note on the sonnet on page 260.) Donne played with thoughts as the poets before him played with images. His restless, subtle mind found pleasure in its own exercise, but his ingenious and sometimes complicated verse-forms and rhythms are saved from appearing merely eccentric by his sincerity and fervency. He exalted thought and feeling by means of new poetic phrases and expressions. The literary standards of his predecessors had little appeal for him. He struck out with boldness and originality, and his finest poems make an impression on the reader's mind that is as fresh and solid as that of the work of our best contemporaries.

P. 11   Song: This pensive lyric is not to be confused with the lyric of amusing conceits of this period, although it may have a conceit or two within it. It is serious, and it mingles sadness with sweetness, skilful expression and mellowness of mood. The pensive lyrics of the poets dubbed metaphysical by Dr. Johnson in derision, often express regret at the flight of time, youth, or friends. Their poetic value lies not so much in their melancholy as in their novelty of expression.

P. 12   On His Blindness: (See the note on the sonnet on page 260.) Owing to much study and writing in poor light, Milton's sight began to fail in 1643. By 1653 he was totally blind. In 1655, at forty-seven, he composed this sonnet and dictated it to a daughter. The rhyme scheme is Petrarchan, but thought and feeling move freely from line to line, unrestricted by the form and enhanced by strong caesuras. The octave ends in the middle of the eighth line rather than at its end. Words like **consider, spent, dark,** and **wide** have double significance when used by a blind man. **talent,** see Matthew 25: 14-30; **exact day-labour,** see John 9:4; **light denied,** the Latin absolute construction serving here in place of a conditional clause, if light be denied; **I fondly ask,** this is the principal clause on which the first seven lines depend; **fondly,** foolishly; **his own gifts,** thousands of angels or messengers; **yoke,** see Matthew 11:30; **post,** travel; **stand and wait,** submit patiently to God's will and purposes. From this sonnet it can be shown that Milton was a man of deep religious feeling, integrity and tenacity of mind, lucid imagination, and remarkable skill in literary composition. He lamented not so much his loss of sight as his inability to serve fully God and humanity by means of his skill as a writer.

P. 12 **Blind Among Enemies:** In the tragic struggle of Samson, the blind champion of Israel, Milton saw a condition similar to his own. Samson was confined in the prison at Gaza and there was forced to labour as in a common workhouse. On festive days he was led forth to sit in the sun where he might bemoan his fate. With the Restoration, Milton's sacrifices for the Commonwealth seemed wasted. He was forced into hiding and reduced to poverty. His books were burned publicly and his daughters rebelled. Blind and scorned, he, like Samson, struggled mightily against his enemies. With passion and restraint he poured into Samson's words some of his own feelings. "Blind Among Enemies" reflects the calm dignity and solitary grandeur of a mighty hero. It convinces because the feeling it expresses is at once intense and restrained. Milton believed that God, by depriving him of sight, intended to deepen his inner vision. In the dramatic poem, *Samson Agonistes*, from which this speech is taken, Milton aimed to set forth the principles of pure Greek tragedy.

P. 13 **The World: Driven by the spheres**, "Time is due to and measured by the revolutions of the spheres" (Bell); **doting**, excessively or foolishly loving; **quaintest**, most ingenious; **flights**, sudden and whimsical changes of mind; **snares**, traps; **statesman**, perhaps an allusion to Cromwell; **brave**, fine; **counting by**, counting on, expecting; **grots**, a short form for grottoes, artificially ornamented retreats; **His bride**, His Church, those elected to salvation (Revelation 21:2-9). Vaughan, a Welsh physician who wrote like Herbert and the English "Metaphysical" poets, was practically forgotten until Wordsworth revived an interest in his intense mysticism. A mystic is one who believes in the spiritual apprehension of truths beyond the understanding – a visionary. The poetry of Vaughan, the mystic, is remarkable for its strong feeling, fanciful imagery, novel verse-forms, and pleasing rhythms.

P. 14 **The Turkey and the Ant:** It is easy to see the faults of others and overlook one's own. A familiar proverb is here presented in the manner of a fable to satirize the behaviour of human beings. A fable is a fictitious anecdote with moral purpose. Its story is its body and its moral is its soul. A fable's style is clear, direct, bold, and simple. No time is spent with description of characters or setting. Simple facts are unadorned. The fable depends for its attractiveness on its message, on the novelty of its improbability, and on its humorous satire. Human qualities are attributed to animals, birds, and things personified. Fables (*fabliaux*) formed an important part of mediaeval literature, and some of these stories in verse – sometimes coarse, often moral and didactic – were known in Scotland in early times. They had, however, little effect on the development of the Scottish ballad. They lack the native strength and magic, the stark tragic sense, the elfin green, and the element of the strange that are peculiar to Scottish balladry. The modern fable is partly the result of the French influence on English literature during the reign of Charles II. The fables of Gay are terse and witty, and reflect some of the literary interests of his day.

P. 15 **A Little Learning: Pierian spring**, the spring of the Muses on Mount Helicon, was produced when Pegasus, the horse of the Muses, struck his hoof into the ground. The Muses were nine goddesses, daughters of Zeus, believed to be the inspirers of the arts, such as poetry and music. **Science**, knowledge. Among Pope's early poems, *An Essay on Criticism*, from which this selection is taken, set him on the path to becoming a popular poet in his time. Under the influence of Horace and Boileau, he set forth principles of literary and moral criticism. Poetry is put to a new use – didactic in mood and manner. The heroic couplet (two rhymed pentameter lines) became the vehicle for critical maxims that have since found their way into common speech. Many people can quote a line of Pope's poetry who never hear his name: "A little learning is a dangerous thing."

P. 16 **An Elegy on the Death of a Mad Dog:** When Gray's *Elegy Written in a Country Churchyard* appeared in 1751, Goldsmith's patience was exhausted with the doleful elegies that were then fashionable. It was time to write an elegy of his own, and in this one he parodies the formal, melancholy elegy, and he lampoons hypocrisy. In form, manner, and mood it contrasts sharply with the "graveyard" poetry that wearied him. The form looks like a ballad, but it is really an imitation of the "military quatrain" popular at that time in French literary circles. The unexpected turn of thought in the last line of each stanza surprises and delights. This "take-off" first appeared as a song in Chapter 17 of *The Vicar of Wakefield*, published in 1766. **Islington**, a village near London in the eighteenth century.

P. 17 **How Sweet I Roamed:** Reputedly composed by Blake before he was fourteen. **Prince of Love**, Cupid; **Phoebus**, Apollo, one of the great divinities of the Greeks, the god of the sun, the god of song and music; **rage**, passion, poetic ardour. Man is given capacity for enjoyment, and then is restricted in its use. He is confined by his own desires. This theme is not uncommon in the lyrics of Blake. On another occasion he wrote:

> He who binds to himself a joy
> Doth the winged life destroy;
> But he who kisses the joy as it flies
> Lives in Eternity's sun rise.

P. 17 **To a Mouse: sleekit**, sleek; **beastie**, the ending *ie* is a common diminutive; **bickering brattle**, confused scamper; **laith**, loath; **pattle**, paddle, a long-handled spade for cleaning the ploughshare; **whyles**, sometimes, occasionally; **maun**, must; **daimen**, odd or occasional; **icker**, ear of corn; **thrave**, a stook of twenty-four sheaves; **lave**, the others that are left; **silly**, flimsy, feeble; **to big**, to build; **foggage**, coarse grass; **baith**, both; **snell**, biting, piercing; **coulter**, a sharp blade attached to a plough to cut the turf in front of the ploughshare; **stibble**, stubble; **But**, without; **hald**, abiding-place; **thole**, endure; **cranreuch**, hoar-frost; **no thy lane**, not alone; **Gang aft a-gley**, often go awry, askew, asquint, amiss. The incident upon which this poem is based took place in November of 1785 at Mossgiel in Ayrshire. When the plough turned up the nest of a mouse and the little creature scampered away through the stubble, John Blane, the ploughboy who led the horse and cleaned the ploughshare at the end of the furrow, ran after it to kill it. Burns called him back to his task, and then fell into a pensive mood. This poem is the result of his meditations, and it reveals the power of the poet's imaginative insight and the depth of his sympathetic understanding. He speaks directly to the mouse, not about it, but the poet's plight is not far from his mind all the while.

P. 19   **Lines Written in Early Spring: periwinkle**, evergreen trailing shrub with light-blue flowers. Wordsworth proclaims a nature of pleasant sounds and sights, but not a nature red in tooth and claw. If all men could see and hear and feel the harmonies in nature, there would be less inhumanity of man to man. This was part of Wordsworth's creed, whether we agree or not, and it is here beautifully expressed in word, image, and rhythm. Blake's "How Sweet I Roamed" deals lyrically with some of nature's attributes, but Blake's conclusions are quite different from those of Wordsworth.

P. 20   **September, 1802:** (See the note on the sonnet on page 260.) "This was written immediately after my return from France to London, when I could not but be struck, as here described, with the vanity and parade of our country. . . ." **Friend**, probably Coleridge, his friend and neighbour in the Cumberland hills. In this sonnet, as in three others written about this time, Wordsworth deplores the fact that the fruits of the industrial revolution are concentrated in the hands of a few wealthy people, and that society is corrupted by materialism. The "good old cause" of the simple life with its sterling virtues is replaced by shallow and frivolous delights in showy furnishings, impressive banquets, and fine equipages. The plunder of one another, greed for money and position, and the vanity of extravagance are the idolatries by which standards are now set. The innocence that is founded in awe, reverence, and esteem for things of the mind and the spirit is gone. Religion which once gave breath and life to family and domestic relationships is no longer respected. With dignity, Wordsworth deplores the conditions he observes, and regrets that people have sacrificed their freedom in this worship of false gods.

P. 20   **Rosabelle: Ravensheuch**, raven's crag, a steep promontory surmounted by a castle and washed by the waters on the north shore of the Firth of Forth; **firth**, bay; **inch**, island; **sea-mews**, sea-gulls; **Water-Sprite**, water-spirit, kelpie, water-horse; **Seer**, wise man who reads signs and forecasts events; **leads the ball**, as his partner in this honoured position she would be the belle of the ball, a place of high social distinction; **at the ring**, riding the ring was a knightly sport, the horseman charging at full speed tried to thrust a lance through a small suspended ring and carry it away. The prize went to the rider who succeeded most often. The sport was a test of horsemanship and marksmanship, and in the test her knight would carry her colours, and if successful, bring honour to her; **Roslin**, Rosslinnhe, the promontory of the linn or waterfall, about ten miles from Edinburgh, a castle and chapel belonging to the family of St. Clair and still preserved as a place of exquisite beauty. In the carvings on the pillars and buttresses, the rose is introduced in allusion to the name, but not the flower; **Dryden** and **Hawthornden** are places in the neighbourhood; at the latter, ancient caves appear in the chalk banks of the Esk River; **panoply,**

275

complete suit of armour representing the figure of the knight lying upon his tomb; **sacristy**, an innermost room in the chapel where the sacred vessels and vestments are kept; **pale**, enclosure, paling or railing surrounding the altar; **battlement**, indented parapet or turret at the top of the wall and enclosing the roof; **pinnet**, pinnacle; **buttress**, (flying buttress) supporting pillar on the outer wall; **fate is nigh**, a reference to a superstitious belief that the chapel appeared on fire as death approached a descendant of William St. Clair, Prince of Orkney, who founded the chapel in 1446; **With candle**, etc., by images and rhythms two forms of burial are here suggested. The elements are exultant in victory over the human being that defied them. In Canto VI of *The Lay of the Last Minstrel*, Harold, the minstrel of the house of St. Clair, sings this song at the feast to celebrate the espousal of Lord Cranstoun and Margaret of Buccleuch. Scott wrote it in imitation of the ancient popular ballad. Another legendary account of "Fair Rosabelle of Rosslyn" will be found in *Tales of Scottish Keeps and Castles* by Elizabeth W. Grierson.

P. 22   **To Night:** (See the note on the sonnet on page 260.) One of the few poems written by this profoundly religious man, "To Night" is regarded as an impressive sonnet. Night is personified and appears to represent all the mysteries that confused the first-born man and inspired wonder and reverence in his breast. The language and the imagery are suggestive and appropriate to the spacious conception of the poet. **Hesperus**, the evening star, dramatically leads the other stars, and night begins its spectacle. The analogy of light and darkness and life and death suggests another – the physical and the spiritual elements in life itself.

P. 22   **La Belle Dame Sans Merci:** "The Beautiful Lady Without Pity." About 1400, Alain Chartier wrote a poem in French that bears this title. An English translation was available to Keats, but he took only the title, and wrote his own poem on the subject. Many attempts have been made to explain this poem, but its meaning cannot be reduced to a statement. It is a combination of romantic feelings and images with a verbal music that fascinates and haunts the mind. It is pure poetry and casts a magic spell. From the first line to the last, not a single detail is out of place in the poet's vision of this knight-at-arms, and every detail bears its own many-sided suggestions. Mystery and a feeling of wonderment pervade the poem, but it was the stained-glass effect of the mediæval imagery that fascinated Rossetti years later and made this poem a model for the Pre-Raphaelite Brotherhood of poets and painters. **knight-at-arms**, a young man raised to Knighthood and commissioned to bear arms, a mediæval ideal of manhood; among other accomplishments, the knight was expected to save damsels in distress; **faery's child**, a small supernatural being in human form, but not subject to human conditions of life and death, possessing magical powers; **wild**, artless, unconventional, spontaneous; **zone**, belt or girdle; **moan**, a form of faery speech; **steed**, not an ordinary horse, but a romantic representation of one; **manna** (hoar-frost), spiritual nourishment; **elfin grot**, remote and enchanted cave or region; **four**, a sacramental number; **no birds sing**, then utter silence and desolation. As elsewhere, the words and rhythm suit the sense. This poem bears a striking resemblance to "True Thomas," an ancient ballad.

P. 23   **Ode to a Nightingale:** "In the spring (1819) a nightingale had built her nest near my house. Keats felt a tranquil and continual joy in her song; one morning he took his chair from the breakfast table to the grass plot under a plum tree, where he sat for two or three hours. When he came into the house, I perceived he had some scraps of paper in his hand, and these he was quietly thrusting behind the books. On inquiry, I found those scraps, four or five in number, the writing was not well legible, and it was difficult to arrange the stanzas. With assistance I succeeded, and this was his 'Ode to a Nightingale.' " – Charles Brown. In this famous and flawless ode, the poet longs for such happiness as the bird enjoys, free from the fret and fever of this world. In imagination he follows it into the dim forest, lit only by moonbeams and made familiar by the recognizable fragrance of sweet flowers. The bird's song is immortal, he thinks, and this thought makes death more tolerable. With the word "forlorn" he comes back to himself, and wonders whether he has been seeing a vision or dreaming a dream. At this time Keats had foreknowledge of his approaching death from tuberculosis. **hemlock,** a poisonous plant which produces death by paralysis; **Lethe-wards.** In the lower world, Lethe was a mythological river. Those who drank from it received blessed forgetfulness of the past; **Dryad,** to each tree the Greeks attributed a divinity of spirit and these spirits were called Dryads; **shadows,** cast by the full moon; **draught,** not earthly wine but poetic inspiration is the means of the poet's transport from the weariness of his present state; **Flora,** the goddess of flowers, here the flowers themselves; **Provençal,** a district in Southern France where lyric poetry flourished in the Middle Ages. In Keats's mind it was associated with love and romantic beauty; **Hippocrene,** a fountain on Mount Helicon, sacred to the Muses; **pards,** leopards that drew the chariot of Bacchus the god of wine; **viewless,** invisible; **embalmèd,** full of balms or perfumes; **eglantine,** sweetbriar or wild rose, often mentioned in pastoral poetry; **Darkling,** in the dark; **requiem,** a hymn sung for the repose of the dead; **alien corn,** see Ruth 2:2; **Charmed magic . . . lands forlorn,** these famous lines suggest the whole world of romance.

P. 26   **Lead, Kindly Light:** This poem sometimes bears the title "The Pillar of the Cloud." It was written at sea between Palermo and Marseilles, in July of 1833, when Newman was thirty-two and passing through a time of great mental and spiritual stress. Like Milton two centuries earlier, Newman, while touring Europe, heard the voice of duty calling him home from his selfish pursuit of personal culture to wage war against the powers of darkness. To enter the conflict and withstand the increasing liberalism of 1833 in England was to him a divine mission. This most beautiful of modern hymns he wrote on a memorable night at sea as a prayer for light to guide him in the coming struggle.

P. 26   **In Memoriam:** a series of 130 elegiac poems, preceded by a prologue and concluded with an epilogue, written between 1833 and 1850 to express various phases of Tennyson's grief, doubts, and faith, in consequence of the sudden and premature death in 1833, at the age of twenty-three, of Arthur Hallam, an intimate friend. At the time of Hallam's death Tennyson was only twenty-four, and the shock to his intelligence and his belief was profound. Tennyson was not alone in his admiration of his friend's gifts of mind and spirit. Hallam's own father described him as an "extraordinary young man." Hallam's college friends "invariably agreed that it was of him above all his contemporaries that great and lofty expectations were to be formed," and that it was he rather than Gladstone who was to be the great man. In 1898, sixty-five years after Hallam's death, Gladstone wrote of Hallam: "At Eton . . . he stood supreme. . . . He was a spirit so exceptional that everything with which he was brought into relation came to be, through this contact, glorified by a touch of the ideal. . . . He resembled a passing emanation from some other and less darkly chequered world." Finally, in 1849, Tennyson decided to publish this series of lyrics in which so much of his sorrow and his faith were expressed, and he wrote an epilogue that really became a prologue to the whole series. It begins:

> Strong Son of God, immortal Love,
> Whom we, that have not seen thy face,
> By faith, and faith alone, embrace,
> Believing where we cannot prove.

Throughout *In Memoriam*, the various aspects of the changing religious beliefs of the time as well as the poet's mental struggles are reflected.

P. 26   In Memoriam LXIV ("Dost thou look back on what hath been?"): The first shock of the poet's bereavement has passed. With quiet regret he can now speculate on the attitude of Hallam in heaven towards the poet left behind on earth. The theme is developed by analogy with two boys, one of whom became an obscure farmer, while the other rose to high office, perhaps prime minister of the nation. This whole poem is one long sentence – a question addressed by the ploughman to the statesman: "Who" in the last stanza refers to "mate" in the stanza preceding. It is the musing ploughman who asks the question with which the poem ends, but the last three stanzas express feelings and thoughts that the ploughman attributes to the statesman. This poem is exquisitely imagined and executed. It was said by an old friend of Tennyson, and never denied by the poet, that this wistful lyric was composed while the author was walking down the Strand, a busy thoroughfare in London. The "golden Keys" refer to state office.

P. 27   In Memoriam CXXIII ("There rolls the deep where grew the tree"): "This is one of many passages in Tennyson which testify to the great effect upon him of the study of geology." On stanza 1, line 4, the author made this note: "Balloonists say that even in a storm the middle sea is motionless." **my spirit,** only in his spirit can Tennyson find a permanent abode. "The transitoriness of Nature's forms shall not shake his faith in immortality and re-union." Nature says, "All is vanity"; the spirit cannot say "Farewell."

P. 28   Prospice: The title in Latin means "Look forward." This poem was written soon after the death of Mrs. Browning in 1861, and the reference in the closing lines is to her. **guerdon,** reward; **arrears,** debts still outstanding for a very happy life. Browning's faith and courage are inspiring, and the cheerfulness of his buoyant, optimistic, fighting heart is contagious.

P. 28   Say Not the Struggle Naught Availeth: This poem was quoted by Sir Winston Churchill in his broadcast to the United States, April 27, 1941. When the hymn was first published in 1862, after the poet's death, it was thought to be his comment on disturbing political conditions in Italy.

P. 29   **Dover Beach: straits**, the straits of Dover between England and France; **cliffs**, the famous chalk cliffs rising out of the sea; **Sophocles**, Greek tragic poet of the fifth century B.C.; **shingles**, beaches. This is Arnold's finest lyric and most-quoted poem. It expresses the note of wistful sadness that runs through his poetry and the feeling of uncertainty and bewildered melancholy that ran through his life. In spite of the poem's dull throb of despair, it is remarkable for its vivid sense of place, its calm restraint, its striving for classical perfection in poetic expression. The second stanza takes up "the eternal note of sadness" and reflects the influence of descriptive passages in Sophocles' drama *Antigone* and Wordsworth's *Lines Composed a Few Miles above Tintern Abbey* where Wordsworth writes:

> For I have learned
> To look on nature, not as in the hour
> Of thoughtless youth; but hearing oftentimes
> The still, sad music of humanity,
> Nor harsh nor grating, though of ample power
> To chasten and subdue. And I have felt
> A presence that disturbs me with the joy
> Of elevated thoughts; a sense sublime,
> Of something far more deeply interfused,
> Whose dwelling is the light of setting suns,
> And the round ocean and the living air,
> And the blue sky, and in the mind of man;
> A motion and a spirit, that impels
> All thinking things, all objects of all thought,
> And rolls through all things.

But in all the confusion of this beautiful world, the only certitude that Arnold could find was in the inspiration of personal love.

P. 31   **Weathers:** The effect of weather on nature and the human spirit is profound. Browning, too, longed to be in England in April. It is a time when birds sing their best, nestlings try their wings, showers are a brief delight. People like to sit out in the sun, girls dress themselves in colourful summer frocks, and everyone dreams of holidays by the sea. There is also another weather, cold and wet, when everything is dull and sodden. In such a season, shepherds fear for their flocks that cannot survive long periods of damp weather without developing disease, especially of the feet. Trees rock in the gales; tides rumble where the sea reaches into the land on the coast of Devon; and rain seems everywhere and everlasting. Even hardy old crows seek shelter, and the poet gladly turns to the warmth of his fireside. The vowels and rhythms of the two stanzas assist in expressing two distinct moods.

P. 31   **When I Set Out for Lyonnesse: Lyonnesse**, a fabled city in the legendary country once inhabited by King Arthur and his Knights of the Round Table and now supposedly submerged off the present coast of Cornwall. The words of the poem are spoken by a young knight of King Arthur's time. **rime**, hoar-frost; **prophet**, one who foretells great events; **wizard**, one who by magical powers forecasts events; **mute surmise**, people could only wonder at the light radiating from his face as a reflection of a strange adventure, but they could not understand it or discover its cause. Any new and wonderful experience is like a visit to Lyonnesse.

P. 32 **Spring and Fall:** Hopkins died in 1889, but his poems, left with Robert Bridges, his literary executor, were not released for publication until 1918. Since that time the creations of this original and inventive mind have had a marked influence on the development of contemporary poetry. This brief lyric gives the reader the sensation, as does much of Hopkins's poetry, that the poet is present and speaking directly to him. Its meaning is not clear at a first reading. It follows the rhythms of speech and should be spoken. Some vowels are accented to show where emphasis falls. Understanding comes as a series of little explosions flashing from his intense contractions. If words cannot be found to convey the naked fact of his experience, he invents them. If his constructions appear strange or awkward, it should be remembered that he would not let the conventions of language stand in his way. **Goldengrove unleaving,** a beautiful and original way of saying that the autumn leaves are falling; **things of man,** this suggests a connection between man and nature, man like the leaves suffers a similar fate; **wanwood leafmeal lie,** the bare woods are carpeted with dead leaves; **the name,** death; **nor mouth . . . expressed,** no one has told or hinted it, but her own heart and spirit had intuitively felt it; **ghost,** the connotation of this word works both ways, suggesting an immortal spirit and a haunting sense of the grave; **blight,** mortality; **you mourn for,** since she is mortal and must die, her grief over the fallen glory of the trees foreshadows her own end. When older, she will understand what she now obscurely feels. The poem is hard and brilliant with thought and feeling.

P. 33 **In No Strange Land:** See Luke 17:21. **fish soar,** the fish and the eagle need not leave their natural elements to find their heaven, and neither need man seek among the spheres for the kingdom of God, because it is everywhere about him and within; **Cry,** pray fervently; **Jacob's ladder,** Genesis 28:12; **Charing Cross,** a thoroughfare in the heart of London; **Gennesareth,** Sea of Galilee. This poem, unpublished during his lifetime, was found among the poet's papers after his death. It is the more remarkable and moving because the poet had personal experience of poverty and misfortune in the **tangible** world. For a time he lived like a tramp, sleeping on park benches at night.

P. 34 **When Smoke Stood Up from Ludlow: Ludlow,** a town in Shropshire; **Teme,** a river nearby. Housman confessed that his lyrics were inspired by the old popular ballads and the songs of Shakespeare. They reflect the stark realism of the former and the subtle melody of the latter.

P. 35 **The Leaders of the Crowd: Helicon,** the home of the Muses who presided over the various kinds of poetry, arts, and sciences. Part of the Parnassus mountain range, Helicon included the fountains of Aganippe and Hippocrene.

P. 36 **For the Fallen:** Binyon's reflections on the death and sacrifice occasioned by the Great War contrast sharply with those of Owen who served with the troops in the line and was killed November 4, 1918, seven days before the Armistice was signed.

P. 38 **The Road: tinks,** tinkers, pedlars; **Little people,** fairies; **What fairy's to touch her that sings as she goes,** a common superstition in Irish folklore; **alannah,** a term of endearment; **bate,** worn out or spent; **Bridgy,** Bridget.

P. 38   **All That's Past: Amaranth,** an imaginary, unfading, and everlasting flower. The memory of what has gone fills the poet's waking dreams with images that fascinate and rhythms that enchant. The present is a part of all that has been and of all that is to be.

P. 39   **The Donkey: fishes flew,** and everything was topsy-turvy in the world; **my secret** and **far fierce hour** refer to and are explained by John 12: 12-15.

P. 40   **Christmas Eve at Sea: "south and soft,"** a reference to an entry made in ship's log; **block,** block and tackle; **reef-points,** little knotted ropes attached to the face of the sail; **silly,** confused (the origin of the word is interesting); **on the hill,** see Luke 2:8. **Rex . . . est,** "The King of the Jews is born"; **Nowell,** Christmas, an exclamation found in old carols.

P. 41   **The Old Ships:** The proper names stand for seaports or islands of the Mediterranean, famous in ancient times. Ææa is a small island off the coast of Italy. The old ships plying the ports of the eastern Mediterranean attracted the attention of the poet, stirred his feelings deeply, and set his imagination on fire. He imagines them, laden with fruit and slaves, gallantly fighting off an attack of pirates long ago. One ship, older and more beautiful than the rest, he imagines may have carried Ulysses home from the Trojan war. The wooden horse is a reference to the device by which the Greeks deceived the Trojans. Finally the poet waits expectantly for the beauty of the old ship to break forth in leaf and flower. Such beauty of image and sound awakens wonder.

P. 42   **Seascape:** A seascape is a point of view at sea as a landscape is a point of view on land. **telegraph,** a manual system of signalling by means of wires and bells between the bridge and the engine-room of a ship; **Mozambique,** Portuguese East Africa; **reis,** in exchange with the pound sterling these Portuguese coins were so depreciated as to be almost valueless; **well-deck,** the lowest portion of the main deck; **The master,** the captain of the ship reads the service for burial at sea from the Church of England's *Book of Common Prayer;* **bo's'n,** boatswain, ship's officer in charge of rigging; **poop,** highest part of deck at stern of ship; **Atlantis,** a legendary island supposed submerged in the Atlantic; **Atlas,** a mountain range in North Africa; **Himalaya,** a mountain range in Northern India.

P. 45   **The Hollow Men: "Mistah . . . dead."** This is a key line in Conrad's *Heart of Darkness.* Kurtz, a European trader, abandons civilization for the African jungle, hoping to obtain wealth and civilize the natives. He, however, succumbs to savage rituals, and as he lies dying, he is given a glimpse into the nature of man. His exclamation is: "The horror! The horror." Kurtz is described as being "hollow at the core." **Old Guy** is a reference to Guy Fawkes' Day in England. Guy Fawkes was executed for plotting to blow up the House of Commons in 1605; the **penny** cry is used on Guy Fawkes' Day (November 5) by children to obtain gifts, as "trick or treat" is used here on Hallowe'en; **death's other Kingdom** is Hell across the river Acheron; **death's dream Kingdom** is the present meaningless "Kingdom" of the hollow men, suspended between the tortures of hell and the bliss of heaven; in Part IV, the **tumid river** is the Acheron, and the **Multifoliate rose** is a reference to Dante's Paradise which takes the form of a rose composed of petals formed from the souls of the blessed; **prickly pear** is desert cactus; **Life is very long** is spoken by another of Conrad's characters in the novel *Outcast of the Islands*. It is spoken to Peter Willems who proves to be "hollow" when he betrays all who trust him.

P. 48   Chorus from *The Rock*: *The Rock* is a play in verse form. The Rock is the Church: "Thou art Peter, and upon this Rock I will build my Church." The poet satirizes our present-day pagan and materialistic outlook, and recommends a return to spirituality.

P. 49   Anthem for Doomed Youth: (See the note on the sonnet on page 260.) About his own poems, Owen made this statement: "This book is not about heroes. Nor is it about deeds or lands, nor anything about glory, honour, or power, except War. The subject of it is war, and the pity of war. The poetry is in the pity. All the poet can do today is to warn, that is why the true poets must be truthful." His pity for others is expressed in the feeling of emptiness and futility reflected in this poem.

P. 50   In Heaven, I Suppose, Lie Down Together: Flying Dutchman, a spectral ship; **Greenwich,** town in Kent, location of the state observatory where standard time of England is calculated; **Antipodes,** regions opposite to our own, the other side of the earth; **anchorite,** hermit-like, secluded or reclusive; **Agag stance,** see I Samuel 15: 32-33; **"Where ...tread,"** "For fools rush in where angels fear to tread" (Pope, *Essay on Criticism*, line 625). On a first reading, this poem may be puzzling, but its mastery is well worth the effort. The more it is read, the more fascinating become its vigorous spirit, verbal power, stretched metaphors, alert allusions, bitter-sweet rhythms, and subtle assonance. The poet is a passionate participant in the adventure of living. He would send his mind in search of new and challenging visions. Some people, like Pilate, cannot recognize truth when confronted by it or they will have no traffic with truth; others accept everything they hear and call it truth. Some cannot think; others will not think. These types represent the traditional horns of a dilemma. But the poet is no longer content with little experiences like stars, separated out from one another, and wherein everything falls pat in conventional pattern in the here and now. He would stretch his mind to apprehend new and larger systems of experience. Such a system might be a new sense of brotherhood of men into which even a recluse would be drawn and in which the dignity and rights of every individual would be recognized. With the New Year some square their shoulders to make a new beginning; others shrug their shoulders in hopelessness or despair. C. Day Lewis, however, rejects both conventional extremes and exerts himself in the pursuit of his own ideal – the discovery of land in a changed world. This, he thinks, is every man's right and duty – to make his personal contribution to the extension of human experience. The poet is dreaming on things to come.

P. 54   The Unknown Citizen: Here the poet satirizes our bureaucratic society, in which the individual is threatened with extinction in a card-index. Soon everyone of us will have a number. The rhythm reminds one of Hopkins's sprung rhythm.

P. 55   Prayer Before Birth: This poem is a mixture of satire and fun that flows from the poet's facility with words and rhythm.

P. 57   The Hand That Signed the Paper Felled a City: The title recalls "The hand that rocks the cradle rules the world." **shoulder,** a powerful shoulder, and not a feeling heart, directs the hand; **chalk,** an allusion to cold mechanical and statistical plans that are made with chalk, "chalk-talk"; **quill,** a primitive pen; **Hands have no tears to flow,** power without mercy, a sharp contrast to the opening of the General Confession "Almighty and Most Merciful Father" in whom might and mercy are in balance. The poetry of Thomas is notable for its originality of theme, startling imagery, spontaneity in turning common words to new uses, and primitive passion to set the reader's mind on edge.

P. 58   A Noiseless, Patient Spider: This is typical of the poetry of Whitman – his interest in ordinary things, "the glory of the commonplace," tremendous vigour, breadth of vision, and lyric ecstasy and wonder. Here he sees a similarity between the activities of the spider and the anxieties in his own soul. Whitman died in 1892, but his influence on poets in Europe, as well as America, is still apparent. This "Lincoln of American literature," this "Good Grey Poet," by reason of the irregularity of the form and the content of his verses, can still qualify as one of our contemporaries.

P. 58   The Snake: Only three or four of Emily Dickinson's poems, now estimated at more than 650, appeared in print during her lifetime. This is one of them, and it appeared in the *Springfield Republican* in 1866. It reveals her intensity of feeling, power of penetration, terseness of phrase, and delicacy of pattern.

P. 59   Wonder Is Not Precisely Knowing: The essence of this poem is the ambiguity of "wonder," and it is ambiguously stated. **his,** suspense is wonder's maturer sister; **adult delight,** compounded of so much bleakness and suspense, adult delight may be a painful delight or a new suspicion, apprehension, and suspense; **gnat,** a small irritating insect made to appear monstrous by the word "mangles"; "gnat," as a possible pun on not, may complete or terminate the negation that is so prominent in the first stanza. Wonder is just wonder; it cannot be defined; its effect cannot be calculated; wonder breeds more wonder. It is an annoying condition of our creature-state. Anyone who has not felt it, has not lived, or no one has lived who has not felt it. The statement, like others in the poem, can be read in two ways.

P. 59   Because I Could Not Stop for Death: Of the poetry of Emily Dickinson, Louis Untermeyer has this to say: "The seal of genius, that unmistakable insignia, is on everything she wrote. Here is that unmistakable idiom, playful yet profound; here are the rapid ascent of images and the sudden swoop of immensities, the keen epithet that cuts to the deepest layer of consciousness, and the paradox on whose point innumerable angels dance." Her cryptic little quatrains appear so effortless that we overlook their irregularities. Intrigued by the ideas they bear, we discover the so-called irregularities to be part of the texture of her thought. Her abundant use of assonance is her way of rhyming.

P. 61   Madonna of the Evening Flowers: your books, the poetess suggests that the Madonna lily has been her companion in her work and has only now suddenly withdrawn; **Te Deums,** the opening of a triumphal hymn, *Te Deum laudamus* ("We praise Thee, O God"). Amy Lowell's sensitiveness to colour and sound makes this scene a painting in miniature. This is called free verse, a manner of verse-writing that Amy Lowell championed in a revolt against traditional forms, and regularity of rhymes and rhythms. She led the "Imagist movement" in poetry, and its members were humorously called "Amygists" by Ezra Pound.

P. 61 **The Road Not Taken:** To conventional forms, Robert Frost gave the naturalness of common speech. Frost's simplicity and understatement are deceptive. In his poems, what at first may appear commonplace may suddenly turn out to be profound and uncommon. This poem was first published in *The Atlantic Monthly*, August 1915, after Frost's return from England in March.

P. 62 **The Wood-Pile: Clematis,** a kind of climbing shrub which, in its wild state, spreads its veins rapidly. Because of its profusion of flowers, it is sometimes called "Traveller's Joy."

P. 65 **Blue Girls: sward,** or swarth, land thickly covered with grass.

P. 67 **somewhere i have never travelled:** See the notes on the other poems of E. E. Cummings, "when god lets my body be," page 145, and "anyone lived in a pretty how town," page 236.

P. 67 **The Last Days of Alice:** This poem compares Alice's plight to the plight of mankind. It ends with a prayer. Alice is, of course, the heroine of Lewis Carroll's *Alice's Adventures in Wonderland* (1865) and its sequel *Alice Through the Looking-Glass* (1872). In the latter, Alice walks through a mirror and into a dream.

P. 68 **The Goal of Intellectual Man:** This poem is both a warning and an explanation. In the second stanza, **goal** is the subject of the verb **is.**

P. 69 **The Death of the Ball Turret Gunner: flak,** anti-aircraft fire. Randall Jarrell has written: "A ball turret was a plexiglass sphere set into the belly of a B-17 or B-24, and inhabited by two .50 caliber machine-guns and one man, a short small man. When this gunner tracked with his machine guns a fighter attacking his bomber from below, he revolved with the turret; hunched upside-down in his little sphere, he looked like the foetus in the womb. The fighters which attacked him were armed with cannon firing explosive shells. The hose was a steam hose."

P. 69 **The Truth:** Of this poem, Randall Jarrell has written: "The little boy who speaks The Truth has had his father, his sister, and his dog killed in one of the early fireraids on London, and has been taken to the country, to a sort of mental institution for children."

P. 71 **The Drunken Fisherman: Stygian,** pertaining to Styx, the river of hate, the chief river of the underworld. According to classical mythology, the shades of the departed were ferried across the infernal river by Charon; **On water the Man-Fisher walks,** see Matthew 4:19; Matthew 14:26; Mark 6:48; John 6:19.

P. 75 **A January Morning:** (See the note on the sonnet on page 260.) **city towers,** Ottawa; **northern hills,** Gatineau Hills; **amethyst,** a reference to the purple haze commonly seen in Laurentian country; **dull as horn,** sombre grey clouds.

P. 76   **The Dreamer:** (See the note on the sonnet on page 260.) **meadow rue** is found in Nova Scotia and south to the Gulf, flowering from July to September, in open swamps and wet meadows. The petals fall early, leaving tufts of whitish stamens that give a feathery appearance to the large flower clusters, a joy to behold.

P. 77   **Père Lalemant:** Father Gabriel Lalemant, a French Jesuit, served as a missionary among the Huron Indians, until he suffered martyrdom at the hands of the Iroquois in 1649, not far from Midland, Ontario, where remains of the mission posts, St. Ignace and St. Louis, are still visible. The opening line of the poem refers to the lifting of the consecrated bread in the celebration of the Mass. **acolytes,** assistants at the rites of the church; **byre,** cow-stable; **Bethlehem,** birthplace of Jesus; **lilies** (fleur-de-lys), the flag of France raised by Champlain when he claimed Canada for the French; **Mont Royal,** Montreal; **Stadacona,** Quebec city; **folds,** outposts where believers are gathered together like sheep in a fold; **roof-tree,** supporting timber; **Sidonian** (see I Kings 5:6), belonging to Sidon, the sister city of Tyre; **Hiram,** King of Tyre, who assisted Solomon in the building of the temple; **confess,** bring to confession; **St. Francis** of Assisi, a monk, founder of the Franciscan order, famed for his kindness to birds and other creatures, all of whom he called his brothers; **scrip,** wallet or satchel.

P. 77   **The Prize Cat:** The terror expressed in the scream of a white-throat caught by a cat resembles, in the poet's imagination, that of an Abyssinian child caught by a leopard. In spite of all the tabby's prize-ribbons and apparent domesticity, its instincts have not changed. Since this poem was written in 1935, it may be interpreted as the poet's bitter comment on Italy's surprise attack on Abyssinia. In that attack a high-ranking Italian airman compared his bombs bursting among Abyssinian children to roses bursting out of bud. Abyssinia is one of the oldest countries on the earth; likewise the tabby's instincts are very old. Italy, the inheritor of Roman art and culture, shocked the world by its attack. **Gads,** spikes, claws.

P. 80   **Toronto Crossing:** A good deal of the nature and character of this woman can be deduced from what she thinks, does, wears, observes, and rejects.

P. 81   **Canada: Case History:** A Case History is common jargon for a full report on a person or a condition. It is supposed to be scientific. The poet here throws out a challenge to Canada to grow up, to be a man, to assert independence in thought and act.

P. 83   **The Still Small Voice:** **Matzoth,** a cake of unleavened bread eaten by the Jews at the Feast of the Passover in April; **paschal,** pertaining to the Passover; **Next Year,** the hopeful response to the call to pilgrimage.

PART TWO

P. 89   The Daemon Lover: In *The Minstrelsy of the Scottish Border*, Scott wrote of this ballad: "It contains a legend, which, in various shapes, is current in Scotland. I remember to have heard a ballad, in which a fiend is introduced paying his addresses to a beautiful maiden; but, disconcerted by the holy herbs which she wore in her bosom, makes the following lines the burden of his courtship: –

> Gin ye wish to be leman mine,
> Lay aside the St. John's – wort and the vervain.

The heroine of this tale was unfortunately without any similar protection." **Daemon** (or Demon), evil spirit or personified evil passion; this tempter approaches in the shape of a former lover; **taffetie**, a kind of silk called taffeta; **drumlie**, gloomy; **cloven**, the split hoof of the fiend; **He strack the top-mast wi' his hand**, the fiend suddenly grew monstrous large and taller than the ship.

P. 91   Hynd Horn: About 1250, an unknown scholar translated into English a French metrical romance, a poem of 1,568 lines, called *Hynd Horn*. Its story soon became popular among a people who loved romantic tales that were full of lively incident and rapidly changing mood. This ballad "Hynd Horn" is not derived from the original romance, but is one of many English and Scottish variations on the theme. Another version begins: "Near Edinburgh was a young son born." In the romance, Hynd Horn is the son of an Eastern king. At fifteen, his father killed and his kingdom lost to the Saracens, Horn, with two princely companions, Fykenhîld and Athulph, is cast adrift in a small boat. In some mysterious way, the vessel is tossed upon a foreign coast and the boys are taken into the court of a king. Horn's beauty and grace win the heart of the King's daughter, Rymenhîld. But the king commands that, before marriage with his daughter, Horn must first redeem his father's kingdom. In Horn's absence, Fykenhîld usurps the affections of the princess, but Horn returns in time to win the maid. The ballad "Hynd Horn" leaves much for the reader's imagination to supply. The refrain, printed in italics, is repeated with every stanza. The first line of it is entirely meaningless except for the melody of its sound. **Hynd**, gentle and courteous; **birk**, the birch; **broom**, a yellow-flowered shrub; **silly**, simple, kind, or good (not an uncomplimentary term in this context); **cloutie**, patched, full of clouts or patches; **shone above**, in the princely clothes he wore beneath the beggar's coat.

Pp. 93-94 The Canterbury Tales: (See the notes to Part I on page 269.)

The General Prologue – Squire: bacheler, bachelor, a candidate for knighthood whose training consisted of service to his liege lord in time of war and devotion to a lady in courtly love in time of peace.

Courtly love was a strict convention of the time; **Juste,** joust, to take part in competitions to prove horsemanship and skill in handling the lance.

Yeoman: Yeman, yeoman, a servant above the rank of a groom; **bracer,** a leather shield for the arm to protect it from scalding by the bow-string; **Cristofre,** an image of his patron saint, St. Christopher, also guardian of travellers, worn as a protection against disaster.

P. 95 **The Magnificat:** See Luke 1:26-55.

P. 95 **The Lord Is My Shepherd:** David, the writer of the Psalms, was once a shepherd boy. When he became king he remembered that God had cared for him as a shepherd cares for his sheep. This psalm is a song of gratitude, trust, and confidence. It opens with pastoral images familiar to the people of Biblical times, and then bursts into a variety of images – a mystic table, a feast of plenty, the oil of friendship and hospitality, streams of goodness and mercy, and finally the house of the Lord to dwell in for all his days. Food, drink, rest, security, refreshment, and honour have been and will be God's gifts to David. The rod is a sign of authority; the staff, a sign of support and direction. This beautiful song has often been called "The Shepherd's Psalm." To a shepherd, all the images would be pastoral.

P. 96 **The Passionate Shepherd to His Love:** This madrigal was first published in 1600 in *England's Helicon,* a poetical miscellany. Isaac Walton described it as "smooth song, which was made by Kit Marlow, now at least fifty years ago; and ["The Nymph's Reply"] an answer to it, which was made by Sir Walter Raleigh in his younger days . . . old-fashioned poetry, but choicely good." Walton inserted both in his *The Compleat Angler* (1653). The spirit of light-hearted gaiety and the extravagance of young love have sustained the popularity of this pastoral through the centuries. **kirtle,** skirt.

P. 97 **Sonnet XXX** ("When to the sessions of sweet silent thought"): (See the note on the sonnet on page 260.) In **sessions** two images are suggested, one of memory summoned as a witness to give evidence in court, and the other of the poet brooding over his thoughts. **expense,** loss; **tell,** count.

P. 98 **Sonnet LXXI** ("No longer mourn for me when I am dead"): (See the note on the sonnet on page 260.) It is not known for whom Shakespeare's sonnets were written, but it is generally agreed that the first one hundred and twenty-six were, for the most part, addressed to a young man who was the poet's patron and friend. In form they are loosely knit, with three distinct quatrains and a summarizing couplet which appears to be tacked on. The long vowels are so placed that the rhythm moves slowly. The tolling of the bell is suggested by the sounds **surly sullen bell. with,** because of. Christina Rossetti's sonnet "Remember me when I am gone away" bears a marked resemblance in theme to Shakespeare's. Many poets have tried in their art to triumph over death.

P. 98 **Sonnet LXXIII** ("That time of year thou mayst in me behold"): (See the note on the sonnet on page 260.) In the first quatrain there is a double metaphor. He compares his condition to that of leafless boughs, and then the condition of the boughs to that of a choir of an abbey that had been wrecked and left to decay. After the disestablishment of the monasteries by Henry VIII, such ruined buildings would be familiar sights. **Death's second self,** the shadow of death; **his,** its, the fire's; **Consum'd,** the fire is consumed by the burning of the fuel that maintains it; **leave,** give up, make the most of the world that you must soon leave. Because of its sequence of related images and its concentration of suggestive power, this is regarded as one of the most remarkable of Shakespeare's sonnets.

P. 99   **Silvia:** A song from *The Two Gentlemen of Verona.* This is the poetry of fancy – dainty and delicate in form and feeling, light-hearted and filled with the spirit of song.

P. 99   **A Hymn to God the Father:** The poet's name was pronounced "Dun," and there is a punning allusion to himself in lines 5, 11, and 17. Although this was written during a serious illness, and in a serious mood, the poet cannot resist the play of wit. **where I begun,** a reference to the original state of man born in sin; **which I,** by which I; **Shall shine,** and thus redeem the poet from his sin.

P. 100   **The Pulley:** The title suggests "that which draws us to God." The pulley is the link between man and God. **span,** a small space, the size of a man; **made a way,** poured down; **rest** (line 10), peace to which the other qualities or blessings are related and without which they are transitory; **rest** (line 14), believe and trust; **both,** both man and God; **rest** (line 16), remainder.

P. 100   **How Soon Hath Time:** (See the note on the sonnet on page 260.) This sonnet first appeared in a letter to a friend, in which Milton tried to justify the fact that at the age of twenty-three he has not yet selected a profession. It is interesting to note that he adopted the Italian sonnet form rather than either the Spenserian or Shakespearean. The content, however, is distinctly his own – the utterance of strong personal feeling with considered restraint and dignity.

P. 101   **On Time:** As his first heading, Milton wrote "set on a clock case." A **plummet** is a weight that moves the works of a clock; **womb** here means belly; **individual** may be interpreted as indivisible.

P. 101   **To Lucasta, On Going to the Wars:** (See the note on "To Althea, from Prison," page 187.) Lovelace, the dashing cavalier, was pleased to call his lady, Lucy Sacheverell, by descriptive titles such as Althea or Lucasta (a contraction of *Lux Casta* meaning "pure light"). This lyric was probably written just after his release from prison, when he was busy raising a regiment to fight for the Royalist cause. He soon crossed to France and was wounded there. His long delay in returning to England probably led Lucasta to believe him dead. When he did return, he found that she had married another. In this song, however, he pays her the compliment of identifying his love and honour for her with the love and honour he bears for his country and his king.

P. 102   **The Peacock, the Turkey, and the Goose:** For comments on the fable, see the note on "The Turkey and the Ant," page 273.

P. 103   **The Quiet Life:** Pope, the acknowledged master of the heroic couplet, wrote very little in the happy form and mood of this poem. This

288

lyric is as genial and musical as the song of a bird. The style of the later Pope is foreshadowed, however, in the neat inversions, terse phrasing, and finished form. It was published in the poet's twenty-first year, 1709, but he asserted that he wrote it when he was twelve years old. Be that as it may, it is an interesting comment on the hurly-burly of life today.

P. 103   **The Winter Morning Walk:** Book V of Cowper's long poem, *The Task* begins with this charming impression of a personal though commonplace experience. The charm resides in the sober and subdued feeling and the gentle, quiet, faithful delineation of things seen. Milton was Cowper's avowed poetic master, and some of the Latinisms and imagery are playful imitations of the master's manner. The subject and the feeling expressed are not classical but romantic, and in Cowper's time quite new and novel. "The whole has one tendency to discountenance the modern enthusiasm after a London life, and to recommend a rural ease and leisure as friendly to the cause of piety and virtue." **sage remark,** doubtless a reference to *Macbeth* (Act V, Scene 5, line 24, "Life's but a walking shadow"); **lean shank,** perhaps a reference to *As You Like It* (Act II, Scene 7, lines 157-61); **bents,** dry stocks of wiry grass; **Deciduous,** yielding, becoming less and less as the farmer cuts around the base of the pile.

P. 104   **The New Jerusalem:** The subtle simplicity of Blake is often misleading. Charmed by the lucid imagery and the exquisite music, the reader may fail to see what his symbols represent. Blake's meaning is elusive because the relationships he envisages are profound. Bow, arrows, spear, chariot, sword – these are all tangible objects that Blake, the artist, could illustrate, but in the mind of Blake, the mystic and the poet, they become symbols of his will and zeal to use his talents to make manifest the kingdom of the spirit.

P. 105   **Epistle to John Lapraik:** These lines are taken from a much longer poem. On an evening before Lent in 1785, Burns, with some cronies, was passing the time singing songs and telling stories. Someone recited a poem. It began:

> When I upon thy bosom lean,
>   And fondly clasp thee a' my ain,
> I glory in the sacred ties
>   That made us ane wha ance were twain.

Burns was much impressed, and when told that it had been composed by "an odd kind chiel" near Muirkirk, about fourteen miles east of where Burns was living, he wrote a letter in verse to its author, entitled *Epistle to John Lapraik, an old Scottish Bard.* The whole of this first epistle to Lapraik, dated April 1, 1785, has twenty-two stanzas. These five stanzas from the epistle set forth some features of Burns's poetic creed, his "crooning to a body's sel." **Muse,** the poet's genius or inspiring goddess; **wha ken hardly,** who hardly knows the difference between verse and prose; **sairs,** serves; **ta'en,** have taken; **shools,** shovels; **knappin'-hammers,** stonebreakers; **hashes,** weaklings; **stirks,** young bullocks; **syne,** then; **Parnassus,** a mountain in Central Greece, sacred to the Muses; **ae,** one; **dub,** puddle.

P. 106   **A Slumber Did My Spirit Seal:** Wordsworth sometimes leaves the reader with an impression of cold reserve and aloofness from the affairs of common men, but beneath his austerity are affection, tenderness, and warm human sympathy. In this brief lyric, his natural reticence actually deepens the pathos of his sorrow at the death of "Lucy Gray." Whether Lucy was a real person or a creature of the imagination is unknown, but we can be sure from the reading of the "Lucy poems" that she was from the age of three "Nature's child." According to Wordsworth's doctrine, the moral influence of nature passed into her and was reflected in the grace and beauty of her form, face, and manners. In the first two lines, he confesses that the shock of bereavement awakened his sympathy with all mankind. For the first time he realizes the inevitability of death. The last two lines move slowly as the poet's imagination contemplates the course of nature and the physical aspects of death. The poem was composed in 1799.

P. 106   **Composed Upon Westminster Bridge:** (See the note on the sonnet, page 260.) To the title of this sonnet, the poet himself appended: "September 3, 1802." He also added: "written on the roof of a coach on my way to France." It is known that Wordsworth spent the month of August, 1802, at and near Calais, France. His sister Dorothy wrote in her diary: "July 30 – Left London between five and six o'clock of the morning outside the Dover coach. A beautiful morning. The city, St. Paul's with the river – a multitude of boats, made a beautiful sight as we crossed Westminster Bridge; the houses not overhung by their clouds of smoke, and were spread out endlessly; yet the sun shone brightly with such a pure light that there was something like the purity of one of Nature's own grand spectacles." Throughout the summer of 1802, the poet "regularly and frequently cultivated" the sonnet. It is possible that in early September, when gathering together a sheaf of sonnets, he put some finishing touches on this sonnet that he had conceived and constructed on the top of the Dover stagecoach on July 30. Wordsworth is reported to have said on another occasion: "It is the *feeling* that instructs the seeing. Wherever there is a heart to feel, there is also an eye to see. . . . People often pity me while residing in a city, but they need not, for I can enjoy its characteristic beauties as well as any." The opening line of this sonnet effectively expresses the poet's quiet conviction. In lines 4 and 5 he creates a vision of freshness. See also Psalm 104: 2: "Who coverest thyself with light as with a garment." **Open unto the fields,** adjacent to the open country south of London, which was then visible from the bridge. The restraint and the falling cadence of the last four lines reflect the depth and power of the poet's feelings.

P. 107   **It Is Not To Be Thought Of:** (See the note on the sonnet on page 260.) This sonnet was first printed in the *Morning Post*, April 16, 1803, and was inspired by a fear of the invasion of England by Napoleon, and by the poet's despair over the state of the country. "The vanity and parade of our own country, especially in great towns and cities, as contrasted with the quiet, and I may say the desolation, that the revolution had produced in France." "**with pomp of waters,**" quoted from Samuel Daniel's *Civil War*, Book 2, where he describes the Thames; **Roused,** see *History of England* for dates 1215, 1381, 1649, 1688, etc.; **bands,** wise restrictions produced by proper laws to prevent freedom from becoming licence; **That** (line 7) same relation as **that** (line 1); **perish,** as seen in some results of French Revolution; **evil,** as check or corrective; **good,** as example; **Armoury**, symbol of warrior's physical prowess; **tongue**, capable of expressing man's deepest emotions and highest hopes; **faith and morals**, beliefs and principles, high ideals; **everything**, in manhood, art, government, all of which uphold true liberty; **first**, noblest; **titles**, such as Mother of Parliaments, Mistress of the Seas, Defender of the Faith, Bulwark of Freedom; **manifold**, qualities of greatness expressed in many forms. The rhythm of this sonnet is tumultuous, like the tumbling current of the poet's thought and feeling.

P. 107   **Proud Maisie:** This suggests much more than the simple words state. Over the pride of youth hangs the mystery of brooding fate. Like many an ancient ballad, it leaves much unsaid but meant, and much to wonder at. **Maisie**, Mary.

P. 108   **Ozymandias:** (See the note on the sonnet on page 260.) In 1818, Leigh Hunt, the journalist and critic, challenged Shelley in friendly competition to see who could write the better sonnet on a given theme. This was Shelley's response. The theme was found in the records of an ancient historian, Diodorus, who quoted the inscription: "I am Ozymandias, King of Kings; if any would know how great I am, and where I lie, let him excel me in any of my works." In his pride and contempt of others, he had erected a statue of himself, the largest in Egypt, probably in the thirteenth century B.C.; **passions**, pride, vanity, cruelty, lust for power; **read**, interpreted; **survive**, outlive; **hand**, of the sculptor; **heart**, of the king: hand and heart are direct objects of the transitive verb, survive; **mocked**, ridiculed by imitation. The sculptor's scorn of scorn has outlived both him and his master. The sonnet begins quietly in a mood of casual story-telling, suggests by its images a scene of deep antiquity, reveals a clash of human passions, rises through staccato effect of octave to sonorous rhythms of the inscription, and then with soft notes and lingering cadences dies away, leaving the reader to reflect on the vain glory of kings and the mutability of life.

P. 108   **On First Looking into Chapman's Homer:** (See the note on the sonnet on page 260.) **Chapman**, an Elizabethan poet whose translation of Homer's *Odyssey* was published in 1614. Keats and his friend Charles Cowden Clarke read together its "famousest passages" at Clarke's home in London on a night in October, 1816. In the early morning, Keats walked the two miles to his own dwelling. At ten o'clock the same morning Clarke received a letter from Keats. It contained this sonnet. **realms of gold**, fields of literature, masterpieces of the literary art; **western islands**, British literature; **Apollo**, in Greek mythology the god of the sun, light – hence the patron divinity of poetry and the arts; **Homer**, Greek epic poet; **serene**, the calm of high thinking and noble feelings; **stout**, stout-hearted, dauntless; **eagle eyes**, a reference to Titian's portrait of Cortez; Cortez conquered Mexico in 1521, but Balboa discovered the Pacific in September, 1513; the error is of little consequence because what the poet wanted was a symbol of the spirit of discovery; **Darien**, a more poetical and suggestive name than Panama. Keats extends the bounds of Darien to include the whole Pacific coast seen from a mountain. The whole poem breathes the spirit of discovery. Because of its artistic completeness, a great poem does not end with the reading of its words; it goes on awakening wonder every time it is read.

P. 109   **To Autumn:** This poem was conceived while Keats was walking through the country-side near Winchester in Hampshire on Sunday, September 19, 1819. Its composition was completed a few days later. Some of its inspiration may have been prompted by Shakespeare's "Teeming Autumn, big with rich increase," but Keats wrote to Reynolds on Tuesday, September 21, as follows: "How beautiful the season is now – how fine the air. A temperate sharpness about it. Really, without joking, chaste weather – Dian skies –I never lik'd stubble-fields so much as now – Aye better than the chilly green of the Spring. Somehow a stubble-plain looks warm – in the same way that some pictures look warm. This struck me so in my Sunday walk that I composed upon it." **maturing sun,** a quality inherent in the sun that causes fruit to ripen; **sallows,** willows; **bourn,** the area of their pasturage.

P. 110   **Rubáiyát of Omar Khayyám: Rubáiyát,** the plural form of a Persian word meaning quatrain; **Omar,** surnamed **Al Khayyám** (the tent-maker), a distinguished scholar and poet (1050-1125). His quatrains were popular throughout the Orient. FitzGerald began to study Persian in 1853, and his translation of Omar's *Rubáiyát* was published in 1857. Critics claim it is more than a translation. It is original, in that it expresses the doubts, spiritual anxieties, and sensuous melancholy of the Victorian age. The spirit of the poem is that of Omar's, but the music is FitzGerald's. Its form and rhyme scheme are as distinctly FitzGerald's, as those of *In Memoriam* are peculiarly Tennyson's. The appetite for rhyme awakened in the opening couplet of each stanza is, after a brief delay or suspension, gratified in the last line. The poem's hedonistic theme is eat, drink, and be merry, and try to make the best of things as they are here and now without thought of tomorrow. The whole poem, which concludes with this excerpt, is usually presented as a series of seventy-five quatrains, a poetic necklace of polished pearls of similar size and quality, arranged without much design or sequential significance. The popularity of this poem suggests that its mood finds an echo in the hearts of most readers.

P. 111   **In Memoriam LIV** ("Oh yet we trust that somehow good"): (See the note on *In Memoriam* on page 277.) Evil will finally in some mysterious way prove to be good. Confronted by the problem of evil in its various forms – disease, death, inherited weaknesses, the sins of the flesh, the will, and the intellect – the poet declares his trust that all will come right in the end, that there is a plan and purpose behind all the accidents of life. Nothing is aimless (line 5), rubbish (line 7), in vain (line 9), fruitless (line 11), or but subserves (line 12). **void,** outer darkness beyond the universe; **pile,** the building; **far off,** the last stanza of the Epilogue reads:

> That God, which ever lives and loves,
> One God, one law, one element,
> And one far-off divine event,
> To which the whole creation moves.

infant, like an infant, his only form of speech is a cry. The fifth stanza of CXXIII reads:

No, like a child in doubt and fear:
But that blind clamour made me wise,
Then was I as a child that cries,
But, crying, knows his father near.

The creed that is taking shape in his mind in LIV was clearly sta
in CXXIII. He no longer looked for God in nature, science, or th
but in the faith and doubts within his own heart and spirit.

P. 111   **In Memoriam CXV** ("Now fades the last long streak of
snow"): Spring revives, and the poet's regret revives with it. **burgeons,**
puts forth young shoots; **maze of quick,** hedge or thicket of hawthorn
bushes, a tangle of quick-growing shrubs; **flowering squares,** sharply
defined fields full of spring flowers; **ashen,** the ash tree; **rings,** with bird-
songs; **living blue,** even the sky appears renewed and alive with new life;
sightless, the lark can still be heard when it is flying too high to be seen;
lea, meadow; **seamew,** gull; **change their sky,** a reference to Horace (I,
Epistle XI, 27): *Coelum non animum mutant qui trans mare currunt:*
"They change their skies, but not their hearts, who travel cross the seas";
becomes, his regret is transmuted into an object of pensive beauty and
a feeling of spiritual growth.

P. 112   **Ulysses:** This poem is founded on the exploits of the Greek
hero Ulysses, as recorded in Homer's *Odyssey.* But in some details it is
based on Dante's *Divina Comedia* (Inferno XXVI, lines 90-142), as
". . . neither fondness for my son, nor piety for my aged father, nor the
due love that should have cheered Penelope, could conquer in me the
zeal that I had to gain experience of the world and of the vices of men
and their valour. I put forth on the deep open sea, with one vessel, and
with that small company which had not deserted me. . . . Consider ye
your origin; ye were not made to live as brutes, but for pursuit of virtue
and of knowledge." In Dante's account, Ulysses sets forth from Circe's
island; but in Tennyson's, from Ithaca. In both accounts, his companions
were old warriors who had fought with him at Troy. According to
Homer's account they had all perished. "*Ulysses* was written (1842) soon
after Arthur Hallam's death and gave my feeling about going forward
and braving the struggle of life perhaps more simply than anything in
In Memoriam." **barren crags,** the unattractive island of Ithaca; **agèd wife,**
Penelope; **mete,** measure out; **scudding drifts,** rifts in low-flying clouds;
Hyades, a cluster of stars that was supposed to presage rain; **three suns,**
three years; **isle,** Ithaca, Ulysses' home; **gods,** the gods often took sides
and fought for or against men; **baths,** ancient astronomers believed that
the stars set every morning in the western ocean; **gulfs,** the vast chasm at
the edge of the world into which the river of Ocean plunged; **Happy Isles,**
the isles of the blessed spirits. They were thought by the ancient Greeks
to lie in the Atlantic. Perhaps they were the Canaries. On these islands of
eternal bliss, the departed spirits of Greek heroes were supposed to dwell:
Achilles, a Greek hero and companion of Ulysses, slain at the siege of
Troy.

P. 114   **My Last Duchess:** The dramatic monologue was one of
Browning's favoured poetic forms, and this is one of his most successful
efforts. The scene is laid in the castle of an Italian nobleman at Ferrara,
a town near Venice in northern Italy. The speaker is the Duke, and the

reader is left to infer from the Duke's words the details of the setting and characterization. The person on the receiving end of this monologue is an envoy from a Count whose daughter's qualifications for marriage with the Duke have just been discussed. When this poem was first published in 1842, it was entitled "Italy." **Fra** (*frater*), brother, a monk with artistic talents, who would not be affected by her charms; **Pandolf,** a name invented by the poet; **a day,** a circumscribed commission; **curtain,** to protect the masterpiece; **but,** except; **favour,** gift, such as a brooch; **all smiles stopped,** she was either put to death or confined in a convent; **Neptune,** a statue of the god of the sea; **Claus,** an imaginary artist; **Innsbruck,** a town in the Austrian Tyrol, famous in the Middle Ages for its metal work.

P. 115   **The Patriot: myrtle,** myrtle leaves were often used to make wreaths with which to honour heroes; Shambles, slaughter-houses; hence, **Shamble's Gate,** the gateway to the place of execution.

P. 117   **Up-Hill:** This has been acclaimed by some as the greatest poem of one of England's sweetest singers. Each simple question moves slowly, sometimes with the effort required for an up-hill struggle; each answer, often shorter by comparison, slides down quickly and easily to its appointed period of thoughtful silence. Each answer contains a double meaning – one obvious, the other somewhat sinister. The grave irony of lines 8, 12, 16, is deepened by the simple words and rhythms that convey it. When the body is carried feet-first to the grave, it will certainly not be kept "standing." The words appear to fall into a pattern that is as inevitable as the music of the *r*'s and *m*'s and *l*'s is delightful. The antiphonal effect of each query and reply harmonizes with the mood of the whole poem. Such art is at once so simple and profound that it awakens wonder. Behind it all is a quiet faith that is as strong as it is tender.

P. 118   **Summer Schemes: fifers,** song-birds; **fane,** temple; **prime** (verb), tune; **quavers,** eight notes in music; **minims,** half-notes; **shakes,** quick repetition of two notes; **thrills,** sudden bursts of quavering notes; **chinks,** clefts. This brief lyric reveals Hardy's austere beauty of phrasing, and his superb craftsmanship.

P. 118   **Great Things: Spinning,** cycling; **Weymouth,** a town on the coast of Dorsetshire; **Ridgway,** a village not far from Weymouth; **"Soul, I have need of thee,"** see Luke 12: 20.

P. 119   **Afterwards:** Here, beautifully expressed, is Hardy's love for fellow human beings, and his quiet joy in companionship with man and nature.

P. 120   **The Windhover:** It requires effort to read this poem, but the result is worth the effort. The poet's mind throughout is possessed by his love of Christ, the fire of his sacrifice, his mastery of the world, the achievement of which makes his glory shine. He caught a glimpse of a **Windhover** (kestrel, falcon, somewhat like a hawk) riding high and joyously in the wind-tossed sky. Profoundly moved by the bird's mastery, grace, and beauty, he called it the favourite (**minion**) of the morning, and the prince (**dauphin**) of daylight. The clean-cut flight of the bird is the result partly of the bird's pride, power, and plumage, and partly of the stress and strain of the big wind in conflict with it. Thus the bird fulfils its life and achieves perfection. **The** greater the obstacles, the greater is the character that overcomes them. The poet is in sympathy with the bird's ecstasy, and we can feel it in the speed and flexibility of the rhythm, and the subtlety of the imagery. Then the poet thinks of his own condition, his **heart in hiding,** or withdrawn in his private vocation, his life hidden from Christ, and he is momentarily overwhelmed by his own love of nature and admiration of physical beauty. In the sestet of this sonnet, the fire of his spiritual passion breaks out "here" and "then." "Buckle" is the keyword, in key position. It carries all three meanings – buckle in, buckle to, and buckle under. His love of nature is consumed in his love of Christ. The beauty of the bird's achievement complements the beauty of Christ's mastery by sacrifice. Both the bird and Christ become his splendid Knight (**chevalier**), radiant in their free and joyous plunge into the dangerous tumult of air and of the world. The conflict makes their beauty shine, even as the ploughshare gleams from cutting the furrow (**sillion**), even as embers glow when ash falls away and they come in contact with the surrounding air, and even as Christ's glory flames in the torture (**gall** and **gash**) of the Crucifixion. **ah my dear** is addressed to Christ. Another famous poet used the same expression:

> I, the unkind ungrateful? Ah my dear,
> I cannot look on Thee.
> George Herbert

In this poem, Hopkins raises one of the most difficult problems for man to solve. Out of his own indecision shines his own conviction. No longer is the **heart in hiding** that has achieved this mastery of complex thought in sonnet form and in living idiom. The reader feels that the poet is present and speaking to him, personally and urgently. Hopkins went out in search of new methods to communicate his sensations. Later he described his "sprung rhythm" (in which a metrical foot may have any number of unaccented syllables) as the "most rhetorical and emphatic of all rhythms." His abundant use of alliteration is so much a part of the texture that it is hardly noticed. Like Shakespeare, Hopkins revealed new resources of the English language. If the reader finds the language of *Windhover* compact, let him recall Lady Macbeth's:

> What thou wouldst highly,
> That wouldst thou holily.

or Macbeth's:

> that but this blow
> Might be the be-all and the end-all here.

Of his own poetry, Hopkins wrote, "Take breath and read it with the ears, as I always wish to be read, and my verse becomes all right." Of *Windhover* he wrote: "The best thing I ever wrote."

P. 122   **Recessional:** This poem was written in 1897, when Queen Victoria's "Diamond Jubilee" was celebrated to mark the sixtieth year of her reign. The poet's prayer would remind the British people not to put their trust in their native strength or courage but in God who gives the victory. "Recessional," a hymn sung by a choir as it withdraws from the chancel of a church at the end of a service; **known of old,** our forefathers knew God to be the source of their strength; **far-flung**, a reference to British troops stationed in distant lands, tropical and otherwise; **awful**, awe-inspiring; **tumult**, of celebration; **captains**, army commanders; **kings**, foreign princes and potentates and colonial ambassadors; **contrite heart**, the kind of sacrifice that God accepts and for which He grants His favour; **far-called**, our naval ships assembled from distant seas return to their posts, and beacon lights of celebration on hills (dunes) and promontory (headland) are extinguished; **Nineveh and Tyre**, once important and magnificent cities in the Middle East, the power of which has now passed away; **Gentiles**, pagan nations as opposed to God's chosen people; **Law**, the word of God; **reeking tube**, smoking gun-barrels; **iron shard**, high-explosive shells; **valiant dust**, native courage.

P. 123   **The Lake Isle of Innisfree:** This is Yeats's most popular poem. It was written in 1891 and had its beginning, according to the poet himself, in the sound of water playing in the window of a chemist's shop in London. A boyhood ambition to live, like Thoreau, close to nature was suddenly revived by the sound, and his thoughts turned to Innisfree (which means "heather isle"), a small island in Lough Gill, County Sligo, Ireland. This poem is the product of his loneliness and longing on that occasion. It is characteristic of the delicate imagery, melody, grace, and strangeness that mark all his early poems. **wattles**, flexible twigs that can be mixed with clay to form a wall; **nine bean rows**, nine is chosen for its sound and for its suggestion of his simple needs. He knows exactly what will suffice in this ideal state. He has had it in mind for a long time; **linnet**, a small singing bird with a quick wing. The poet implies that he will go to this enchanted world in the mood of a prodigal son.

P. 124   **Ghoul Care: Ghoul**, an evil spirit mentioned in Eastern tales of the Middle Ages, supposed to prey on corpses; **fiend**, the devil in the form of a huge bat flying in the wood; **Pit**, hell; **whelps**, the devil's imps; **hags**, demons, one is reminded of Macbeth's exclamation: "How now, you secret, black, and midnight hags!"

The poet's recipe for the good life is security, peace, and happiness. His conscience is like a lizard's shining eye, clear, cold, calculating, and steadfastly watchful, like a heavily laden bee busily engaged in its proper work, and like the light-hearted goldfinch happy in its security. Thus kept clean of evil, the poet's soul is a pleasant greenwood of peace and spiritual well-being. It was the fabled virtue of the lizard to awaken sleepers when a serpent was creeping up to sting them. The bee has long been a symbol of industry. The goldfinch has been called the faithful bird. These three "charms" are as ancient as superstition itself.

P. 124   **The Scribe:** In ancient times a man who could write and keep records was called a scribe; **tarn**, a small, deep, dark lake far up in the hills or mountains of England; **Leviathan**, sea-monster, here used to represent the largest of creatures; **honey-fly**, the bee, here used to represent the smallest of creatures. There is something about God and man that cannot be reduced to simple words.

P. 125   **Fare Well: Traveller's Joy**, wild clematis, a climbing shrub commonly known in Britain by this name.

P. 127   **Sea-Fever:** This is probably Masefield's most popular lyric. It first appeared in 1913 in *The Story of a Round-House and Other*

Poems. Like many other famous poems, it has been set to music, and it has inspired parody.

P. 129   **Dreamers:** (See the note on the sonnet on page 260.) Contrary to the beliefs of some people when the Great War began, modern soldiers are not monsters of uncontrolled ferocity but rather natural human beings with all the foibles and fancies and simple tastes of average persons.

P. 130   **Futility:** This poem was written during the Great War, and the poet asks why the sun ever awakened the earth from a cold star to life, and why clay grew into tall men to respond to the light and warmth of the sun, only to end in the destruction and annihilation of war.

P. 131   **In Westminster Abbey:** This is an excellent example of the use of irony.

P. 134   **Do Not Go Gentle into That Good Night:** This is a villanelle addressed to the poet's dying father. A villanelle is a poem of five three-line stanzas with a final quatrain. Only two rhymes are used, and some lines are repeated. It imposes on the poet a strict metrical discipline and the need to avoid the effect of monotony or artificiality. It is a genuine test of a poet's skill and power. The natural man clings stubbornly to life and struggles against death. The philosophical man accepts death, as Thomas believes, with cold comfort. The poet would urge his father to put up a good fight, to live as long as possible, to continue to rebel against stultifying conventions. David Thomas, the poet's father, was a gentle, dignified, and dedicated schoolmaster who yearned some day to be a poet. The son's tribute to the father is tender and beautiful.

P. 138   **Meeting-House Hill:** This is free verse as written by one of its most vigorous exponents in the first quarter of the twentieth century. It illustrates the fact that images and impressions can be painted with words as well as with a brush.

P. 142   **The Student:** The following annotations are Marianne Moore's. They show how memorable phrases from her wide reading and observation are fitted, mosaic-like, into the text of this poem. **"In America."** *Les idéals de l'Education Française*; lecture, December 3, 1931, by M. Auguste Desclos, Director-adjoint, Office National des Universités et Écoles Françaises de Paris. **The Singing Tree.** "Each leaf was a mouth, and every leaf joined in concert." *Arabian Nights. Lux et veritas* (Yale); *Christo et ecclesiae* (Harvard); *sapiet felici.* **"Science is never finished."** Professor Einstein to an American student; *New York Times.* **Jack Bookworm** in Goldsmith's *The Double Transformation.* **A variety of hero:** Emerson in *The American Scholar*: "there can be no scholar without the heroic mind"; "let him hold by himself; . . . patient of neglect, patient of reproach." **The wolf.** Edmund Burke, November, 1781, in reply to Fox: "there is excellent wool on the back of a wolf and therefore he must be sheared. . . . But will he comply?" **"Gives his opinion."** Henry McBride in the *New York Sun*, December 12, 1931: "Dr. Valentiner . . . has the typical reserve of the student. He does not enjoy the active battle of opinion that invariably rages when a decision is announced that can be weighed in great sums of money. He gives his opinion firmly and rests upon that."

P. 144   **Dead Boy:** This poem is an ironic, nostalgic statement of the effects of a boy's death on associates and relatives.

P. 145   **when god lets my body be:** Cummings has been described as "a modern of the moderns," Striving for originality, he puts the resources of English to the test. It is sometimes difficult to distinguish between craftsman and clown in his manipulation of oddities, but after the reader has unscrambled the syntax and disentangled the rhetoric, he discovers that the striking images and phrases are held together by a strong thread of romantic feeling.

P. 147   **Death of Little Boys:** An individual experience of death is extended to a universal statement about death. The poem was first published in *The Nation* in 1925 and has been popular ever since.

P. 149   **The Woman at the Washington Zoo: embassies,** like those of India and Pakistan. Of this poem Randall Jarrell wrote: "Late in the summer of 1956 my wife and I moved to Washington . . . every day I would drive to work through Rock Creek Park, past the zoo. I worked across the street from the Capitol, at the Library of Congress. . . . The woman talking is a near relation of women I was seeing there in Washington. . . . She is a kind of aging machine-part. . . . I felt that one of these hundreds of thousands of government clerks might feel all her dresses one dress, a faded navy blue print, and that dress her body. . . . Inside the mechanical official cage of her life, her body, she lives invisibly; no one feeds this animal, reads out its name. . . ." **the white rat,** the woman herself. See Brooks' and Warren's *Understanding Poetry* for a detailed examination of this poem.

P. 150   **Death from Cancer:** This is one of four poems under the general title "In Memory of Arthur Winslow." Here the landmarks of Boston are seen against a mythological background. **Phillips' House,** a hospital; the **crab,** the constellation and sign of Cancer in the Zodiac; **Charon,** in classical mythology, Charon ferried the shades of the departed across the river Styx to Hades; **shells,** very light, long and narrow racing rowboats; **coxes',** or coxswains' – a coxswain steers or has charge of a racing shell; **Jesus walks the waves,** Matthew 14: 26, Mark 6: 48, John 6: 19; **Acheron,** "the River of Sorrows" in Hades.

P. 150   **Advice to a Prophet:** In this poem the prophet is a contemporary who envisions the desolation of the world by nuclear weapons. **Xanthus,** the ancient name of the Scamander river; this "gold-red river," according to Homer, was scalded by Hephaestus, the Greek god of fire.

P. 152   **How One Winter Came in the Lake Region: Lake Region,** the region of the Great Lakes. The poet had in mind the shore of Georgian Bay, near Wiarton.

P. 153   **Late November:** (See the note on the sonnet on page 260.) This sonnet, in black and white, shows what can be achieved by a poet who sees clearly and records sincerely. Against the sombre background and within the subdued emotion, the reader hears only the shouts of woodsmen filing by, and he sees only the gleam of distant lamps. **uplands** are highlands or hillsides, especially in the region around Ottawa.

P. 154   **Low Tide on Grand Pré:** In Longfellow's poem *Evangeline* the name Grand Pré, meaning "Great Meadow," is given to the low lands lying about the Minas Basin in Nova Scotia. At low tide these vast "barren reaches" extend so far out to the water's edge that the scene is most impressive. **He,** the sun; **Acadie,** a familiar form of Acadia, the name given to those parts of Nova Scotia settled by the French in 1632 and from which the French were expelled in 1755 for refusal to take the prescribed oath of allegiance to the British King; **birch,** birch-bark canoe; **time was ripe,** time was at an end. When this poem was published in 1893, it attracted attention in both Canada and the United States. It served as the literary foundation-stone on which Carman's international reputation as a lyric poet was built. In spite of the intense personal note sounded in the poem, faint overtones of the history of "Evangeline's people" can be heard echoing in the poet's mood.

P. 155   **At the Cedars:** This poem was published in 1895 in *The Magic House and Other Poems.* Some critics consider it to be one of the greatest of Canadian poems. **cant-dogs** are cant-hooks, short, strong, wooden poles with movable iron hooks, used by lumbermen to roll logs.

P. 157   **In Flanders Fields:** (See the note on the rondeau on page 260.) This famous poem, first appeared anonymously in *Punch,* December 8, 1915. It was composed in May of that year, "literally born of fire and blood during the hottest phase of the second battle of Ypres." McCrae, a surgeon, attached to the First Brigade Canadian Artillery, was posted at a dressing-station near the Yser canal. From his dugout entrance he could see close at hand the white crosses, row on row, of a military cemetery, and in the distance the smouldering city of Ypres. For seventeen days, wrote McCrae "gun-fire and rifle-fire never ceased for sixty seconds." **Flanders,** a very old name once applied to parts of Holland, Belgium, and northern France. During the Great War it was used to designate generally that part of Belgium through which ran the Allied lines; **our place,** our graves from which we, the Dead, now speak; **The torch,** the symbol of our fighting spirit. In Scott's *The Lady of the Lake,* Canto III, the Highland clans were summoned to battle by runners who passed a fiery cross from one to another; **poppies,** the wild poppy is a common weed in Flanders. Its bright red bloom makes it very noticeable. The reference here is to the poppy as a source of a drug reputed to have the power to induce sleep. This poem is additionally interesting because it is written in the form of a rondeau.

P. 158   **The Song of the Ski:** **Arab Boy,** the Arabs are reputedly quick in their movements; **bacchanal,** a reveller dancing in honour of the Greek god of wine; **sybarite,** an inhabitant of the Greek colony of Sybaris in Italy famed in ancient times for its luxury and indulgence. It should be noted that the poet is here describing the thrills of a natural rather than an artificial ski-jump.

P. 159   **The Little Sister of the Prophet:** This poem presents a critical incident in the boyhood of a prophet. The brother's vision stands in stark contrast to the sister's desire and the mother's advice. **curds,** a substance like cottage cheese; **byre,** cow-stable; **head-tyre,** head-dress.

P. 162   **The Mulleins:** (See the note on the sonnet on page 260.) These common weeds grow to a height of four or five feet. The leaves are large and woolly, and the flowers are yellow and clustered in a head. The stalks are sturdy and straight, and often may be seen in winter standing rigid above the snow in abandoned pastures and along fences.

P. 164   **Atlantic Door:** This poem, like "Pacific Door" by the same poet, is a warning to anyone who would enter Canada by sea. The poem is remarkable for its creation by image and structure of the immensity and supremacy of the ocean, its massive indifference to the human sacrifice that has tumbled into its massive maw. In spite of all the human blood that has been poured into it, its crests still break white and exultant. **cobra . . . and mongoose,** natural and traditional enemies; **lascars,** seafaring cut-throats from India; **Gilbert,** Sir Humphrey Gilbert, a famous Elizabeth "Sea-Dog," who raised the English flag on Newfoundland in 1583; **Jellicoe,** an admiral of the British fleet during the First World War; **Hood,** Britain's largest and fastest capital ship at beginning of the Second World War. It blew up and sank in May, 1941, off Greenland; **Titanic,** the finest passenger liner of her time. On her maiden voyage in April, 1912, she struck an iceberg in the Atlantic and sank with a loss of fifteen hundred lives; **narwhal,** a horned, Arctic, whale-like monster.

P. 166   **For All Who Remember: convoys,** a reference to the sailors who risked their lives to provide protective escort for ships laden with men and materials crossing the Atlantic during World War II; **columns,** a reference to the soldiers who, wearing capes as protection against poison gas, went into the front line of attack against the enemy; **stuff's away,** a reference to the parachutists who were dropped over enemy territory.

P. 166   **Simeon Takes Hints from His Environs:** Christians are often unaware of the extent to which the symbols, speech, and behaviour associated with their faith leave their mark on customs and environment. To a Jew living in a Christian environment, even the angels appear to be Judaeophobes. Only one course is left open to Simeon, so far as life in this world is concerned, and that is to forsake the faith of his fathers and become a Christian. The poet's complaint is neither caustic nor self-pitying; it is a plea for tolerance and love.

PART THREE

P. 175   **Binnorie:** (See the note on the ballad on page 259.) Although the origin of this ballad is unknown, some features of its story are found in Scandinavian folk-tales. A similar ballad, in which a singing flute is made from a lady's thigh-bone, exists among the Negroes of the West Indies. More versions of this ballad have been found than of any other, and it has appeared under a half-dozen different titles with as many different refrains. In Scott's *The Minstrelsy of the Scottish Border*, it bears the title "The Cruel Sister." Its popularity is not hard to understand. The story is direct and simple and moves rapidly. The rhythm is strong, the folk-lore arresting, and the tragedy stark. **Binnorie**, the refrain printed in italics is repeated with every stanza; **bour**, bower or lady's room; **abune**, above; **sair**, sorely; **swam**, floated; **soummin'**, floating; **draw your dam**, draw off the water from your mill-race; **gowden**, golden; **girdle**, belt or sash; **braw**, splendid; **breast-bane**, breast-bone; **by lane**, alone or by itself.

P. 177   **The Braes of Yarrow:** (See the note on the ballad on page 259.) According to Scott's account in *The Minstrelsy of the Scottish Border*, this ballad, titled by him "The Dowie Dens of Yarrow," is reputedly based on an incident in the early history of the Scottish Border. One guess is that the hero of the story was a knight called Scott, the Baron of Oakwood. Sir Walter Scott found several versions of this ballad popular among the inhabitants of Etterick Forest. The story of the family's feud, malice, and treachery had its beginning in the decision of a lord to endow his daughter on marriage with half his property. His son bitterly resented this settlement and made plans to kill his brother-in-law. **Braes**, the hillsides; **Yarrow**, a tributary of the Tweed in the Border country; **lawing**, the bill, the reckoning; **dawing**, dawning, morning; **marrow**, mate, husband; **dowie**, sad, doleful; **kaim'd**, combed; **brand**, sword; **Tennies**, name of a farm below Yarrow kirk; **den**, wooded hollow; **stubborn**, obstinate, cowardly; **thorough**, through; **leafu'**, lawful; **heather green**, unlucky to dream of anything green (dreams worked by opposites); **read**, interpret; **haud**, hold.

P. 179   **The Canterbury Tales:** (See the notes to Part I on page 269.)

     The General Prologue – Prioress: Prioressè, a head-nun in a convent, a presiding superior; **Saintè Loy**, Saint Eligius (French *Eloi*), a courtly saint who refused to swear. This was a very mild oath, compared with those used by most ladies of the time; **Stratford-attè-Bowè**, the convent of St. Leonard's, near London. Because it lacked aristocratic affiliations, the nun, who spoke boarding-school French, was anxious to give the impression of good breeding and delicate social manners. It is left to the reader to decide whether Chaucer's depiction of the Prioress is intended to be complimentary or satirical; **smalė houndės**, this fondness for little dogs was a fashion of the time. Nuns had to be restricted from bringing their lap dogs into church. Chaucer was shrewdly amused that these dogs should be fed on choice morsels such as bread made with the finest flour when some human beings had little enough to eat; **gauded al with grenė**, every eleventh bead (gaudee) was large and coloured green.

P. 180   **I Will Lift Up Mine Eyes:** The essence of this psalm is contained in a title that it has sometimes been given: "The Lord, Thy Keeper." It is among the first in a series of psalms commonly known as psalms of ascent, or degrees. They may be the songs of the captives returning from Babylon to Jerusalem, or the songs of the pilgrims going up to Jerusalem for the annual feasts, when they may be called Pilgrim or Festal Songs. The rhythm of this song is appropriate for a marching hymn. Judged by its position in the series of psalms and the principal images it contains, this psalm may have been inspired by the first sight of the environs of the sacred city. First a personal note is struck, and then, as so often happens in the psalms, its application is made universal. In the firm faith of being heard, David here supplicates divine help and comforts himself and others with the assurance of God's infallible protection and direction. It has been said of this psalm that it contains "the quintessence of all that is most attractive, and most unanalysable, in sacred lyrics." Inspired by its simple grandeur, John, Duke of Argyll, composed the lovely hymn, beginning:

> Unto the hills around do I lift up
> My longing eyes.

P. 181   **Remember Now Thy Creator:** This is one of the most familiar and beautiful of all Biblical poems. It is part of "Ecclesiastes" and is attributed to King Solomon in his old age. "Ecclesiastes" is an inquiry into the chief good — what can render a man happy. From personal experience, Solomon proclaims that all knowledge and wisdom, apart from true religion, are vain. He counsels us to make, so far as it is consistent with the fear of God, a cheerful and charitable use of things as they are, without expectation of permanent delight in such transient earthly pleasures as prosperity and power. He exhorts us to do good abundantly and affectionately, to live peaceably, meekly, and reverently. True happiness springs from a love of God. Because of the images of old age and the sublimity of the whole conception, this passage is memorable in any translation.

P. 181   **When Icicles Hang by the Wall:** At the end of Shakespeare's comedy *Love's Labour's Lost*, which is a satire on utopias, two songs are heard — almost as after-thoughts in the burlesque play devised for the entertainment of the ladies. One celebrates the cuckoo as a symbol of spring; the other is sung by a representative of winter, who sounds the characteristic notes of the owl. In the second lyric, the poet gathered together the homely sights, sounds, and feelings typical of winter in the country. Dick, Tom, Joan, and Marian are common country names. Winter is both grave and gay. **nipped**, a tingling sensation; **foul**, choked with snow and ice; **staring**, intense stare, the essential characteristic of the owl's appearance; **greasy**, the right epithet for one preparing greasy meats in greasy pots; **keel**, stir and skim to prevent boiling over; **parson's saw**, preacher's moralizing, probably the poet's jibe at ponderous and "long-winded" harangues; **brooding,** like brooding hens that puff themselves out to create with their feathers a non-conducting layer of warm air; **crabs,** crabapples bubbling and bouncing about in spiced ale.

P. 182   **Sonnet CVI** ("When in the chronicle of wasted time"): (See the note on the sonnet on page 260.) This is another of the complimentary sonnets addressed to the poet's young patron. Shakespeare was not afraid to express whatever he felt. **wasted,** passed away; **wights,** creatures, human beings; **blazon,** the descriptive details of a coat of arms; **master,** possess; **for,** because.

P. 183   **Sonnet CVII** ("Not mine own fears, nor the prophetic soul"): (See the note on the sonnet on page 260.) Attempts have been made to link this sonnet with the death of Queen Elizabeth on March 24, 1603; with the peaceful accession of James VI of Scotland; with the consequent collapse of fear of rebellion and civil war; and the release of the Earl of Southampton from the Tower, April 10, 1603. All these events may have been in the poet's mind, for they could explain such phrases as "mortal moon" and "peace proclaims." But it is simpler and safer to take this poem for what it is, a love sonnet intended to celebrate an ideal friendship. Some estrangement may have threatened the friends, but it has now been removed. The eclipse is over, peace reigns again, love enjoys its "balmy time," even Death must come to terms. It must be remembered when reading Shakespeare's sonnets that he was the literary heir to clearly defined conventions of courtly love lyrics. But he seldom drew heavily on the inheritance.

P. 184   **Sonnet CXLVI** ("Poor soul, the centre of my sinful earth"): (See the note on the sonnet on page 260.) In this famous sonnet Shakespeare breaks away from convention and expresses a fundamental belief concerning the relationship of soul and body. The soul is compared to a citadel, and the body of sinful earth, to its fortifications. Out of the body arise rebellious forces that humble and weaken the soul. Since the body has so short a lease on life, why should it be pampered at the soul's expense? Rather starve the body to feed the soul; purchase ages in heaven by selling worthless hours on earth; cheat death of its power by enlarging the soul's dominion. The grim phrases and the battering-ram of questions add to the virility of this sonnet. In some editions *fool'd by* is replaced by *amidst.*

P. 183   **The Parting:** (See the note on the sonnet on page 260.) It is easy to accept the opinion that this is one of the most famous sonnets ever written. It appeals to the heart of every disappointed lover, and unrequited love is not an uncommon experience. The poet breaks with the conventions of the sonnet of his time. The short, decisive phrases are as natural as speech itself. The rhythm is the rhythm of words, rather than the rhythm of verse, and the words move with the changing moods of the poet. True love cannot give up loving. This is suggested by the difficulty encountered in voicing the syllables "last gasp." The figures grouped round love's bedside were personified by textual editors in the eighteenth century and have remained so ever since. This is sonnet sixty-one in a cycle of sixty-four written between 1594 and 1619. This sonnet appeared first in the final edition in 1619. The whole sequence was given the title *Idea* in imitation of a famous French sonnet sequence in which Plato's divine idea of beauty was symbolized.

P. 184 **Death the Leveller:** The masque or lyrical-dramatic play *The Contention of Ajax and Ulysses*, from which this pensive lyric is taken, has long since been forgotten, except by scholars studying the decline of Elizabethan drama. The proud and the humble are made equal by the great Leveller. Death closes all, but it has no power over the spiritual realities of truth, beauty, and goodness. **blood**, birth or the rights pertaining to noble lineage; **state**, station in life as a result of wealth or power; **Sceptre and Crown**, symbols of authority and power; **scythe and spade**, both peasants and princes are represented by their characteristic accessories. This device is called metonymy; **laurels**, here used as symbols of victory on the battlefield; **tame but one another**, death still remains the victor, even the conquerors are conquered; **murmuring**, this suggests two meanings – faltering and protesting; **garlands**, such rewards are not substantial; **actions**, only deeds and words done or spoken in love survive and continue to renew themselves. The validity of the metaphor in the final couplet relieves the poem of any note of bitterness. This poem must have been known in England about 1642, since it has been reported that King Charles sang it to annoy Cromwell.

P. 184 **A Thanksgiving to God for His House:** A man of worldly interests and appetites, Herrick was a clergyman. As vicar at Dean Prior in Devonshire, he became gradually accustomed to his task and enamoured of the joys of the countryside. **spars**, beams; **meat**, food; **buttery**, pantry; **unflead**, not damaged by flies or dampness (a Shropshire word); **pulse**, pottage made from peas or beans; **worts**, cabbages; **purslane**, lettuce; **mess**, portion; **beloved beet**, the poet's favourite vegetable; **wassail-bowls**, bowls of spiced ale; **soils**, fertilizes; **teeming**, productive; **conduits**, channels or ducts; **render**, give in return; **incense**, a perfume from burning spices or gums used to represent prayer; **by Thee**, the contrite heart leaves the judgement to God. This poem is a prayer in praise of the gifts of God. It expresses the happiness of contentment – the joy to be found in simple, little things.

P. 186 **On Shakespeare, 1630:** This is a remarkable poem for a man of twenty-two to write, when Shakespeare's genius was just beginning to dawn upon the world. Although Milton had been writing verse since he was ten years of age, this was his first poem to appear in print. It was prefixed to the second folio of Shakespeare's plays in 1632. **relics**, bones; **weak**, dull; **lifelong**, lasting; **unvalued**, value that cannot be estimated; **Delphic**, the celebrated seat in ancient Greece of the oracle of Apollo, god of sun and song. The suggestion here is that Shakespeare's inspiration came directly from this mythical divinity and patron of the arts; **marble**, by means of language, Shakespeare's powerful imagination overwhelms our fancy and establishes conceptions in us firmer and more far-reaching than monuments in stone.

P. 186 **I Did But Prompt:** (See the note on the sonnet on page 260.) In August, 1642, civil war between Cavaliers and Roundheads broke into the open in England. On June 14, 1643, Parliament appointed committees to control the licensing of books. Milton, the Puritan and admirer of

304

Cromwell, became the inspired champion of the cause of liberty, but when Parliament placed restrictions on the freedom of the press, Milton rebelled. He threw all his classical learning, political ardour, and religious zeal into the attack. He feared his own party would become more tyrannical than the party it sought to depose. In this sonnet, he vehemently attacks the lesser minds of his opponents. It shows what a poet can do with his indignation, especially when laws of libel do not exist to restrain his wrath. **hinds**, rustic servants; **Latona**, the Roman name of the Greek Leto, mother of Apollo (god of the sun) and Diana (goddess of the moon). According to legend, she knelt by a fountain with her infants in her arms to quench her thirst and was insulted by some Lycian clowns who were immediately turned into frogs.

P. 187   **To Althea, from Prison:** For delivering to the Long Parliament a petition on behalf of the people of Kent, asking that King Charles I be restored to his rights, Lovelace, a gay Cavalier, was committed to Gatehouse prison at Westminster on April 30, 1642. There he wrote this spirited lyric to his divine Althea (Lucy Sacheverell), whom he also called Lucasta, a contraction of *Lux Casta* in Latin ("pure light"). The imagery is varied and flits as wantonly as a bird in flight. **grates**, prison bars; **wanton**, fly without restraint; **allaying Thames**, diluting water; **careless**, without worry; **flames**, love of king; **committed**, caged; **Enlargèd**, free; **curl the flood**, stir the sea into turbulent waves; **Stone walls**, this famous stanza begins with a spondee and two strong vowels that mark decisively the change of mood from one of fancy and quaintness to one of sincerity and earnestness. It is a triumph of mind over matter, imagination over reality; **hermitage**, places of quiet retirement. Here he can enjoy more freedom than have birds, fish, winds, and angels.

P. 188   **Song of the Emigrants in the Bermudas:** Here Marvell imagines he hears a Puritan refugee (from religious persecution in England) singing praises to God as he rows along the coast of an island in the Bermudas. The poet's imagination heightens the contrast between conditions in the old land and the new. Perhaps because he is writing from reports of friends who had been in the Bermudas, he is free to let his fancy range. His favourite verse form, the eight-syllabled couplet, moves with the rhythm of rowing. The "song" is like a chant. **listening winds**, the singer was free to sing what and how he liked; **stage**, landing-place; **prelates' rage**, a term of reproach intended to stigmatize the heads of the Church of England; **enamels**, makes green and bright (no fog); **in care**, in His care of them; **close**, as in a treasure chest; **Jewels**, the rich ruby seeds of the pomegranates; **Ormuz**, an island in the Persian Gulf, a centre of trade in precious stones; **apples**, probably pineapples since each stock bears fruit once, so perfect they could not be repeated, here was heaven on earth; **by His hand**, not by hand of Solomon or a merchant prince; **ambergris**, a substance formed in the stomach of sick whales, from which perfumes are made; **we rather boast**, we prefer to boast and give thanks to God for deliverance; **pearl**, in Matthew 13: 45-6 the Kingdom of Heaven is referred to as "a pearl of great price"; **vault**, the sky; **Echo**, carry their faith, gratitude, devotion, and hope to other lands; **holy and cheerful**, these are the dominant characteristics of their abounding praise. If Marvell, the passionate Puritan, is interpreting their reports correctly, the emigrants must have been people with strong intellectual powers and fine tastes. Marvell's sympathetic insight into the beauty of nature is both intense and spontaneous.

P. 189   **The Hare with Many Friends:** (See the notes on the fable "The Turkey and the Ant," p. 273.) In Gay's time, the public taste for satire, parody, and burlesque was very strong. In 1727, when this poem was written, Gay, a patron-seeking poet, was labouring under a heavy burden of poverty, and he appealed to influential friends for help. The "hounds" in this poem are doubtless his creditors, and it has been suggested that the "Bull" may be Sir Robert Walpole himself. In 1728, Gay's *The Beggar's Opera* was enthusiastically received, and his fortunes were improved. His *Fables* will long be remembered for their sense of reality, lightness of touch, and ability to make the style reinforce the content of his argument. George Orwell's *Animal Farm* is proof of the continued popularity of the fable.

P. 190   **'Tis Hard to Say:** (See the note on "A Little Learning" on page 274.) In his twenty-third year, Pope published his long poem *An Essay on Criticism* from which this passage is taken. His glittering couplets, clear and compact, dazzled the readers of his day. His inexhaustible cleverness and instinct for perfection of form still impress the readers of our time. **partial to their wit,** carried away by their own cleverness or smartness as proof of their creative power.

P. 191   **The Tiger:** In *Songs of Innocence* appeared "The Lamb"; in *Songs of Experience*, "The Tiger." Blake was becoming more aware of the power of evil in the world. Hell could not be divorced from Heaven, nor the flesh from the spirit. It is easy to be deceived by the simplicity of Blake's poetry.

P. 194   **Three Years She Grew:** (See the notes on "Lines Written in Early Spring," p. 275, and the sonnet.) This is one of a group of poems commonly known as "the Lucy Poems." Whether Lucy was a real or an imaginary personage is not known, but it is hard to believe that the grief of the poet felt at her supposed death was invented. In this poem, the poet expresses his favourite doctrine of the moral influence of nature on the passive mind and character of one who lives in sympathetic communion with her birds, trees, flowers, streams, sunrise, sunset, and starlight. **law and impulse,** restraining and kindling force; **lawn,** an open glade in the woods; **insensate,** not endowed with sense; **round,** dance. A sense of the very influence that the poet attributes to nature is felt by the reader in the simplicity of his language and the muted melody of his verse.

P. 195   **London, 1802:** (See the note on the sonnet on page 260.) This poem belongs in a group of sonnets written immediately after the poet's return from France to England in September of 1802. Wordsworth feared the expanding despotism of Napoleon and lamented the political and social wantonness, the pride and vanity of the people of England. Here he addressed Milton, the great advocate of freedom and virtue, the austere example of England's greatness in thought and art, with the hope that his countrymen might reaffirm their ancient heritage. **fen,** low marshy land, the metaphor suggests material corruption and spiritual stagnation; **altar,** religious faith; **sword,** military prowess; **pen,** creative literature; **Fireside,** family life; **hall,** main room in a castle where men assembled to discuss affairs of state; **bower,** room set aside for the ladies; **inward happiness,** spiritual peace as a source of greatness, "pure religion breathing household laws," all that gives life unity and purpose; **manners,** a sense of dignity in all conduct; **star,** pure and splendid, aloof from petty pursuits; **lowliest duties,** Milton taught Latin to a few assistants.

P. 195   The World Is Too Much with Us: (See the note on the preceding sonnet.) Wordsworth's poems reflect not only the spirit of the man himself but also the spirit of the times. **Nature,** we see nature only as a source of material things, something to be exploited, and not as a giver of joy to the spirit; **sordid boon,** the seeming contradiction in this figure of speech, called oxymoron, arrests the attention. Since we have given ourselves up to delight in sordid gain, our hearts are out of tune with nature's beauty; **Pagan,** primitive man saw spiritual beings everywhere in nature and worshipped them; the Greeks did likewise, and in their mythology **Proteus** and **Triton** were the deities of the sea. The poet says he would rather be a pagan who is moved by nature's wonders than a self-interested person who has no feeling for natural things. **Proteus,** the prophetic old man of the sea who tended the sea god's flocks (Poseidon's seals) and rose at mid-day from the sea to sleep on the rocks. **Triton,** son of Poseidon, who with his trumpet, a sea-shell, soothed the restless waves at his father's command.

P. 196   Kubla Khan: In Coleridge's account of how he composed the poem, he tells that he took an opiate and fell asleep in a chair just as he was reading Purchas' *Pilgrimage* – "Here the Khan Kubla commanded a palace to be built, and a stately garden thereunto. And thus ten miles of fertile ground were enclosed with a wall." He slept for about three hours, and during that time he had "the most vivid confidence that he could not have composed less than from two to three hundred lines . . . without any sensation or consciousness of effort." When he awakened, he started to write down the lines that appear in the poem. Unfortunately, a business caller detained him for about an hour and when he returned to his task, most of the remainder of the vision had gone. **momently,** at every moment; **dulcimer,** a stringed instrument played with two padded hammers.

P. 197   Bonnie Dundee: (See the note on the ballad on page 259.) Among Scott's dramatic pieces is *The Doom of Devorgoil.* In Act II, Scene II of it, this song is sung by Leonard, a Ranger, who supposedly learned it from an old minstrel. When John Graham of Claverhouse, Viscount Dundee, a handsome and spirited supporter of James II, failed to influence the Scotch Convention of Estates at Edinburgh in 1688 against the acceptance of William of Orange and the rejection of James, he mustered fifty cavaliers and rode out of the city and into the Highlands. There he organized the Jacobite forces to restore the House of Stuart to the throne. At Killiecrankie, July 27, 1688, his army routed the English, but Dundee was killed in the battle. In this song, the refrain is repeated after every stanza. **Lords of Convention,** assembled to further the interests of William of Orange; **Claver'se,** Claverhouse was the name of Dundee's estate; **crowns to be broke,** skulls to be cracked; **bonnet,** tam-o'-shanter; **West Port,** the west gate of the city; **rung backward,** in reverse of a regular chime as a signal of alarm; **Provost,** mayor;

douce, wise and prudent; **sanctified bends of the Bow,** Bow Street, narrow and winding and leading to the West Port, was inhabited by pious Presbyterians, Covenanters, who would be opposed to Dundee and his cause; **ilk carline,** every old woman; **flyting,** scolding; **pow,** head; **couthie and slee,** friendly and sly; **Whigs,** a term applied in Scotland to the Presbyterians who had been associated with the morose Roundheads; **Grassmarket,** once a place of execution at the foot of Bow Street; **West,** where the Whigs were strong; **cowls,** a hooded head-dress worn by the dour Whigs in the southwestern part of Scotland; **spits,** swords; **gullies,** knives; **close-heads,** openings to side streets and blind alleys; **Castle rock,** seat of Edinburgh Castle; **Gordon,** the Duke of Gordon, commander of the garrison, held the Castle for King James; **Mons Meg,** a large cannon, supposed to have been cast at Mons, Belgium; **marrows,** mates; **shade,** spirit; **Montrose,** James Graham, Marquis of Montrose, fought for King Charles I in the Civil War, and was hanged in the Grassmarket, 1650; **Duniewassals,** gentlemen of the secondary ranks of the Highland aristocracy who lived north of Pentland Hills and Firth of Forth; **target,** round shield; **barkened,** tanned with bark; **usurper,** William of Orange; **Ravelston's cliffs, Clermiston's lee,** western environs of Edinburgh.

P. 199   **Chillon:** (See the note on the sonnet on page 260.) Someone described a sonnet as "impassioned utterance dignified by the artistic restraint imposed by the form." This one is noble and sublime and, along with Byron's longer poem *The Prisoner of Chillon*, it established Byron, on the continent at least, as the champion of liberty. This sonnet might be compared to Wordsworth's, which begins "Two Voices are there, one is of the Sea." The Castle of Chillon stands near Montreux at the eastern end of Lake Geneva. There, in 1530, a Swiss patriot, François de Bonnivard, prior of St. Victor's Priory, near Geneva, was imprisoned for political reasons by the tyrannical Duke of Savoy. At Chillon today, tourists may see in the dungeon the actual pillar to which Bonnivard was chained and the flag-stones worn by the prisoner's feet during the six years of his imprisonment. With the change in Swiss political fortunes in 1536, he was released.

P. 199   **When I Have Fears:** (See the note on the sonnet on page 260, Shakespeare's in particular.) This great poem was written in January, 1818, months before Keats contracted, on the Isle of Mull, the violent cold that rapidly developed into tuberculosis. He did not meet Fanny Brawne until October or November of the same year. He knew at this time that his brother Thomas was suffering from the disease, but his own death warrant had not yet been issued. **charact'ry,** letters in printed form; **garners,** storehouses; **fair creature,** any young woman as a symbol of Love's shaft; **faery,** magic; **unreflecting,** indulgent. Life may end for the poet before his teeming brain has delivered its rich cargo. In the presence of this thought, Love and Fame seem transitory.

P. 200   **Bright Star:** (See the note on the sonnet on page 260.) This was Keats's last poem. It was written in September, 1820, as he passed down the Channel on board the ship that was bearing him to Italy. It was written on a blank page in Shakespeare's *Poems*, facing "A Lover's Complaint." Thirteen months before, at Winchester, he had told Fanny Brawne that he had two luxuries to contemplate – her loveliness and the hour of his death. "Oh, that I could have possession of them both in the same minute." In this poem he appears to have achieved both. The grandeur of the octave is equalled by the calm of the sestet. The whole sonnet is a hymn of immense stillness. Like life, it is a cry of intense longing from a heart as warm and sacred as the light of love. The writing of this sonnet seemed momentarily to ease for the poet "the burden of the mystery." **Eremite**, hermit, beadsman.

P. 200   **Ode on a Grecian Urn:** (See the note on the ode on page 260.) As Keats's physical health began to fail, his passion for beauty became more intense, and his imagination more concerned with its own integrity. In the British Museum he found in Greek vases and marble pieces the loveliness his heart desired. It was at this time that he wrote this rapturous ode and his sonnet "On Seeing the Elgin Marbles." His spirit seemed as much at home in Hellenism as in the Mediævalism reflected in "La Belle Dame Sans Merci." Efforts to find the particular urn or vase that inspired Keats have been unsuccessful. His "urn" is probably a composite of the beauty he perceived in many objects of Grecian art. As we read it, a succession of beautiful, sculptured scenes passes before our eyes. The scenes appear to be alive because we see them through the feelings and reflections that they awaken in the poet. In one scene, we see a rout of fleeing maidens and pursuing men, a youth playing his pipe beneath the trees, a maiden almost caught by her bold lover. In another we see a procession following a priest and a sacrificial victim. The forest altar and the deserted streets of the little town, like some other details of the interwoven scene, are visible only to the poet's imagination. This beauty, wild rapture, and serene happiness are permanent. By contrast, human passion cloys and human passion is fleeting. **unravished**, preserving its beauty and purity; **foster-child**, nursed by them; **Sylvan historian**, telling tales of woods as well as men; **Tempe . . . Arcady**, Tempe is a picturesque valley near Mount Olympus, and Arcady (Arcadia) a district in Southern Greece renowned in mythology and classical poetry for its pastoral beauty, quietude, and simplicity and gentleness of life; **Heard melodies are sweet**, but Keats rates the imagination above the senses, and art above reality; **Attic**, Athenian; **brede**, a variant of braid, a garland, an interweaving of forms into a design; **Pastoral**, a conventional poetry that celebrates the rural innocence of dwellers in the out-of-doors, shepherds and herdsmen.

P. 201   **How Do I Love Thee?:** (See the note on the sonnet on page 260.) This is "one of the noblest poems ever written on Love." It is the forty-third in a cycle of sonnets that Elizabeth Barrett wrote in 1845. After her marriage in 1846, she showed them to Browning, and they were finally published in 1850 under the title *Sonnets from the Portuguese,* which implied they were translations. But the intimate character of their sentiment could not be disguised, and it turned out that the title may have been suggested by Browning's playful reference to his wife as "my little Portuguese" because of her olive skin. When these sonnets were written, Elizabeth Barrett was an invalid confined to her father's home in Wimpole Street in London. After her secret marriage and escape to Italy, which is the subject of Rudolf Beiser's successful play *The Barretts of Wimpole Street*, her health greatly improved. The reference to death in the last line of this sonnet was very real, because in 1845 her expectation of good health was very poor.

P. 202   **In Memoriam XXVII** ("I envy not in any moods"): (See the notes on *In Memoriam* on page 277.) The secret that the poet has discovered in his grief over Hallam's death is that the virtue of life is love. He will not envy any ease that is due to want of sensibility; **takes his licence,** lives without law because untroubled by promptings of a higher nature; **field of time,** earthly life; **stagnates,** like a stream clogged with weeds; **want-begotten rest,** contentment that is due to a vacuum or deficiency; **I hold it true,** this decisive conviction reveals the poet has reached a definite stage in his belief.

P. 202   **In Memoriam CI:** ("Unwatch'd the garden bough shall sway"): In this exquisite poem, the poet expresses his regret at leaving the home of his boyhood and early manhood, the rectory at Somersby. He wonders if the stranger will come to love the place as he has; and he knows that his own memory of it must gradually fade away. **brook,** it must have been an object of special affection in his childhood. The germ of the poem "The Brook," published in 1855, five years after *In Memoriam*, may be in these lines; **lesser wain,** this constellation has the pole star as its axis. This sight and the sound of the unseen brook must have had a special appeal for the young Tennyson; **gird,** the brook circles the grove; **hern and crake,** water birds; **blow,** like a flower; **labourer,** who does not move away, but belongs to the landscape.

P. 203   **Home-Thoughts, from Abroad:** Although Browning lived most of his life in sunny Italy, he cherished a love for England and her scenery. This poem was probably written in 1838, and has since never ceased to be admired for its warmth of feeling, delightful images, and the freshness of its melodious rhythm; **unaware,** unexpectedly; **sheaf,** group of saplings round the trunk of the elm; **twice over,** the thrush repeats his phrases; **look rough,** thick and shaggy with the dew upon them; **dower,** a gift to the children; **melon-flower,** a coarse, showy Italian flower. The poem is remarkable for the particular tokens of spring that the poet took to be characteristic.

P. 204   **Peace: Caermarthen,** a holiday resort in Wales; **Camden Hill,** a borough in the City of London; **Verdi,** Italian composer of well-known operas; **Vance,** a music-hall singer of popular songs; **morning Herald,** a London daily newspaper.

P. 205   **In Time of "The Breaking of Nations":** "Thou art my battle axe and weapons of war; for with thee will I break in pieces the nations, and with thee will I destroy Kingdoms" (Jeremiah 51: 20). Nations may be destroyed, dynasties disappear, and the history of wars be forgotten, but seeding and harvesting, the tilling of the soil, the wooing of maid by man, will remain as long as the earth lasts. Love and simple acts performed in faith and hope of harvest will survive all hates and petty vanities. This was written in 1915 and published in 1917, while World War I was in progress. **couch-grass,** twitch or quick-grass, a prolific and persistent weed, gathered root and stock and burned in the autumn; **wight,** an old English word meaning, in this context, man or sweetheart.

P. 206   **Nature's Questioning:** In contrast to Hopkins's religious fervour, to Browning's optimism and Wordsworth's idealism, there stands the sombre doubting Hardy. Beneath Hardy's so-called pessimism lies a profound sympathy with struggling humanity and a love of nature in all her moods.

P. 207   God's Grandeur: (See the notes of Hopkins's "Spring and Fall" and "Windhover.") Hopkins was a devout man with a passionate love for the handiwork of God as revealed in nature. In language, image, rhythm, he was – an originator. "The dearest freshness deep down things" comes to the surface in his poetry. His poems are hymns of praise to the grandeur and glory of God's creation. In spite of man's disobedience, contrariness, and the smudge and smell and smear and barrenness he has left upon the earth, the Holy Spirit broods over the world and renews its beauty. The generations are destined to aimless "trodding," so long as they refuse to heed and reckon with His will.

P. 207   Smooth Between Sea and Land: runes to grave, charms or incantations in cryptic verse-form to engrave upon the sand.

P. 208   L'Envoi: A dedication, a postscript, a sending forth of a poem on its way; **tubes,** paint containers.

P. 209   Before the World Was Made: Here is simplicity that does not deceive the reader but reveals the poet's craftsmanship. As the girl puts on mascara, powdered chalk, lard, or iron rust, she claims even with a little arrogance that she is neither vain nor deceitful, but merely trying to discover the ideal beauty and ideal personality to which she is entitled, but which she has somehow lost in the vicissitudes of time. Perhaps she can reclaim a portion of that beauty and love by diligently searching for them in mirror after mirror to see if all be right.

P. 209   An Irish Airman Foresees His Death: Kiltartan, a village in Galway where Yeats lived.

P. 210   The Listeners: First published in 1913, this poem has, because of its appeal to the imagination, been popular ever since. At first it appears to be a ghost story or a strange adventure, but a knowledge of de la Mare and his poetry assists greatly in the interpretation of individual poems. "Nature itself resembles a veil over some further reality of which the imagination in its visionary moments seems to achieve a more direct evidence." Thus wrote de la Mare, and many of his poems find their geography in that mysterious borderland between the real and the imaginary. Robert Frost admired this poem.

P. 211   Tewkesbury Road: The road runs to Tewkesbury, a town in Gloucestershire, England.

P. 212   Cavalier: In both Scotland and England during the Civil War and later, the name Cavalier was applied to the highspirited defenders of Charles I or his memory. **feathers,** plumes in their helmets; **blue,** Royalist colour; **bannerol,** small banner attached to cavalry lance; **Rupert,** nephew of Charles I, who came to England to lead the Royalist cavalry. After nearly three hundred years, the dash and courage of the Cavaliers could still fire the imagination of Masefield.

P. 214   In the Cool of the Evening: "And they heard the voices of the Lord God walking in the garden in the cool of the day." Genesis 3: 8.

P. 214   **To a Poet a Thousand Years Hence: Mæonides**, a name by which Homer was known to the ancients, for he was reputed to be the son of Mæon. Homer in his old age was blind and poor. Flecker claims that poets, from the first to the last, understand one another because their fancies (imaginations and intuitive creative powers) blow down the ages from one to another.

P. 215   **Snake:** This poem is based on an actual experience of the poet while living at Taormina, Sicily, in 1922. Some lines move quickly; some slowly; and some stand still. The poet has succeeded in communicating his innermost thoughts and feelings at this strange encounter. **carob,** a common evergreen tree found in countries bordering the Mediterranean; **Etna,** the famous active volcano on the east coast of Sicily; **thrice adream,** as if three stages removed from reality, like a god retiring to his own region; **albatross,** the Ancient Mariner received the great sea bird as a good omen, but finally shot it, and then suffered for his cruel and evil deed. See S. T. Coleridge's *The Rime of the Ancient Mariner.*

P. 218   **The Dead:** (See the note on the sonnet on page 260.) This sonnet was inspired by the poet's experiences during World War I. It expresses the tragic futility of war.

P. 219   **Journey of the Magi:** In "The Hollow Men" Eliot reached the bottom of emptiness and desolation. Life had no meaning or value. At forty he began the long journey back to faith and declared himself a "classicist in literature, royalist in politics, and Anglo-Catholic in religion." This poem stands at the turning-point between disbelief and belief. It is partly a fable-like recounting of Matthew 2: 1-12. **the Magi,** members of a Persian priestly caste, the "Three Wise Men from the East" who brought gifts to the infant Jesus; **sherbet,** a refreshing drink; **this was all folly,** this was a foolish journey; **Finding the place,** the inn at Bethlehem in which Mary and Joseph could not find a room; **like Death,** a new belief in Christ meant death to all their old pagan beliefs; **old dispensation,** the pagan beliefs accepted by their people, but doubted and rejected by them; **alien,** estranged; **another death,** any change, physical or spiritual, that could relieve him of his present misery.

P. 220   **Arms and the Boy:** In this famous poem, another poet of World War I expresses the pity he felt at seeing innocent youth sent into the devilish business of war. For regular rhyme the poet substituted assonance.

P. 221   **On Another Theme from Nicolas of Cusa:** Nicolas of Cusa (1401-1464) was a Roman Catholic cardinal and philosopher who was born in Cusa, near Trier in Germany. He anticipated Copernicus by holding that the earth revolved about the sun.

P. 222   **Ballad:** Under this unassuming title, the poem appeared in *New Verse*, December, 1934. With the first line, the reader is thrust into the action, and he may anticipate a straightforward story. It is not, however, a connected story. The poem is a series of facets on what war does to people. It begins quite innocently, but it ends by wrecking society. **scarlet,** the redcoats, regular peace-time troops; **cunning,** knows how to sell to friend or foe, to make money out of war. The title suggests comparison with both old and new ballads.

312

P. 224   **Fern Hill:** Some Critics acclaim this poem to be the finest Thomas wrote. The essence of all the joy and happiness of a boy spending a summer holiday on a farm is concentrated in it. **Fern Hill** is located near the village of Laugharne (larn) in South-western Wales. The poet gives this name to a hillside farm with pasture lands overlooking the estuary of the river Towy. Here the poet spent boyhood summers with an aunt and uncle. In his nostalgic recollections, the farm becomes a Garden of Eden before the Fall, and time, an angel with a flaming sword. The poem is an imaginary journey from innocence to experience, from grace to corruption, and from unity to dissolution. The imagery passes from light and heat and joy to dark and cold and a sense of foreboding. The poem might be called "An Elegy in Praise of Lost Youth." It may be compared to other great threnodies in English, such as Milton's *Lycidas*, Gray's *Elegy*, and Shelley's *Adonais*. A **dingle** is a wooded hollow; **heydays** are exalted times; **below a time**, out of and before this time, **windfall light**, the falling light of day and also the light blown away by the wind of time; **nightjars** are birds that fly with a whirring sound; **ricks** are haystacks; **first, spinning place** suggests the beginning of creation when the earth was formed; **house high hay** means haystacks that are as high as a house.

P. 226   **Naming of Parts:** This is an amusing parody of a sergeant-instructor's diction and callous lack of concern with the raw recruit who is a person with feelings and imagination.

P. 227   **Verses at Night:** The poet sees as in a nightmare the terrors of man's past, and his future scarred with disease and extinction. Against this backdrop, he hears his small daughter whimper in her cot, and shouts his denial of the visions he has seen. But his defiance, he suspects, is vain. **metaphrast**, one who alters the sense of something; **preterites**, words in the past tense.

P. 228   **Indian Summer:** The uniqueness of this poem and the quality of Emily Dickinson's genius are highlighted by comparison with other poems on the same subject in this book.

P. 229   **The Railway Train: stanza**, a pattern of sound; **Boanerges**, surname of two sons of Zebedee, James and John, so called because of their fiery zeal; sons of thunder; see Mark 3: 17, in this context the word means thunderous voice.

P. 231   **Stopping by Woods on a Snowy Evening:** This popularly admired lyric may, by its simplicity, deceive the reader. Its theme is as profound as its language and rhyme scheme are ingenuous. The poet wonders whether he should heed the call of personal delight in beauty, or obey the call of duty to others.

P. 232   **Chicago:** One of the largest industrial cities in the United States, famous for its live-stock yards, grain elevators, and railway yards. It was a symbol of American capitalism at the turn of the century. At different times in his early career, the poet worked in the city as a milkman and a newspaper reporter.

P. 235   **To the Stone-Cutters:** In the midst of life's frustrations and defeats come occasional brief moments of peace and joy. In spite of all human struggle, or as an ironical comment on it, beauty in some form will mysteriously remain, even when no one remains to behold it – not even a pessimist.

P. 235   **Piazza Piece:** This is a vital, new sonnet on the old theme of Death and the Lady. (See the notes on the sonnet on page 260.)

P. 236   **Bells for John Whiteside's Daughter:** This poem understates the cruel irony implicit in the death of a young, active girl.

P. 236   **anyone lived in a pretty how town:** Once the reader has adjusted to the unusual use of language and syntactical structure in Cummings's poetry, he can settle down to explore its themes. **anyone** is any male and **noone** is "anyone's" wife or mother. They live happily together as the seasons pass in this unusual town. Words are used to create patterns of sound, and the tolling measure of the refrain heightens the harmony of the relationship of these two unusual people whose only routine is found in the seasons and in their love for one another. Indirectly the poem is a comment on the sterile lives lived by masses of people submerged in a sea of artificial conventions. The poem might be called "A Lyric in Praise of Non-Conformity."

P. 240   **A Camp in the Prussian Forest:** "An American soldier is speaking after the capture of one of the German death camps. Jews, under the Nazis, were made to wear a yellow star. The star of David is set over Jewish graves as the Cross is set over Christian graves." – Randall Jarrell.

P. 241   **As a Plane Tree by the Water:** Lowell's poem is a satiric condemnation of Boston, a modern American city with an important past. **Plane Tree by the Water,** the plane tree is any of a genus of large trees with broad leaves: the American sycamore or buttonwood. Psalm 1: 3, "And he shall be like a tree planted by the rivers of water, that bringeth forth his fruit in his season; his leaf also shall not wither; and whatsoever he doeth shall prosper." **Lady of Babylon,** Revelation 17; **Babel Tower,** the allusion is to Genesis 11, where according to the narrative, the children of men tried to build a tower that would reach to heaven, but Jehovah to prevent its completion, "confounded their language" so that they could not understand one another. Nothing could be heard but a confused uproar; **Bernadette,** Bernadette Soubirous (1844-1879) was a French peasant girl born at Lourdes, France. Her vision of "Our Lady of Lourdes," who told her to make known the miraculous healing powers she would give the water there, resulted in the shrine of Lourdes. In 1866, Bernadette joined the Sisters of Charity at Nevers. She was canonized in 1933. The story is told by Franz Werfel in his *The Song of Bernadette*; **Massabielle,** the name of the grotto where Bernadette saw her vision; **walls of Jericho,** Joshua 6: 20.

P. 242   **The Beautiful Changes: Queen Anne's Lace,** a common field weed, with flat round clusters of small white flowers; **Lucernes,** the lake of Lucerne is in central Switzerland.

P. 242   **High Flight:** (See the note on the sonnet on page 260.) This sonnet was written on the back of a letter to his mother in September, 1941, while John Gillespie Magee, Jr., was in training with the R.C.A.F.

314

in England. On December 11, 1941, at the age of nineteen, he was killed in action. To honour his memory, his sonnet has been made the official poem of the Air Force, and is posted in pilot-training centres throughout the British Commonwealth.

P. 244   **We Live in a Rickety House: tracts** are pamphlets filled with moral and religious precepts for the guidance of the wayward; **grog** is an intoxicating liquor.

P. 245   **Winter Uplands:** (See the note on the sonnet on page 260.) This was Lampman's last poem, the final testament to beauty of this "Canadian Keats." Its conception began in the countryside about the city of Ottawa. On the evenings of January 29 and 30, 1899, he completed its composition, and the poet's last line is the poet's last word. On February 8, 1899, he was stricken with a severe pain in the lungs; on February 10, he died. Nothing Lampman wrote was more typical of him or more characteristic of his poetic genius than this sonnet.

P. 246   **Evening:** (See the note on the sonnet on page 260.) **upland slopes**, hillsides; **Flickering**, darting irregularly in pursuit of flies; **peevish**, its call is harsh and complaining; **night-hawk**, a close relative of the whip-poor-will; **Beats up**, circles higher; **lucent**, the light of the sunset still lingers in the upper air; **griding**, a rasping sound is made by the air rushing through the quill-feathers; **homely**, associated with the familiar things of home; **Pandean**, Pan was the god of flocks and shepherds among the Greeks. He loved music, and invented the shepherd's flute. According to myth, Pan, when taking leave of an old haunt, gathered up the frogs at the water's edge and "blew into their velvet throats." They have repeated his music ever since.

P. 246   **Indian Summer:** After the first severe autumn frosts, summery weather often returns to eastern Canada in the form of warm hazy October days and cool nights with clear, full moon. This season is commonly known as Indian Summer. **sumachs**, in autumn the leaves of the sumach tree turn crimson, and the clumps of seeds turn dark red. All these sights and sounds are typical of Indian Summer.

P. 247   **Vestigia: Vestigia** in Latin means footprints.

P. 247   **The Half-Breed Girl:** With imaginative insight and sympathetic understanding, the poet probes the heart and feelings of a girl who is half Scot and half Indian. He imagines that her misery stems from her dual yearnings. She cannot be wholly Scot or Indian, and death would be preferable to her divided life. **reek**, smoke; **loch**, lake; **shealing** (shieling), cottage; **the tangle of the poles**, at the peak of the wigwam where the poles are braced against one another to hold the structure erect.

P. 249   **The Fundamentalist:** The term is here used, reproachfully, of those who would usurp God's judgement seat and legislate according to their personal tastes and opinions.

P. 250   **The Lamp of Poor Souls:** Before the Reformation, a **Lamp of Poor Souls** was kept burning continually in churches to remind parishioners to pray for all souls who had departed to another world. The poetess here imagines a poor mother praying for her dead child, and expresses her faith and emotion with unique insight and profound tenderness. This poem appeared first in *Scribner's* magazine, September, 1909.

P. 251   **Frost:** In all its patterns, frost is here used as a symbol of changing forms. In the full glare of the sun, all imaginative designs melt away, and only the bare, bleak, empty pane of glass remains streaked with dripping fire. The straight lines of the sash suggest the outline of the Kremlin, the seat of government in Czarist and Communist Russia. **Armies,** a reference to Napoleon's invading forces; **fane,** temple.

P. 251   **Sea-Gulls:** The poet finds language inadequate to describe the beauty and the grace of gulls in wild flight, but by poetic image and rhythm he can suggest to the reader's imagination something akin to their beauty and grace. There are a number of remarkable differences between the structure and the effect of the first eight lines and those of the last seven. The power of language to describe things may be limited, but its power to suggest things is infinite.

P. 252   **The Reticent Phrase:** The title means the phrase that holds back, reluctant to come into existence. Anyone who has tried to find an original phrase will apprehend something of this poet's experience of the process by which phrases are tempered. **excalibur,** the sword of King Arthur.

P. 252   **Canada: North's green fires,** Northern Lights; **Bow,** tributary of the South Saskatchewan, flowing from the mountains eastward through Alberta; **Daulac** (or Dollard), an intrepid Frenchman who in 1660 with a small band diverted an attack by the Iroquois on Montreal by stubbornly fighting a delaying action at the Long Sault rapids on the Ottawa River. Although Daulac lost his life, his courage amazed the Iroquois, and forced them to change their plans; **Lampman,** a Canadian poet whose love for the beauty and grandeur of his native countryside and towering forests has made his poetry memorable.

P. 253   **Winter Saturday:** The poet compares a family of prairie folk headed for town in their Ford on a wintry night to a caterpillar changed into a cocoon; then in the light of the town into moths; and finally into a chrysalis. The interplay of vowel sounds creates a pleasant dreamy and drowsy atmosphere.

P. 254   **Resurrection in October: Seigneur,** feudal lord, lord of the trees that he has decked with autumn robes; **cavalier,** Seigneur Death; **their** refers to ghosts of reawakened life; **stubborn,** the leaves, for instance, did not wish to let go; **We are alive,** man has no dormant period, he must press on with living and achieving and without display of pride or splendour. In the autumn harvest, man's plans for spring begin again.

P. 256   **Portrait:** Details selected from the girl's environments, as she works in a library, serve to reveal her qualities, and indirectly to reflect a phase of life today.

BIOGRAPHICAL NOTES

ABSE, Dannie (1923-   ) was born in Wales and now lives in Golders Green, London, where he practises medicine. During World War II he served with the Medical Corps of the Royal Air Force. In the mid-'fifties he became one of the founders of a new movement in poetry whose members were dubbed "mavericks."

AIKEN, Conrad (1889-   ) was born in Savannah, Georgia, to which he has recently returned after spending many years variously on Cape Cod, in New York, and on the Sussex coast of England. In his youth at Harvard, he was a member of the class of 1911, which included such men as T. S. Eliot, Robert Benchley, and Walter Lippmann: all later to become, like himself, famous in the literary world. As well as volumes of poetry, he has produced short stories, plays, and novels.

ARNOLD, Matthew (1822-1888) was born in Laleham, England, and died in Liverpool. Eldest son of Dr. Thomas Arnold, famous Headmaster of Rugby, he was educated at Rugby and Balliol College, Oxford. After graduation he served for four years as a private secretary and for ten years was professor of poetry at Oxford. In 1851, he was appointed Inspector of Schools, and this position he held for thirty-five years. During his tenure of office, he had a profound influence on the course of education in England. In addition, he was an accomplished literary critic, essayist, and poet. His poetry is characterized by subdued tones, high and questioning purpose, and fine workmanship.

AUDEN, Wystan Hugh (1907-   ) was born at York, the son of George Auden, M.D., and was educated at Christ Church College, Oxford. At university his political sympathies were with the Left, and he was associated with a group of young poets, some of whom, like Louis MacNeice, have become as famous as himself. After graduation and a brief sojourn in Germany, he took up school teaching at Malvern, 1930-1935. During the Spanish Civil War, he drove an ambulance for the Loyalist forces. In 1939, he was awarded the King's Poetry Medal. Since 1939, he has been a citizen of the United States and has held chairs of poetry at several universities. A prolific writer, possessed of great energy and versatility, he has won respect for his wit, satire, and even cynicism, and among his honours are a Pulitzer Prize and the Merit Medal of the National Academy of Arts and Letters. He has been described as a man of extraordinary insights, and his themes are as unpredictable as they are provocative.

BENÉT, Stephen Vincent (1898-1943) was born in Bethlehem, Pennsylvania, and educated at Yale. At seventeen, he published a small book of poetry. In 1928 he published *John Brown's Body*, a long narrative poem, for which he was awarded the Pulitzer Prize. Some of the interpolated lyrics in this longer poem are wrought with fine artistic skill.

BENÉT, William Rose (1886-1950), Stephen's older brother, was born at Fort Hamilton, New York Harbour. After graduation from Yale, he served in turn as a freelance writer, a magazine editor, and an officer in the U.S. Air Service in World War I. After the war, he became one of the editors of *The Saturday Review of Literature*. His poetry is remarkable for its imaginative sweep and sonorous rhythms. Ingenuity and versatility are characteristics of his work. Like his brother, he has been a recipient of the Pulitzer Prize.

BENSON, Nathaniel (1903-1967) was born in Toronto and educated at the University of Toronto. After a few years of school teaching in the Toronto area, he joined the staff of an advertising agency in New York. Some years ago, he returned to Toronto as a secondary school teacher of English. Possessed of great facility in the use of words, combined with pleasing felicity of expression, he published several volumes of poetry and plays throughout a long writing career.

BETJEMAN, John (1906-   ) was educated at Marlborough and Oxford, where he was a contemporary of Auden and MacNeice. He is a versatile writer whose interests extend from architecture *Ghastly Good Taste* (1933) to poetry *Old Lights for New Chancels* (1940), *New Bats in Old Belfries* (1945), and on to guide books such as the *Shell Guide to Shropshire* (1951). In recent years his *Collected Poems* has become a best-selling volume. *Summoned by Bells* is his autobiography in verse.

BINYON, Laurence (1869-1943) was born at Lancaster, England, and educated at Oxford. In 1890, he was awarded Newdigate Prize for Poetry. In 1893, he was appointed head of the department of printed books in the British Museum, a post that he held until his death. He was an authority on Asiatic art, and in 1933-4 was Norton Professor of Poetry.

BIRNEY, Earle (1904-   ) was born in Calgary and educated at the Universities of British Columbia, Toronto, California, and London. He has taught at colleges in Utah, British Columbia, and Toronto. During World War II, he served with the Canadian armed forces in Europe, later publishing some of his observations and experiences overseas in a novel *Turvey*. Capable of presenting his ideas in striking images and with terse expression, he reveals himself as a person with an original and independent mind and with a poet's genuine concern for the fate of art and men.

BISHOP, Elizabeth (1911-   ) was born in Worcester, Massachusetts, and now lives in Brazil. She was educated at Vassar College and has published a number of short stories and two volumes of poetry. *A Cold Spring* was awarded the Pulitzer Prize for poetry.

BLAKE, William (1757-1827), the son of a hosiery shop-keeper, was born in London, and died there. He had no formal education, but as a child was apprenticed to an engraver, and later became a member of the Royal Academy. He found his own way into the delights of art and literature, and before he was twenty years of age he had written a series of amazing poems, at once simple and profound. Many of his poems were etched on copper plates and published like engravings. Artist and poet, Blake possessed two great gifts, one of vision and the other of lyric expression.

BOGAN, Louise (1897-   ) was born in Livermore Falls, Maine, and now lives in New York. She attended Boston University. For some years she has been poetry critic for *The New Yorker*. Her *Collected Poems* in 1954 was awarded the Bollingen Prize.

BOOTH, Philip (1925-   ) was born in New Hampshire and now lives in Syracuse, New York. He was educated at Dartmouth, where he gained a varsity letter as a member of the ski team. In World War II, he served as a pilot in the U.S. Air Force. He has taught at Dartmouth and Wellesley, and is now on the staff of the University of Syracuse.

BRIDGES, Robert (1844-1930) was born at Walmer, Isle of Thanet, and died at a village near Oxford. He was educated at Eton and at Oxford where he became a close friend and confidant of Gerard Manley Hopkins. He began his career as a surgeon in a London hospital, but after seven years in the practice of medicine, he gave it up to devote all his time to the writing of prose and poetry. He was a man of great learning and culture, a skilful craftsman, and a master of the light lyric. In 1913, he was appointed Poet Laureate.

BRONTE, Emily (1814-1848) was born in Yorkshire at Thornton but spent most of her life in the village of Haworth in close proximity to the desolate, storm-ridden moors of that area. The three sisters – Emily, Charlotte, and Anne – were daughters of a clergyman, and all became novelists. Indomitable courage in the face of adversity, disease, and loneliness formed the background for their writing and imaginings. Emily's *Wuthering Heights* and Charlotte's *Jane Eyre*, both published in 1847, are classics.

BROOKE, Rupert (1887-1918) was born at Rugby, son of an assistant master at that famous school. After graduation from Cambridge, he travelled extensively in America. During World War I, he was commissioned in the Royal Naval Division. On his way to the Dardanelles, he died of blood-poisoning and was buried at Scyros, Greece. Edward Thomas, a fellow poet, said of him, "A golden young Apollo to look at, he was part of the youth of the world." Virility of mind and spirit, lofty vision, and depth of feeling reflected in his poetry a man of exceptional gifts.

BROWN, Audrey Alexandra (1904-   ) was born in Nanaimo, British Columbia, where she still resides. Her first book of poems, *A Dryad in Nanaimo* (1931), was popularly received, and since then she has contributed poetry and prose to periodicals. In 1946, she received the Lorne Pierce Medal from the Royal Society of Canada for her distinguished service to Canadian letters.

BROWNING, Elizabeth Barrett (1806-1861) was born in Durham, England, and died in Florence, Italy. Owing to a spinal injury at the age of fifteen, she was a semi-invalid for most of her life. She married Robert Browning in 1846 and escaped to Italy, leaving behind a tyrannical father and the life of a recluse in Wimpole Street. As a poet, she was famous before her husband, and on Wordsworth's death in 1850, she was seriously considered for the position of Poet Laureate. Much of her work emphasizes moral and social ideals, and her *Sonnets from the Portuguese* are as inspiring as any love poems in the language. "O lyric love, half angel and half bird" may be her husband's tribute to her.

BROWNING, Robert (1812-1899) was born in Camberwell, London, and died in Venice. He was educated by tutors, by reading in his cultured father's study, and by travel in Italy. A hearty fighter, he enjoyed the struggle toward perfection more than the attainment of the goal. In his dramatic poems, he turned ideas into persons and depicted the crises in the lives of men and women. His optimism, confident faith, and eager zest for the fullness of life are reflected in the thought, feeling, and form of his poetry. The art and life of Italy were an intellectual stimulation to both Brownings and the inspiration of their greatest poems.

BRUCE, Charles (1906-   ) was born in Shoreham, Nova Scotia, and educated at Mount Allison University, Sackville, New Brunswick. As a newspaper man, he has worked in Halifax and New York. In recent years, he headed the Canadian Press, Toronto, from which he retired to devote all his time to writing. Among his publications are the following volumes of poetry and prose: *Wild Apples, Tomorrow's Tide, The Flowing Summer*, and *The Township of Time*.

BURNS, Robert (1759-1796) was born in Alloway, near Ayr, Scotland, and died in Dumfries. His schooling was meagre, but his reading of Shakespeare and Pope was extensive and appreciative. His short life was marked by toil, poverty, and a love of good fellowship with the lads and lassies of his shire. Between the ages of seven and seventeen, hard labour on his father's poor farm at Mount Oliphant nearly killed him. Popular rustic Scottish songs became the models for his own love lyrics addressed to various young women who stirred his passion. The first collection of his poems was published at Kilmarnock in 1786, *Poems Chiefly in the Scottish Dialect*, and it made Burns famous immediately as the poet of the common heart of all humanity. He loved liberty and hated sham. In spite of the misery that came upon him as a result of poverty, his own emotional extravagance, and rheumatic fever, his singing heart could not be stilled. In the poetry of this inspired plowman, an important aspect of the romantic revival is embodied.

BYRON, George Gordon, Lord (1788-1824) was born in London and educated at Harrow and Cambridge. At the age of eleven, he became heir to a baronial title and a large estate, Newstead Abbey. After extensive travel on the continent, he published the first two cantos of his long narrative poem *Childe Harold's Pilgrimage* (1812). "I awoke one morning to find myself famous," said this self-styled "grand Napoleon of the realms of rhyme." In the House of Lords, he defended the common workers, and was at first thought to be an able politician. Married in 1815, separated within a year, he left England in 1816, a disappointed and disgruntled man, a rebel against authority and public opinion. After a brief life of dissipation in Italy, he gave himself and a part of his fortune to the cause of Greek liberty against Turkish oppression. He died of fever at Missolonghi, Greece. His personal scorn can be felt in most of his poetry, and his depiction of nature in her magnificent moods, places his fame securely among the romantic poets of his day.

CALVERLEY, Charles (1831-1884) was the son of the Reverend H. Blayds who had the family name changed to Calverley in 1852. He was educated at Harrow, Oxford, and Cambridge, and was called to the Bar in 1865. In 1866, a fall on ice changed him from an athlete to an invalid. A scholar, musician, and writer of humorous verse, he is here remembered as one of the greatest parodists among English poets. *Verses and Translations* (1862) and *Fly-leaves* (1872) are his best-known publications.

CAMPBELL, Roy (1901-1957) was born in Durban, the son of Dr. Samuel George Campbell. At fifteen he joined the South African Infantry for service in World War I, but was apprehended and sent back to school. After the war, he attended Oxford and between the wars lived in Wales and in France, accepting and enjoying the rough active life of country people. At one time he was a professional bull-fighter and horse-dealer. During the Spanish Civil War he was war correspondent of *The Tablet* (London). In the second War, he was permanently disabled. His death was the result of a motor accident on a road in Spain. Between 1924 and 1946 he published six volumes of poetry, and in 1949 his *Collected Poems* appeared.

CAMPBELL, Wilfred (1861-1919) was born in Kitchener, Ontario, the son of a Church of England clergyman. After graduation from University College, Toronto, and Harvard University, he entered the ministry and engaged in parish work in New England and in New Brunswick, from which he retired in 1891 to join the staff of the Bureau of Archives at Ottawa. He published three volumes of poetry and two historical novels. Some of his finest nature lyrics reflect the deep impression that his boyhood experiences at Wiarton, Ontario, made upon him.

CAMPION, Thomas (1567-1619) was born in London, England, and educated on the continent. A man of many accomplishments, he was a practising physician, a musician, and a writer of songs and masques. He was a leader in the rapid development of music as an art (both vocal and instrumental) in Elizabethan times. Like Shakespeare's songs, the songs and music of Campion are still popular.

CARMAN, Bliss (1861-1929) was born in Fredericton, New Brunswick. After graduation from the University of New Brunswick, Edinburgh, and Harvard, he entered journalism in New York but soon retired to give full time to writing. His first collection of poems *Low Tide on Grand Pré* appeared in 1893. Thereafter he published twenty-two volumes of poetry. At the time of his death at New Canaan, Connecticut, he was regarded as Canada's "poet laureate." He was Greek in his love of the beautiful and in his search for perfection. He was Canadian in his love of nature. He was deft in his creation of imaginative and melodious lyrics.

CHALMERS, Patrick R. (1872-1942) was born in Aldbar, Forfarshire, Scotland. Educated at Rugby, he later pursued a career in banking. He was a regular contributor to *Punch*. His bright and cheerful lyrics, often in dialect, reveal an insight into human nature that is as whimsical as it is urbane.

CHAUCER, Geoffrey (1340?-1400) was born in London and died there. Chaucer acquired the elements of a good general education from his various occupations. Son of a wine-merchant, he was at different stages in his career a page at court, a solicitor, a ransomed prisoner of war, a yeoman, an esquire, a knight, and a member of parliament. He was sent on diplomatic missions to Flanders, France, and Italy, where he possibly met Boccaccio and Petrarch. A glance at a collection of his poems will reveal that Chaucer was well read in the literature of his time and a born teller of tales. His most famous work is *The Canterbury Tales*, a series of descriptive-narrative poems based on the experience, real or imaginary, of a pilgrimage made by a group of people from London to the shrine of Thomas à Becket at Canterbury. An alert and kindly observer of all types of people, he depicted with clarity, good humour, and simplicity both the typical and the individual characteristics of the men and women of his day. The reader of *The Canterbury Tales* does not need to go far on this pilgrimage before he realizes why Chaucer has been called "the father of English poetry and perhaps the prince of it."

CHESTERTON, G. K. (1874-1936) was born in London, England, and died there. He was educated at St. Paul's School and the Slade School of Art. Essayist, novelist, playwright, and poet, he ranged in his writings over a wide variety of aims and forms, from art criticism to the detective story. As a professional literary man and a champion of the established order, he sought by novelty of style to refurbish ancient truths.

CIARDI, John (1916-   ) was born in Boston and now lives in Metuchen, New Jersey. He attended Bates College, Tufts College, and the University of Michigan. He has taught at the University of Kansas City, Harvard, and Rutgers. In World War II, he served as an aerial gunner. At present he is poetry editor and columnist with *The Saturday Review*. He is a strong advocate of the modern idiom in poetry.

CLOUGH, Arthur Hugh (1819-1861) was born in Liverpool, England, and died in Florence, Italy. At Rugby he came under the influence of the famous Dr. Thomas Arnold, and at Oxford, where he became a tutor, he made a close friend of Matthew Arnold who later made Clough the subject of his elegy *Thyrsis*. A great experimenter in metrical forms, he is remembered best for a few sad and beautiful lyrics.

COHEN, Leonard (1934-   ) was born in Montreal and attended McGill University. He has since published several volumes of verse, two novels, *The Favourite Game* (1963) and the controversial *Beautiful Losers* (1966), and become a popular singer.

COLERIDGE, Samuel Taylor (1772-1834) was born at his father's vicarage of Ottery St. Mary in Devonshire and died at the home of an admirer, Dr. Gillman, in Highgate, London. After his father's death, Coleridge at the age of nine was sent to live with his uncle in London and was entered in the charity school of Christ Hospital. Later he attended Jesus College, Cambridge, for two years, but grew weary of university life and withdrew to follow a life of vacillation and the pursuit of opium. With Southey he founded a scheme for a Pantisocracy, a utopian colony on the banks of the Susquehanna in America. With Wordsworth he planned and published a joint volume called *Lyrical Ballads* in which Coleridge's efforts were directed to "persons and characters super-natural, or at least romantic." His main contribution was the remarkable long ballad *The Rime of the Ancient Mariner*. Owing to a strange paralysis of will, the promise of his youth went unfulfilled. In spite of misfortune, frustration, and illness, he managed, however, to produce lasting proof of his poetic genius.

COWPER, William (1731-1800) was born at Great Berkhampstead, Hertfordshire, and died at East Dereham. After graduation from Westminster, he entered law, but owing to fits of melancholy, he was forced into country retirement where he was cared for by devoted friends. Some of his finest poems were written at the behest of appreciative acquaintances. His delicate and sensitive nature expressed itself in both hymns and humorous verses that are still popular. Rural scenes, as subjects for poetry, were uncommon in his day. Cowper's descriptions of woods, brooks, plowmen, teamsters, letter carriers, and domestic animals show acute powers of observation and sympathetic insight. His manner of expression has freshness and charm that mark him as a poet of striking originality in his time.

CUMBERLAND, Robert W. (1895-   ) was born in Aylmer, Quebec, a son of the manse, and the only child of James and Nancy Cumberland. He was educated at Queen's University and at Columbia University. For thirty-five years he was professor of English at Cooper Union, New York, a post from which he retired in 1963. *Verse and Translation*, published in 1922, reveals him as a poet of keen sensitivity and genuine sympathy with fellow mortals.

CUMMINGS, Edward Estlin (1894-1962) was born in Cambridge, Massachusetts, the son of a professor of English at Harvard. He became the "Peck's Bad Boy of American Poetry." An eccentric stylist, impudent satirist, and romantic sentimentalist, he proclaimed his individuality through the years. As a lifelong iconoclast, he was an enemy of systems, regimentation, and restrictions of all kinds.

DAVIES, William Henry (1870-1940) was born in Newport, Monmouth-
shire, Wales. He had little education and had to live by his wits.
Extricating himself from a poor apprenticeship, he embarked for America
where he tramped and "rode the rods" about the United States and
Canada. Attempting to board a moving train at Renfrew, Ontario, he
lost his right foot. He returned to England and during convalescence
took up writing. With money saved from working at odd jobs and
peddling small-wares, he paid for the printing of his first book *The Soul's
Destroyer and Other Poems*. George Bernard Shaw commended the
poetry, and Davies' future was assured. His *Autobiography of a Super-
Tramp* (1907) made him famous, and he continued to write poetry and
prose until his death. His special gift was a child-like simplicity and
directness. He looked upon the common things of life with the rapture
of a child discovering them for the first time. His sense of wonder was
acute.

DE LA MARE, Walter (1873-1956) was born in Charlton, Kent, a descendant of a Huguenot family. He was educated at St. Paul's School,
London. Unable to attend college, he worked for nearly twenty years as
an accountant in the London Office of the Standard Oil Company. He
published *Songs of Childhood* in 1902, and since 1908 has lived by his
writing. He is "the poet of dim suggestions, of fugitive thrills; he evokes
the wondering of a child, and communicates the feeling of invisible
presences." He is an adventurer in the realms of the imagination and a
master craftsman with a sensitive ear for suggestive sounds and descriptive rhythms. Among contemporary poets, he stands supreme as a writer
of gentle wistful lyrics on themes that are often profound.

DICKINSON, Emily (1830-1886) was born in Amherst, Massachusetts,
and died there. At seventeen she entered South Hadley Female Seminary,
but rebelled and returned to the seclusion of her father's sedate and
cultured home. There she lived the life of a recluse and wrote most of her
short cryptic poems on bits of paper sent as notes to close relatives and
acquaintances. Only three or four of her poems were printed during her
lifetime; but since her death, hundreds of her poems have been discovered
in odd corners of the old home and published as literary discoveries. By
reason of her spontaneous and epigrammatic terseness, her clear, cool
precision in the choice of words, her whimsical rhythms, and her warmth
and intensity of feeling, she made a distinct contribution to the art of
poetry in the English language.

DONNE, John (1573-1631) was born in London, England, and educated at Oxford and Cambridge. He enlisted for foreign service with Essex to the Azores and later became private secretary to the Lord Keeper of the Great Seal. Dismissed, he turned to pamphleteering and was rescued from poverty by a forgiving father-in-law. At forty-two he took holy orders, and became one of the most eloquent preachers of his day. His poetry and the enigma of his personality have been the subjects of much controversy. In both, the trivial mingled with the sublime, the flesh with the spirit, theology with love, and startling conceits with rough vigour. Donne was a strange mixture of many attributes of genius.

DRAYTON, Michael (1563-1631) was born in Warwickshire, England, and died in London. From his earliest youth he wished to be a poet. While serving as a page in Polesworth Castle, he was introduced to popular songs and ballads by the local minstrel. He was a facile and ready writer, full of fancy, and given to some graceful and dreamy rhythms. Among his fellow poets, to which group Shakespeare belonged, Drayton, for all his ambition, energy, and innovation, did not attain major rank. His memory has been kept alive by a few songs and sonnets that for sincerity of natural feeling and artistic excellence have not been surpassed.

EBERHART, Richard (1904-   ) was born in Austin, Minnesota, and educated at Dartmouth College. After graduation, he went round the world "in search of truth." He attended Cambridge University where he received his M.A. degree. Returning to the United States he began a course of study at the Harvard Graduate School. After service with the navy in World War II, he began a career in business, becoming vice-president of an industrial firm, but recently he has spent much of his time on lecture tours of universities. Of his own poems, he states that they are "biased and canted toward the spiritual," "thrusts of imagination," "attempts to give pleasure in spite of pain," and "phases of understanding." Between 1959 and 1961, he was consultant on poetry to the Library of Congress.

ELIOT, Thomas Stearns (1888-1965) was born in St. Louis, Missouri, of Puritan New England stock, educated at Harvard, the Sorbonne, and Oxford, taught in a boy's school in London, worked in a bank, and finally entered publishing as literary editor for a publishing house. As a naturalized British subject, he lived in London almost continuously for the past forty years, and during that time he published a considerable amount of poetry and literary criticism and a number of plays. In all forms he proved himself to be a close observer of life and a sensitive craftsman. His work attracted a great deal of attention on both sides of the Atlantic. Some of his poetry has been severely criticized for its unusual substance and structure, but it has seldom failed to excite interest. It is serious, profound, and challenging.

FINCH, Robert (1900-   ) was born in Freeport, Long Island, New York, of British parentage. After graduation from the University of Toronto and the Sorbonne, Paris, he became professor of French at University College, Toronto. An accomplished musician, painter, and poet, he has published four volumes of short poems that are as brightly polished as new-minted coins. To read any one poem is to encounter the terseness and tension of an alert and subtle mind.

FITZGERALD, Edward (1809-1883) was born near Woodbridge, Suffolk, England, the son of a well-to-do country gentleman. He was educated at Cambridge and became a close friend of Thackeray and Tennyson. Most of his life he lived in quiet retirement and in the exercise of a scholarly talent for translating Spanish, Persian, and Greek literature into English. In translating a masterpiece he aimed to communicate not only the meaning of the original, but also what he considered its effect on the readers to be. In translating the *Rubáiyát*, for instance, he entered so deeply into the spirit of the piece that he made from it a new poem. His adaptation of Omar's thinking about life and death found ready acceptance in minds that were growing weary of Victorian smugness and respectability. His polished quatrains and dreamy rhythms made Omar's speculations delightfully impudent and refreshing. Many people who would sneer at Omar's mysticism and frown on his hedonism have succumbed to the spoil of FitzGerald's poetry. The continued popularity of the Rubáiyát is assured because it strikes a note that stirs a response of some kind in everyone.

FLECKER, James Elroy (1884-1915) was born in London, England, and died at Davos Platz, Switzerland. He was educated at Dean Close School, Cheltenham, where his father was headmaster, and later at Trinity College, Oxford. At Cambridge, he studied Oriental languages in preparation for the consular service. He was appointed British consul at Constantinople, later at Smyrna, and later at Beirut. Though he suffered all his short life from the enervating effects of tuberculosis, he proved, by the success that he made of his work as consul, that poets are not impractical dreamers. *The Golden Journey to Samarkand* (1913) and *The Old Ships* (1915) reflect his appreciation of the art of the Middle East and his love for the quiet country lanes of his native land. His metrical drama *Hassan* is a work of great technical perfection in the craft of using words, rhythms, sights, and sounds to suggest a world of romance to the imagination. He disliked the rough verbal realism of some of his contemporary poets.

FROST, Robert (1874-1963) was born in San Francisco, California. His parents were school teachers. When Robert was ten, his father died, and his mother brought her small family east to Massachusetts to the old Frost homestead. After attending the high school at Lawrence, Robert went for short periods to both Dartmouth College and Harvard University. Finding college life uncongenial, he withdrew to become mill-hand, school teacher, farmer, and poet. Seeking a change of environment, he took his family to England where he lived for three years and published his first book of poems *A Boy's Will* (1913) and a second *North of Boston* (1914). He was recognized as a new voice with a distinct and unique tone in literature, and returned to America to find himself famous. For nearly forty years, he practised farming, writing, and lecturing to audiences, in and out of colleges, in all parts of America. His poetry is rooted in the common experiences of rural life, and beneath the simple facts of his observations and his plain language, moves a wisdom that is firm and sure of itself and so shrewd that it is called honest. Of himself, Frost has this to say: "If I must be classified as a poet, I might be called a Synecdochist; for I prefer the synecdoche in poetry – that figure of speech in which we use a part for the whole." And again he wrote: "To me, the thing that art does for life is to strip it to form."

GAY, John (1685-1732) was born near Barnstaple, England, and died in London at the home of the Duke of Queensbury, his friend and sometimes patron. An indolent, improvident, but witty man of the world, Gay often turned to wealthy friends and patrons of the arts for money and sustenance. His first collection of poems, published in 1720, brought him one thousand pounds, but in the collapse of the South Sea Company, he lost everything. Among his friends he numbered the greatest writers of his day – Pope, Swift, Addison, and Steele. He wrote a number of satirical dramas, but his fame rests on his *Fables* (1727) and *The Beggar's Opera* (1728). His fables were inspired by the French poet La Fontaine and written at the request of the Princess of Wales (later Queen Caroline) for her little son William, Duke of Cumberland. For its realism, his poetry was original in his day. His language was "poetical without being too elevated, and familiar without being too low."

GIBSON, Wilfrid Wilson (1878-1962) was born in Hexham, Northumberland, and received his education at private schools. In 1912, he went to London to live. Later he spent time in a speaking tour of the United States, and in service with the Army Service Corps in World War I. He has published a dozen books of poems. First the war and later the economic depression of the 'thirties made a deep impression on the man and his writings.

GOLDSMITH, Oliver (1728-1774) was born in Pallasmore in County Longford, Ireland, and died in London. His father was a poor Anglican curate and schoolmaster. He attended school at Elphin and Athlone and graduated from Trinity College, Dublin, at the bottom of the list. Homely, awkward, and irresponsible, he failed in everything he attempted as a young man but distinguished himself by wandering from place to place in England, Scotland, and on the Continent, playing his flute at country dances. In France, he met Voltaire, and was greatly influenced by him. When he returned to England, he took up hack writing and reviewing, met Dr. Samuel Johnson, and turned over to him the manuscript of a novel he had written. Johnson promptly sold the manuscript to a publisher for sixty pounds and paid Goldsmith's rent. That was the beginning of *The Vicar of Wakefield*, and of the fame of a great novelist, playwright, poet, and essayist." "He touched nothing that he did not adorn."

HARDY, Thomas (1840-1928) was born in the village of Upper Bock-hampton, near Dorchester, in Dorsetshire, the son of a stone mason. He was educated at the local schools, was apprenticed to an architect, and in 1863 won the prize and medal of the Institute of British Architects for his essay on "Coloured Brick and Terra-Cotta Architecture." For about ten years he practised as an architect in London and continued to write poetry as a hobby. George Meredith, then a publisher's reader, recommended that he turn from poetry to prose, and encouraged him in his early efforts. *Under the Greenwood Tree* (1872) fell into the hands of Frederick Greenwood, editor of *Cornhill Magazine*, and Hardy's future was assured. He left his profession and devoted himself to writing. Half a dozen great novels followed, and then in 1896 he returned to his first love, poetry, and wrote only poetry until the end of his long life, spent among the Wessex hills. Hardy saw man as a victim of chance, and life as a struggle against fate. He found inspiration in obscure people and in humble places. He denied the charge of pessimism sometimes made against him. He has attracted generations of readers by his lyric skill and by the earnestness and tenderness exhibited in his epic and dramatic handling of great human themes. He said: "If way to the better there be, it exacts a good look at the worst."

HERBERT, George (1593-1633) was born in Montgomery Castle in Wales, of noble parentage, and died at Bemerton, in Wiltshire. After graduation from Cambridge, he decided against a career at court, took orders instead, and became rector of Bemerton. A kind, devout, and saintly man, he was greatly beloved by his parishioners and was known to some as "Holy George." He was a friend of Bacon and Donne, and was deeply influenced by the latter. Religious fervour and subtle fantasy mingle as gracefully in his poetry as do the tastes of the courtier and the cleric in his life. He even infused a quaint symbolism into his hymns.

HERRICK, Robert (1591-1674) was born in London, educated at Cambridge, and died at the vicarage of Dean Prior in Devonshire. Encouraged by friends, he gave up the gay life of an irresponsible youth on the streets of London, and settled down regretfully to the quiet life of a remote parish where he learned to love country ways and wiles. His poems are usually light and delicate, sprightly, and whimsical. A thoroughgoing Epicurean, he has been described as "the most frankly pagan of English poets." Some of his songs and love lyrics are among the best in the language.

HESKETH, Phoebe (1909-   ) was born in Preston, Lancashire. She was educated at Cheltenham Ladies' College. She served as editor of the *Bolton Evening News* from 1943 to 1945, and her contributions of poetry and criticism may be found in the *Times Literary Supplement*, *Time and Tide*, *Listener*, *Contemporary Review*, and *Poetry Review*. Some of her books of verse are: *Lean Forward, Spring, No Time for Cowards, Between Wheels and Stars, The Buttercup Children.*

HODGSON, Ralph (1871-1962) was born in Yorkshire, worked for a short time in a publishing house in London, and for twenty years was a lecturer in English literature at Sendai University, Japan. In 1941, he was awarded the Polignac Prize by the Royal Society of Literature for two poems "The Bull" and "The Song of Honour." Since 1939, he lived in the United States, mostly at his retreat, half farm and half bird sanctuary, near Canton, Ohio, where he indulged his love for the out-of-doors and his hobby of raising bull-terriers. The writing of poetry was an avocation with him, and he published only what he considered first-rate. His exquisite lyrics have a grace and freshness, a sincerity and spontaneity.

HOOD, Thomas (1799-1845) was born in London and spent most of his life working as a journalist in that city. First, in 1821 to 1823, he was assistant editor of *The London Magazine*. He became well acquainted with De Quincey, Lamb, and Hazlitt. In 1840, he was made editor of the *New Monthly Magazine*, and this post he retained until his death. "He was a man who seemingly could not help being cheerful" in spite of his precarious health and limited wealth. He left behind a few poems of superior quality.

HOPKINS, Gerard Manley (1844-1889) was born in Stratford, Essex, and died in Dublin. He was educated at Highgate, and at Balliol College, Oxford. At twenty-two he became a Roman Catholic and was received into the Society of Jesus. This decision was perhaps his reaction to the religious doubts and scientific speculations of his day. He preached and ministered at Liverpool and Birmingham, and was appointed to a church near Oxford. From there he went to the chair of Greek at Dublin University. He worked among the poor in Dublin, and died there of typhoid fever. He left all his writings to Robert Bridges, an old friend of college days, and appointed him his literary executor. Not until 1918 did Bridges release *The Poems* to the public. Since then the influence of his intensely original mind and poetry has been deep and continuous. He invented what he called "sprung rhythm." The novelty of his expression is inseparable from the novelty of his thought and passion. In his "spiritual-sensual" poetry, his love of God is identified with his love of all beauty.

HOUSMAN, A. E. (1859-1936) was born near Bromsgrove, Worcestershire, and died at Cambridge. Graduating from Oxford, he entered the Civil Service and served for ten years in the Patent Office. From 1892 to 1911, he was professor of Latin at University College, London, and from 1912 to 1936 he held a similar post at Cambridge. He published three small but significant volumes of poetry: *A Shropshire Lad* (1896), *Last Poems* (1922), and *More Poems* (1936). Some of his exquisite lyrics were inspired by the Scottish Border ballads and were written during a period of convalescence in Shropshire. Their grim simplicity, conciseness, subtle irony, and melody place Housman among the finest writers of lyric verse in the language.

JARRELL, Randall (1914-1965) was born in Nashville, Tennessee. After graduation from Vanderbilt University, he taught at Sarah Lawrence and Kenyon College, the Universities of Texas, Illinois, Indiana, Cincinnati, and Princeton. In 1942, he enlisted in the Air Force. Praised as a novelist, critic and poet, he was until his death Professor of English at the Women's College of the University of North Carolina. His poems are swift, suggestive, and intense. Louis Untermeyer said of him: "He has so much sympathy with suffering innocence and so much persuasive pity that the heart is moved long before the mind can appreciate the poet's skill."

JEFFERS, Robinson (1887-1962) was born in Pittsburgh, Pennsylvania, and received his early education at local schools and in Switzerland and Germany. He graduated in medicine from the University of Southern California and in forestry from Washington University. Living on a legacy, he was able to devote his time to writing and through the years published eighteen books of poetry. An individualist, a pessimist, Jeffers found life a series of frustrations, a dark passage lit only by flashes of beauty.

JOHNSTON, George (1913-   ) was born in Hamilton, Ontario. He was educated at the University of Toronto and Mount Allison University, Sackville, New Brunswick, where from 1946 to 1949 he was assistant Professor of English. He is now a Professor of English at Carleton University, Ottawa. He published *The Cruising Auk* (1959), a collection of his own poems.

KEATS, John (1795-1821) was born in London, England, and died in Rome, Italy. He was educated at Enfield school, and apprenticed to a surgeon, but turned to literature under the influence of Hunt, Hazlitt, and Shelley. His poems reflect the eager, sensitive, and sensuous imagination of youth. In love with beauty, he dressed his goddess in rich phrases and exquisite rhythms. "Poetry must surprise by a fine excess," he declared, and his own masterpieces bear testimony to the soundness of his artistic judgement. His instinct for the right word, image, colour, and sound seemed infallible. And his letters attest to his intuitional powers. In four troubled years, he produced some of the finest poems in the English language, and he ranks as one of England's greatest poets.

KIPLING, Rudyard (1865-1936) was born in Bombay, India, of British parentage, and died in Burwash, Sussex. He was educated in England at the United Service College at Westward Ho in North Devon. After graduation he returned to India as a journalist. His published works include poems, tales, novels, and children's stories. A man of great virility, he endowed the characters he created, his Tommies and his natives, with such spirit that they live in print.

KIRKCONNELL, Watson (1895-   ) was born in Port Hope, Ontario, and educated at Queen's University and at Oxford. He has travelled widely in Europe and has lectured and written on a variety of subjects. His *European Elegies* contains translations of poems from about forty different languages. In recent years he has been President of Acadia University, Wolfville, Nova Scotia, a post from which he retired in 1964. He is currently active as a translator and reviewer.

KLEIN, Abraham Moses (1909-   ) was born in Montreal and educated at McGill University. He practises law in Montreal. He has been a leader of Canadian Young Judea and editor of *Canadian Jewish Chronicle*. An authority on Hebrew language and history, and interpreter of Jewish life, he contributes both prose and poetry to periodicals. *The Rocking Chair and Other Poems* was published in 1948.

LAMPMAN, Archibald (1861-1899) was born in Morpeth, Kent County, Ontario, and died in Ottawa. After graduation from Trinity College

School, Port Hope, and from Trinity College, Toronto, he entered the Civil Service at Ottawa. He published two volumes of poetry which for their quality and distinctiveness placed him among Canada's major poets.

LAWRENCE, David Herbert (1885-1930) was born in Eastwood, a colliery town in Nottinghamshire, and was educated at High School and University College, Nottingham. He taught in a country school for two years before turning to writing for a living. His published works include novels, short stories, travel sketches, and poems, some of which aroused sharp criticism and made his life and work a subject of controversy. A pagan at heart and a lover of the primitive life, he let his instinct be his guide. Whatever he did, he did well, completely absorbed in the task at hand, no matter how trivial or humble it might be.

LAYTON, Irving (1912-   ) was born in a small town near Bucharest in Roumania and as a very young child was brought to Canada. Montreal has been his home ever since, and in 1939 he was graduated from Macdonald College with a B.Sc. in Agriculture and in 1946 from McGill with an M.A. in Economics and Political Science. He is now on the staff of Sir George Williams University. Since graduation he has produced on an average a book a year, either poetry or short stories. He thrives on controversy and apparently enjoys the chastisement of literary critics. His poems are collected in *A Red Carpet for the Sun* (1959) which has been well received by both the critics and the general reader.

LE PAN, Douglas (1914-   ) was born in Toronto and educated at the University of Toronto Schools, the University of Toronto, and at Oxford. During World War II, he served in the ranks for a time, and later joined the staff of the Canadian Department of External Affairs. He left the Canadian Diplomatic service to become professor of English at Queen's University. He has just been appointed Principal of his old college, University College, University of Toronto. In 1948, his first book of poems *The Wounded Prince and Other Poems* was published with an introduction by C. Day Lewis. His first novel, *The Deserter*, was published in 1964.

LEWIS, C. Day (1904-   ) was born in Ballintogher, Ireland, and was educated at Sherbourne School and Wadham College, Oxford. He has taught in various schools and colleges. A friend of Auden and Spender, he has devoted his time since 1935 to literature and politics, in both of which he is a revolutionary. Under the pseudonym "Nicholas Blake," he published a number of detective stories, but his fame rests securely on his poetry.

LEWIS, Clive Staples, pseudonym of Clive Hamilton (1898-   ), is the author of *The Screwtape Letters*, *Beyond Personality*, and other books on Christianity and Christian behaviour, which excel in both wit and depth. His writings have had a profound influence on thought and behaviour in England and throughout the English-speaking world.

LOVELACE, Richard (1618-1658) was born in Woolwich, a suburb of London, England. He was educated at Oxford, inherited four large estates in Kent, risked everything in the Civil War on the Royalist side and lost, and was twice imprisoned for political reasons. A gay cavalier, "the most amiable and beautiful person that eye ever beheld," he died of tuberculosis in utter poverty in a cellar in a London slum. His memory lives in a few neatly turned and tender lyrics.

LOWELL, Amy (1874-1928) was born in Brookline, Massachusetts, and died there. She was educated privately and travelled widely. She possessed and used what is called "family background," and led a group of young poets who called themselves Imagists. She was an experimenter in both the form and the techniques of verse.

LOWELL, Robert (1917-   ) was born in Boston, Massachusetts. He attended St. Mark's School, Harvard, Kenyon College (where he taught briefly), and Louisiana State University. At Kenyon, he was influenced by his teacher, John Crowe Ransom. Twice, in 1943, he attempted to enlist for war service, but he was rejected; later, when he was drafted, he refused to serve on the grounds that his country was then out of danger and that the bombing of civilians was unprincipled murder. For five months, he was imprisoned as a conscientious objector during World War II. Later, he taught at Kenyon College and Boston University. His *Lord Weary's Castle* (1946) was awarded the Pulitzer Prize. His poetry is complex: involved allusions, congested images, elliptical structures, and sudden transitions demand the reader's careful consideration. Beneath the formalism of his verse is a deep, sometimes violent, protest against the corruption of the times. It is a poetry, at once inventive, passionate, and powerful.

MAGEE, Jr., John Gillespie (1922-1941) was born in Shanghai, China, where his parents were missionaries. He was educated at Rugby and Yale. He enlisted in the R.C.A.F. at Montreal in October of 1940. On active service in Britain, he was killed in December, 1941.

MARLOWE, Christopher (1564-1593) was born in Canterbury and educated at Cambridge. He is now considered the most important of Shakespeare's predecessors. Sidney, Shakespeare, Jonson, and Drayton praised him for his poetic gifts. He was stabbed to death in a London tavern where he quarrelled with Ingram Frizer over the payment of a bill.

MARRIOTT, Anne (1913-   ) was born in Victoria, B.C., and lived there till 1945. Although she is often regarded as a Prairie writer because of her convincing "The Wind Our Enemy" and "Prairie Graveyard," her farm experience was limited to "a couple of summer holiday visits I made to relatives in Saskatchewan." Today she, her husband, and family live in North Vancouver.

MARVELL, Andrew (1621-1678) was born at the Rectory of Winestead, Yorkshire, where his father was clergyman and schoolmaster, and was educated at Cambridge. Although he was an ardent Puritan, he had friends among the Cavaliers. He was a friend of Milton and an assistant to Milton who was Latin Secretary to Cromwell; he was also a favourite of Charles II. The contrasts apparent in Marvell's friendships, tastes, and interests are reflected in the content and the style of his poetry.

MASEFIELD, John (1878-1967) was born in Ledbury, Herefordshire, the son of a lawyer. At fourteen he took to sea on the *Conway*, a sailing ship, and set forth on a life of wandering. He worked in Luke O'Connor's saloon in New York and in a Yonker's carpet factory. Discovering a delight in the works of Chaucer, Shakespeare, Milton, and Keats, he decided to return to England and to take up writing as a career. Since the publication of *Salt-Water Ballads* in 1902, he wrote more than seventy books of poems, plays, novels, tales, and essays. During World War I, he served with the Red Cross. On the death of Robert Bridges in 1930, he was chosen Poet Laureate. The realism of his long narrative poems *The Everlasting Mercy* and *The Widow in the Bye Street* shocked the readers of 1912. There is a virility in Masefield's sentiments and idealism that is salty and racy.

MILLAY, Edna St. Vincent (1892-1950) was born at Rockland, Maine, and graduated from Vassar in 1917. Her first poem "Renascence" was published in *The Lyric Year*, 1912. In 1920, she published a collection of poems *A Few Figs from Thistles: Poems and Four Sonnets*. For some years she was connected with the Provincetown Players, both as a dramatist and as an actress.

MILTON, John (1608-1674) was born in Cheapside, London, England, and died there. He was educated at St. Paul's School and at Cambridge, travelled on the Continent, and studied in Italy. He championed liberty, was appointed Latin Secretary to Cromwell, but at the Restoration was forced into retirement. In his poetry are joined high purpose, grandeur of theme, dignity of word and manner, loftiness of imagination, and great scholarship. He ranks as one of England's greatest poets.

MOORE, Marianne (1887-   ) was born in St. Louis, Missouri. After graduation from Bryn Mawr College in 1909, she taught commercial subjects at the United States Indian school in Carlisle, Pennsylvania, from 1911 to 1915. She also worked as an assistant in a branch of the New York Public Library. From 1925 to 1929, she was editor of *The Dial*, a famous literary magazine. Her *Collected Poems* (1951) won the Bollingen Prize, the National Book Award, and the Pulitzer Prize. Her early poems are easy to understand, but her later work is sometimes puzzling. Her effects result from a combination of observation, fact, quotation, image, and odd data pieced together in a montage-like manner. Her own detailed annotations to her poems help explain the references. Her poems are mathematically exact and logical; her images, unforgettable. Though she has been called "the pet of the intelligentsia," she herself modestly declared, "I can see no reason for calling my work poetry except that there is no other category in which to put it. Anyone could do what I do."

MUIR, Edwin (1887-1959) was born at Kirkwall in the Orkneys and educated at the grammar school there. For a time he was employed as a clerk by various ship-building firms in Glasgow, but in 1919 he went to London to try his hand as a free-lance journalist. After serving as editor of at least one paper, he went to Prague as Director of the British Institute. Later he became Warden of Newbattle Abbey College. He published fiction, criticism, and biography in addition to three volumes of poetry.

McCRAE, John (1872-1918) was born at Guelph, Ontario, and died at Wimereux of pneumonia while on active service as a medical officer with the Royal Army Medical Corps in World War I. As a young man he had served as a lieutenant with the artillery in South Africa. After graduation from the University of Toronto and Johns Hopkins University in Baltimore, he joined the staff of the Medical School at McGill. His faultless rondeau "In Flanders Fields" was first published in *Punch*, December 8, 1915, but his small volume of verse, bearing the same title, was not published until 1919.

MacDONALD, Wilson (1880-   ) was born in Cheapside, Ontario, and educated at Woodstock College and McMaster University. He published many volumes of poetry, some of which he illustrated himself. He has lectured a great deal in both Canada and the United States.

MacKAY, L. A. (1901-   ) was born at Hensell, Ontario, and educated at the University of Toronto and at Oxford. He is professor of classics at an American university, and has published one book of satirical verse, *Viper's Bugloss*, under the pseudonym of "John Smalacombe."

McLACHLAN, Alexander (1818-1896) was born in Scotland and came to Canada as a young man to settle on a farm near Guelph, Ontario. Before coming to Canada, he experienced the degrading life of the mills and slums of Glasgow, and his sympathy with the poor and the depressed is reflected in some of his verse.

MacLEISH, Archibald (1892-   ) was born in Glencoe, Illinois. He was educated at the public schools of Glencoe, Yale University, and Harvard Law School. He practised law in Boston, but gave it up for literary pursuits. His *Conquistador* (1933), a narrative that has been called "a triumph in sonority and sustained power," won the Pulitzer Prize. He has been an editor of *Fortune*, the Librarian of Congress (1939), and Under-Secretary of State. His poetic dramas, *Panic* and *J.B.*, his radio and television plays, and volumes of essays, mark him as an inventive spirit. His stylistic subtleties, keen perception, highly charged images, nostalgic tone, use of ordinary language, and experiments in tension, stamp his poetry as his own. In 1949, he was appointed Boylston Professor of Rhetoric and Oratory at Harvard.

MacNEICE, Louis (1907-1963) was born in Belfast, Ireland. He attended Merton College, Oxford, and later taught Greek in London. He belongs to the "English group" that includes Spender, Lewis, and Auden. Much of his poetry dealt with the political and social issues of his day.

NEWMAN, John Henry (1801-1890) was born in London and died at Edgbaston, Birmingham. Educated at Oxford, he took holy orders first in the Church of England, and later in the Roman Catholic Church, becoming a Cardinal. A great scholar and a brilliant analyst, he attacked the liberalism of his day in essays that are masterpieces of clear thinking. He was revered even by his opponents for his saintly character.

NOWLAN, Alden (1933-   ) was born at Windsor, Nova Scotia. In 1952, he moved to New Brunswick where he was News Editor of the Hartland *Observer*. A prolific writer, he has produced several volumes of poetry and short stories: *The Rose and the Puritan* (1958), *A Darkness in the East* (1959), *Under the Ice* (1961), *Wind in a Rocky Country* (1961), *The Things Which Are* (1962).

O'SULLIVAN, Seumas (1879-1958) was born in Dublin, Ireland, as James Starkley, and contributed prose and poetry to Irish periodicals under the pseudonym "Seumas O'Sullivan." *New Songs*, edited by George Russell ("A.E."), was published in 1902, and *Poems* in 1912. He was a poet of the Celtic twilight.

OWEN, Wilfred (1893-1918) was born at Oswestry, Shropshire, and was killed in action November 4, seven days before the Armistice. He was educated at Birkenhead Institute and at the Unversity of London. He taught school in France, and when the war broke out he joined the Artists' Rifles, and was awarded the Military Cross for gallantry in October 1918. His poems were collected and published with an introduction by Siegfried Sassoon in 1920. His poems are a comment on the tragedy and pity of war. "He pitied others; he did not pity himself," wrote Sassoon. He admired the poetry of Keats. He tried to enrich his own poetry by seeking substitutes for rhyme.

PAGE, P. K. (1917-   ) Patricia Page was born in England and was brought to Canada as a very young child. Her education began in St. Hilda's School in Calgary. Later she lived in Ottawa and Montreal. In 1950, she married W. A. Irwin who entered the Department of External Affairs. In recent years she has lived with her family abroad. Two books of poetry have won wide acclaim, *As Ten as Twenty* (1946) and *The Metal and the Flower* (1954).

PICKTHALL, Marjorie (1883-1922) was born near Cheswick, England, and died in Vancouver. In 1890, at the age of seven, she came to Canada with her parents, and was educated at Bishop Strachan School, Toronto. Working as a librarian in Victoria College, Toronto, she contributed verse to a local newspaper, *The Mail and Empire*. In 1913, she published a collection of poems, *The Drift of Pinions*, which was widely acclaimed. During World War I, she lived in England, but after the war she returned to Canada and took up residence in British Columbia. She published novels, short stories, and several volumes of poetry. Of her poetry, a reviewer had this to say, "The work was the product of genius undefiled and radiant, dwelling in the realm of pure beauty and singing with perfect naturalness its divine message."

POPE, Alexander (1688-1744) was born in London, and died at Twickenham, England. He was educated privately, and because he was a Roman Catholic, he could not at that time be admitted to a British university. Pope was a dwarfish little figure with many handicaps to overcome, but he became the greatest poet of his time. He perfected the heroic couplet. He made it the instrument of the bitterest satire and resentment against people and practices that offended him. Many of his phrases and couplets are so neatly turned that they have become common proverbs, such as "To err is human; to forgive divine" and "Fools rush in where angels fear to tread."

POUND, Ezra (1885-   ) was born in Hailey, Idaho, and his first book of poems appeared in Venice in 1908. Since then he has published over ninety volumes of poetry, criticism and translation, particularly the translation of poetry. While still a young poet he lived in London and later in Paris, and since 1924 he has considered Italy his home. He returned there in 1958 after fourteen years in St. Elizabeth's Hospital in Washington, D.C. His championship of the work of other poets has only been equalled by his influence on them.

PRATT, Edwin John (1883-1964) was born at Western Bay, Newfoundland, and died in Toronto. He was educated at Methodist College, St. John's, and at the University of Toronto. In 1920, he was appointed to the teaching staff of Victoria College, where he remained as a professor of English until appointed Professor Emeritus in 1953. His first volume of poetry *Newfoundland Verse* was published in 1923, and since that time he published a book of poetry almost every other year — a remarkable achievement in both quantity and quality. A racy virility is a characteristic of his poetry, as it was also of his personality. His style reflects the tempo and the temper of his mind. He feared and loved the sea as only one can who has felt its power and seen its beauty.

RANSOM, John Crowe (1888-   ) was born in Pulaski, Tennessee. He received his B.A. at Vanderbilt University in 1909; then went to Oxford as a Rhodes scholar. In 1914, he returned to Vanderbilt to teach English. For many years, since 1937, he has been Professor of English at Kenyon College, Ohio. He was founder and editor of the *Kenyon Review*. His books of criticism have been highly acclaimed, and his influence on several distinguished younger poets such as Robert Lowell and Randall Jarrell is well known. Ransom, "master of the ironic," writes about people with originality, surprise, and a "curiously involved speech." Some poems have such obscure allusion that they are almost unintelligible without footnotes.

REANEY, James (1926-   ) was born on a farm near Stratford, Ontario. He attended Stratford Collegiate Institute and the University of Toronto where he received an M.A. in 1949 and a Ph.D. in 1958. He is now a member of the staff of Middlesex College, University of Western

Ontario. The titles of a few of his publications reflect his interests: *The Red Heart* (1949), *A Suit of Nettles* (1958), *Twelve Letters to a Small Town* (1962), *The Kildeer and Other Plays* (1962).

REED, Henry (1914-   ) was born in Birmingham, England, and now lives in London, where he works as a free-lance writer for newspapers, magazines, radio, and television. He has published only one volume of poetry, *A Map of Verona* (1946).

ROBERTS, Sir Charles G. D. (1860-1943) was born at Douglas, York County, New Brunswick, and died in Toronto. He was educated at Fredericton Collegiate and the University of New Brunswick, and for a time taught school. From 1885 to 1888, he was professor of English and French literature in King's College, Windsor, Nova Scotia. From teaching he turned to journalism, and finally to writing as a full-time occupation, interrupted only by service in World War I. He published several historical novels, many animal stories that are now famous for their accuracy of observation and lucidity of style, and sixteen volumes of poetry that gave him an international reputation. His brother Theodore and his cousin Bliss Carman were also poets and men of distinction in the realm of Canadian letters.

ROBINSON, Edwin Arlington (1869-1935) was born at Head Tide, Maine, and died in New York. He was educated at Gardiner High School, and after two years at Harvard was forced to leave because of his father's health. In 1897, he published a small book of verse *The Children of the Night*. He worked as an inspector in the New York subway, and was saved from starvation by President Theodore Roosevelt who became interested in his poetry and gave him a clerkship in the New York Custom House. His best volume is perhaps *The Man Against the Sky* published in 1916. He is famous for a collection of pen-portraits of American characters, in which his lyricism is touched with both irony and tenderness.

ROSSETTI, Christina (1830-1894) was born in London, England, and died there. She was the daughter of an Italian scholar, poet, and reformer who was living in exile in England. She was the sister of Dante Gabriel Rossetti. Because of her intense piety and passionate devotion to her beliefs, she twice refused offers of marriage, preferring the life of a recluse. She was a member of the Church of England. Many of her lovely lyrics are devotional in nature, traditional in form, and imaginative and melodious in expression. She ranks with Elizabeth Barrett Browning as one of England's greatest women poets.

SANDBURG, Carl (1878-1967) was born at Galesburg, Illinois, of Swedish parents. He left school at thirteen, and in the next few years worked as a milkman, a stage-hand, a truck handler in a brickyard, a dish-washer, a house-painter, and a harvester. In 1898, he joined the Sixth Illinois Volunteers and served in Puerto Rico. On his return to Galesburg, he entered Lombard College, where he was editor of the college paper, captain of the basketball team and janitor of the gymnasium. In 1907, he left college and joined the staff of the *Chicago Daily News*. His first collection of twenty poems, *In Restless Ecstasy*, appeared in 1904 and was followed by several volumes of verse: *Chicago Poems* (1916), *Cornhuskers* (1918), and *Smoke and Steel* (1920). Sandburg was a literary descendant of Walt Whitman. His poetry expressed his personal energy and exaltation. In language and rhythms, it can be brutal or tender, slangy and "bull-necked" or delicate, poignant, and even mystical.

SANTAYANA, George (1863-1952) was born in Madrid, Spain, and died in Rome. Brought to Boston at the age of nine, he was educated in the Boston schools and at Harvard. He became an American citizen and was appointed to the staff of Harvard in the department of Philosophy in 1889, where he remained until 1912, and had among his students T. S. Eliot and Conrad Aiken. After 1914, he lived in England, France, and Italy. In addition to notable volumes of philosophy, he wrote poetry that is traditional in form and dignified in thought and feeling. Some of his sonnets rank with the best in the language.

SASSOON, Siegfried (1886-1967) was born on a country estate in England, the son of an English mother and a father who was descended from Persian Jews. He was educated at Cambridge, published his first poems at the age of sixteen; enlisted for service in World War I; rose to rank of captain in the Royal Welsh Fusiliers; was awarded the Military Cross for gallantry; served in Palestine; and published *Counter-Attack*, a collection of war poems, in 1918. These poems expressed his bitter hatred of war. "For war is hell and those who institute it are criminals," he wrote. His later poetry became more reflective.

SCOTT, Duncan Campbell (1862-1947) was born in Ottawa and educated at local public schools and at Stanstead College, Quebec. He entered the Civil Service in the Department of Indian Affairs at seventeen, became head of the department in 1913, and retired in 1932. He published ten volumes of poetry and two books of short stories. An intimate friend of Archibald Lampman, he shared Lampman's love of the Canadian northland. His poetry reflects the craftsmanship of an artist and a musician in the use of words and rhythms.

SCOTT, Sir Walter (1771-1832) was born in Edinburgh, Scotland, and died at Abbotsford, his country estate on the Tweed. He was educated for a career in law, but turned to literature and the collecting of border ballads. He published his first great original poem *The Lay of the Last*

Minstrel in 1805, and his second *The Lady of the Lake* in 1810. In 1814, his first great novel *Waverley* appeared, and in the next eighteen years he produced more than twenty novels which are now acknowledged classics. His poems reflect his intense love of Scottish history and romance.

SERGEANT, Howard (1914-   ) was born in Hull, Yorkshire. He was educated at the College of Commerce. From 1949 to 1954 he was Company Secretary for Jordan and Sons Ltd., Publishers. He served as Advisory Editor for the British Commonwealth on the Editorial Board of the Borestone Mountain Poetry Awards. He was founder and editor of *Outposts*. His criticism may be found in the *Times Literary Supplement, Observer, Fortnightly, New Directions,* and *Saturday Review.* Also he has edited *An Anthology of Contemporary Northern Poetry,* and *New Poems, 1953.* Some of his own publications are: *The Headlands, Tradition in the Making of Modern Poetry* (Volume I), *The Cumberland Wordsworth, A Critical Survey of South African Poetry.*

SHAKESPEARE, William (1564-1616) was born at Stratford-on-Avon, England, and died there. Educated at the local grammar school, he went to London to seek his fortune. There, he joined a company of actors, began refurbishing old plays, and then writing and producing his own. His fame rests firmly today on the thirty-seven original dramas and his sequence of one hundred and fifty-four sonnets. He is England's greatest playwright, and one of the greatest dramatic and lyric poets of all time.

SHAPIRO, Karl (1913-   ) was born in Baltimore, Maryland. He attended the University of Virginia and Johns Hopkins University and later served with the Army in the South Pacific for four years. He has been editor of *Poetry: A Magazine of Verse*, and has published a volume of poetry, *Essay on Rime* and a volume of essays, *In Defense of Ignorance*. He has lived in Lincoln, Nebraska, where he was professor of English at the University of Nebraska.

SHELLEY, Percy Bysshe (1792-1822) was born at Field Place near the village of Horsham, Sussex, and was educated at Eton and Oxford. From Oxford he was expelled because of his strong nonconformist attitude and his writings. He disliked authority and dictation of any kind. Highly imaginative and emotional, he produced some of the finest lyric poetry in the English language. While sailing a small boat in the Gulf of Spezia, Italy, he was drowned.

SHIRLEY, James (1596-1666) was born in London, England, and died there. He was educated at Oxford, took orders, but left the church and took up teaching. Then he turned to the writing of plays: before the theatres were closed in 1642, he had written about thirty plays. Driven from his home by the Great Fire of London, both he and his wife died of shock and exposure.

SOUSTER, Raymond (1921-   ) was born and educated in Toronto. During the war he served in the Royal Canadian Air Force, and since 1945 has worked in his native city as a banker. During the past fifteen years, he has produced nearly a dozen books and his poems have been collected in *The Colour of the Times* (1964). He is well known among the poets and other literary people both in Canada and the United States.

SPENSER, Edmund (1552-1599) was born in London, England, and died there. Educated at the Merchant Tailor's School and at Cambridge, he was appointed secretary to the Earl of Leicester, and then to the Lord Deputy of Ireland. Although he spent most of the last eighteen years of his life in Ireland, his heart was with his friends and scholarly interests in England. Because of his strong sense of form in poetry, his clear imagery, and his rich melody, he has been called the "poet's poet."

STEPHENS, James (1882-1950) was born in Dublin, Ireland. He was too poor to receive much formal education and worked as a typist in a lawyer's office. Some of his early poems came to the notice of George Russell ("AE") who encouraged him to devote himself to writing. His best known novel is *The Crock of Gold*, published in 1912, and in the same year appeared his second volume of poems, *The Hill of Vision*. In 1925, he was popularly received in the United States as a lecturer and reader of his own poetry. His poetry is notable for its spontaneity and whimsicality.

TATE, Allen (1899-   ) was born in Winchester, Kentucky. He was educated in private and public schools in Louisville, Nashville, and Washington, D.C. After graduation from Vanderbilt University in 1922, he became a free-lance literary critic. He was one of the founders of *The Fugitive*, a magazine that influenced the careers of several writers identified with the "new criticism." Today he is professor of English at the University of Minnesota and one of America's finest literary critics. It has been said of his poetry that he rewrites a poem so often that it loses its original edge. Though the poem gains allusiveness, it lacks a directness many readers require.

TENNYSON, Alfred, Lord (1809-1892) was born in Somersby, Lincolnshire and died at Aldworth, his home near Haslemere in Surrey. After graduation from Cambridge, he devoted himself through a long life to poetry. On the death of Wordsworth in 1850, he was appointed Poet Laureate, and in 1884 he was raised to the peerage. The history of his life is recorded in the dates of his numerous publications. His poetry reveals his exquisite sense of beauty, high moral purpose, precision in the use of words and felicitous rhythms, and ability to match sound with sense.

THOMAS, Dylan (1914-1953) was born in Swansea, Wales, and died in New York. He attended the Swansea Grammar School, and later contributed poems, stories, and reviews to English, Welsh, and American periodicals. In 1934, he published *18 Poems*, and in 1936, *25 Poems*. His *Collected Poems* appeared shortly after his death. There is in his poetry a vigour and a spontaneity that compels attention. He tumbles images, sounds, and ideas upon the page and leaves the bewildered reader to work out the sequence impelled by the poet's urgency. At the time of his death, Thomas was one of the most original poets of our time.

THOMPSON, Francis (1859-1907) was born in Lancashire and died in London. Son of a medical doctor, he was being prepared to follow in his father's practice. When he failed hopelessly in his medical examinations, he set out for London where the drug habit, poverty, and misery awaited him. In a feeble attempt to keep alive, he peddled small wares in the streets. Some verses and articles that he sent in to a periodical, *Merry England*, brought him to the attention of its editor, Wilfrid Meynell, who befriended and encouraged him. Thompson was capable of poetic ecstasy, and he wrote some of the most passionately religious poems in the language.

VAN DOREN, Mark (1894-   ) was born at Hope, Illinois, and educated at the University of Illinois and at Columbia. He taught English at Columbia and became literary editor of *The Nation*. As well as his volumes of poetry, he has produced a number of important books of literary criticism. His *Collected Poems 1922-1938* was awarded the Pulitzer Prize.

VAUGHAN, Henry (1622-1695) was born in Brecknockshire, Wales, and died there. Educated privately, he went to London to study law but turned to medicine, and practised it all his life at Newton by Usk in Wales. In his writing, he was greatly influenced by George Herbert and John Donne, and his own poetry is said to have made a great impression on Wordsworth. His poems often read like meditations. His imagination was at once warm and spacious.

WALLER, Edmund (1606-1687) was born at Coleshill, Buckinghamshire and died at Beaconsfield. A Cambridge graduate, a wealthy courtier and an adroit politician, he could adapt his views and his verses to the needs of the moment. His poetry was very popular in his day, and many of his lyrics are still admired for their grace and charm.

WHITE, Joseph Blanco (1775-1842) was born in Seville, Spain, of Irish stock, and died in Liverpool. Moving to England in 1810, he tried teaching and journalism without much success, and was finally given a pension by the government. He was a profoundly religious man who was never free from doubts. He sought for a faith that he was never able to find. Coleridge pronounced the sonnet "To Night" "the most grandly conceived sonnet" in the language.

WHITMAN, Walt (1819-1892) was born in West Hills near Huntington, Long Island, and died at Camden, New Jersey. His opportunities for formal education were meagre. At eleven he went to work as an errand boy, and then by turns worked as a carpenter, typesetter, and journalist. His first collection of poems, *Leaves of Grass*, published in 1885, attracted immediate attention, and today it is regarded as one of the most important books in American letters. He celebrated the interests, experience, and points of view of the "working people," and has been called the "poet of the common man."

WILBUR, Richard (1921-   ) was born in New York. After graduation from Amherst College, he served in Europe with the infantry. He returned to Harvard for graduate work and had taught English there, at Wellesley College, and Wesleyan University. Among his publications are: *The Beautiful Changes and Other Poems* (1947), *Ceremony and Other Poems* (1950), *Things of This World* (1956), *Poems, 1943-1956* (1957), *Advice to a Prophet* (1961).

WILLIAMS, William Carlos (1883-1963) was born in Rutherford, New Jersey, where he was a practising pediatrician. He took his degree in medicine at the University of Pennsylvania. Besides poetry, he wrote short stories, novels, and plays. A strong advocate of a distinctly American idiom in poetry, he has had a profound influence on younger writers.

WOLFE, Humbert (1885-1940) was born in Milan in Italy and died in London, England. Educated at Oxford, he joined the Civil Service in 1909, and died in that service of a heart attack brought on by overwork. Of more than a dozen volumes of poetry, the best are *Kensington Gardens* (1924) and *Requiem* (1927). The fabric of his light lyrics is woven from delicate fancies and whimsical ironies.

WORDSWORTH, William (1770-1850) was born in Cockermouth in the Cumberland District of England and died at Rydal Mount near Grasmere. He was educated at Hawkshead Grammar School and at Cambridge. Under the influence of his intimate friend Coleridge, he decided to devote himself to poetry, and jointly the two friends published *Lyrical Ballads* (1798) with an important preface on the theory of poetry. From that date until his death, the record of his life is a series of literary achievements. On the death of Southey in 1843, he was appointed Poet Laureate. Living most of his life among the solemn hills of the beautiful English Lake District, he developed a strong sense of the mystical relations between man and nature. Much of his best poetry reflects his preoccupation with this theme. With Shakespeare and Milton, he ranks today as one of England's greatest poets.

YEATS, William Butler (1865-1939) was born at Sandymount in Dublin, Ireland, and died at Roquebrune, near Nice, in Southern France. He was educated at Godolphin School, Hammersmith, and at Erasmus Smith School, Dublin. He lived for many years in London, but his poetic inspiration had its source in Irish legends and folk-lore. He was one of the leading organizers, playwrights, and producers of the Irish National Theatre in Dublin, known as the Abbey Players. He is loved as a poet whose lyricism is characterized by wistful, haunting melody and Celtic mysticism, but remembered as the writer who managed to bridge the gap between the late nineteenth and the twentieth centuries. In 1922, he became a senator of the Irish Free State, and in 1924 he received the Nobel Prize for literature.

YOUNG, Francis Brett (1884-1954) was born at Hales Owen, Worcestershire, and educated at Epsom College and at the University of Birmingham where he graduated in medicine. Besides serving as a medical officer in World War I, he managed between 1913 and 1922 to write and publish eight novels. His poetry revealed him as a writer with unusual powers of imagination, sympathy, and technical skill.

SELECTIONS LISTED BY AUTHOR

LIST OF BOOKS

ON POETRY

Its Interpretation, Appreciation,
and Enjoyment

Adams, Hazard, THE CONTEXTS OF POETRY, *Little, Brown & Co., 1963.*

Bridges, Robert, THE NECESSITY OF POETRY, *Oxford, 1917.*

Brooks, Cleanth, and Robert Penn Warren, UNDERSTANDING POETRY, *Holt, Rinehart and Winston, New York, 1960.*

Brown, E. K., ON CANADIAN POETRY, *Ryerson, 1943.*

Brown, Victoria V., THE EXPERIENCE OF POETRY IN SCHOOL, *Oxford, 1953.*

Bullough, Geoffrey, THE TREND OF MODERN POETRY, *Oliver & Boyd, 1934.*

Chute, Marchette, GEOFFREY CHAUCER OF ENGLAND, *Dutton, New York, 1946.*

Danby, John F., APPROACH TO POETRY, *Heinemann, 1940.*

Diltz, B. C., PATTERNS OF SURMISE, *Clarke, Irwin, Toronto, 1962.*
THE SENSE OF WONDER, *McClelland & Stewart, Toronto, 1953.*

Drew, Elizabeth, DISCOVERING POETRY, *Norton & Co., N.Y., 1933.*
THE ENJOYMENT OF LITERATURE, *Norton & Co., N.Y., 1935.*
POETRY: A MODERN GUIDE TO ITS UNDERSTANDING AND ENJOYMENT, *Dell, New York, 1959.*

Empson, William, SEVEN TYPES OF AMBIGUITY, *Chatto & Windus, 1930.*

Gilkes, Martin, INTRODUCTION TO MODERN POETRY, *Blackie, London, 1935.*

Gurrey, P., THE APPRECIATION OF POETRY, *Oxford, 1935.*

Hamilton, G. Rostrevor, POETRY AND CONTEMPLATION, *Cambridge, 1937.*

Harris, L. S., THE NATURE OF ENGLISH POETRY, *Dent, London, 1931.*

Henn, T. R., THE APPLE AND THE SPECTROSCOPE, *Methuen, London, 1951.*

Housman, A. E., THE NAME AND NATURE OF POETRY, *Cambridge, 1933.*

Kreuzer, James R., ELEMENTS OF POETRY, *Collier-Macmillan, Canada, 1955.*

Leavis, F. R., NEW BEARINGS IN ENGLISH POETRY, *Chatto & Windus, 1932.*
REVALUATION, *Chatto & Windus, 1936.*

Lewis, C. Day, POETRY FOR YOU, *Copp Clark, Toronto, 1945.*

Linenthal, Mark, ASPECTS OF POETRY, *Little, Brown & Co., 1963.*

Lyon, P. H. B., THE DISCOVERY OF POETRY, *Arnold, London, 1930.*

Murray, J. Middleton, ASPECTS OF LITERATURE, *Cape, London, 1934.*

Norman, Charles, POETS ON POETRY, *Collier Books, New York, 1962.*

O'Donnell, Margaret J., FEET ON THE GROUND, *Blackie, London, 1946.*

Perrine, Laurence, POETRY: THEORY AND PRACTICE, *Harcourt, Brace & World, New York, 1962.*
SOUND AND SENSE, *Harcourt, Brace & World, New York, 1963.*

Phelps, Arthur L., CANADIAN WRITERS, *McClelland & Stewart, Toronto, 1951.*

Ridley, M. R., POETRY AND THE ORDINARY READER, *Dent, London, 1938.*

Rosenthal, M. L., and A. J. M. Smith, EXPLORING POETRY, *Macmillan, New York, 1955.*

Sparrow, John, SENSE AND POETRY, *Constable, London, 1934.*

Tillyard, E. M. W., POETRY DIRECT AND OBLIQUE, *Chatto & Windus, London, 1934.*